Rhetoric of InSecurity

This book demands that we question what we are told about security, using tools we have had for thousands of years.

The work considers the history of security rhetoric in a number of distinct but related contexts, including the United States' security strategy, the "war" on Big Tech, and current concerns such as cybersecurity. Focusing on the language of security discourse, it draws common threads from the ancient world to the present day and the near future. The book grounds recent comparisons of Donald Trump to the Emperor Nero in a linguistic evidence base. It examines the potential impact on society of policy-makers' emphasis on the novelty of cybercrime, their likening of the internet to the Wild West, and their claims that criminals have "gone dark". It questions governments' descriptions of technology companies in words normally reserved for terrorists, and asks who might benefit.

Interdisciplinary in approach, the book builds on existing literature in the Humanities and Social Sciences, most notably studies on rhetoric in Greco-Roman texts, and on the articulation of security concerns in law, international relations, and public policy contexts. It adds value to this body of research by offering new points of comparison, and a fresh but tried and tested way of looking at problems that are often presented as unprecedented. It will be essential to legal and policy practitioners, students of Law, Politics, Media, and Classics, and all those interested in employing critical thinking.

Victoria Baines is Visiting Fellow at Bournemouth University's School of Computing. She has held visiting research fellowships at the University of Oxford and lectured at Stanford University. Trained as a Classicist with a specialism in rhetoric in Roman literature, she worked as a law enforcement intelligence analyst and a technology company executive before returning to research. Her research touches on public policy, threat representation, surveillance, cyberspace and internet governance, and futures methods. She regularly contributes to media coverage on the misuse of social and emerging technologies.

Law, Language and Communication

Series Editors

Anne Wagner, *Université du Littoral Côte d'Opale*, France and Vijay Kumar Bhatia, formerly of *City University of Hong Kong*

This series encourages innovative and integrated perspectives within and across the boundaries of law, language and communication, with particular emphasis on issues of communication in specialized socio-legal and professional contexts. It seeks to bring together a range of diverse yet cumulative research traditions in order to identify and encourage interdisciplinary research.

The series welcomes proposals – both edited collections as well as single-authored monographs – emphasizing critical approaches to law, language and communication, identifying and discussing issues, proposing solutions to problems, offering analyses in areas such as legal construction, interpretation, translation and de-codification.

Titles in the series

International Arbitration Discourse and Practices in Asia
Edited by Vijay K Bhatia, Maurizio Gotti, Azirah Hashim, Philip Koh and Sundra Rajoo

Phraseology in Legal and Institutional Settings
A Corpus-based Interdisciplinary Perspective
Edited by Stanislaw Gozdz Roszkowski and Gianluca Pontrandolfo

Fiction and the Languages of Law
Understanding Contemporary Legal Discourse
Karen Petroski

Law and Imagination in Troubled Times
A Legal and Literary Discourse
Edited by Richard Mullender, Matteo Nicolini, Thomas D.C. Bennett and Emilia Mickiewicz

Social Media in Legal Practice
Edited by Vijay Bhatia and Girolamo Tessuto

For more information about this series, please visit: www.routledge.com/Law-Language-and-Communication/book-series/LAWLANGCOMM

Rhetoric of InSecurity

The Language of Danger, Fear and Safety in National and International Contexts

Victoria Baines

Routledge
Taylor & Francis Group
LONDON AND NEW YORK

First published 2022
by Routledge
2 Park Square, Milton Park, Abingdon, Oxon OX14 4RN

and by Routledge
605 Third Avenue, New York, NY 10158

Routledge is an imprint of the Taylor & Francis Group, an informa business

British Library Cataloguing-in-Publication Data
A catalogue record for this book is available from the British Library

Library of Congress Cataloging-in-Publication Data
Names: Baines, Victoria, author.
Title: Rhetoric of insecurity : the language of danger, fear and safety in national and international contexts / Victoria Baines.
Description: Abingdon, Oxon ; New York, NY : Routledge, 2021. | Includes bibliographical references and index.
Identifiers: LCCN 2021001200 (print) | LCCN 2021001201 (ebook) | ISBN 9780367463076 (hardback) | ISBN 9781003028062 (ebook)
Subjects: LCSH: Security, International. | National security. | Rhetoric–Political aspects.
Classification: LCC JZ5588 .B3524 2021 (print) | LCC JZ5588 (ebook) | DDC 355/.033–dc23
LC record available at https://lccn.loc.gov/2021001200
LC ebook record available at https://lccn.loc.gov/2021001201

ISBN: 978-0-367-46307-6 (hbk)
ISBN: 978-1-032-03084-5 (pbk)
ISBN: 978-1-003-02806-2 (ebk)

DOI: 10.4324/9781003028062

Typeset in Galliard
by Taylor & Francis Books

For Jeff, and his counsel always to get to the point.

Contents

Illustrations

Figure

Tables

Preface

Over the course of the last 20 years, I have increasingly come to the conclusion that one never really stops being a Classicist. Study of the Greco-Roman world, its history and literature, exposes one to tales and events that are the bedrock of Western civilisation. Thus inculcated, Classicists are destined for the rest of their natural lives to spot echoes of epic poetry, tragedy, and other ancient literary forms in contemporary culture. It is an irresistible compulsion.

After completing my doctorate on the Roman satirist Juvenal, I embarked on a career as an intelligence analyst in law enforcement. As well as finding myself suddenly required to write in a more concise style than that to which I had become accustomed in academia, my focus changed from second-century Rome to crack cocaine and heroin trafficking, child abuse, and cybercrime. But in many respects my work consisted of the same core tasks – to take text apart, make sense of it, and present my findings to others.

I also discovered that I couldn't help but be alert to how authorities, myself included, communicated on issues of crime and security: not only the substance of their press releases, reports, and speeches, but also the techniques they used to present them. As an author of threat assessments for national and international law enforcement organisations, I am doubtless guilty of having contributed to threat inflation. In hindsight, I was perhaps not always as mindful as I could have been about the potential impact on citizens of the public, sanitised versions of these documents.

A subsequent spell as a US technology company executive put me on the receiving end of safety and security rhetoric. First-hand experience of how governments and media outlets shaped the popular narrative on Big Tech, how those companies responded, and the impact of both activities on policy- and law-making afforded a privileged insight into the dynamics of public discourse: who gets to speak, who is listened to, and how this is mediated. A realisation that security stakeholders repeatedly talked past each other propelled me to return to research, this time to shed light on conceptual and rhetorical gaps with the ultimate aspiration of closing them.

As an expression of this aspiration, this book is therefore more than a love letter to a Classical education, although it is undoubtedly also such. It is an invitation to all comers to grasp and work with the tools of Classical rhetoric to deconstruct modern policy-making and media representations of security concerns. Its analytical targets have been selected based on my research background (Roman depictions of danger), direct exposure to their operations (online safety and cybersecurity), and their suitability as a corpus of study (national security strategies).

My thanks go to Corneliu Bjola and the Oxford Department for International Development for hosting me during my Visiting Research Fellowship; Tom Greeves for insight into political speechwriting; Nicholas Cole for guidance on John Quincy Adams; Andy Phippen for numerous 'sounding board' moments in what has otherwise been a year of unusual disconnection; and Llewelyn Morgan, for reminding me that Classicists know more than anyone about rhetoric.

V.J.B. 2020

Introduction

What is rhetoric?

"Rhetoric" is a contested word. Often we see or hear it used pejoratively, as when commentators or political opponents dismiss a public figure's speech as "mere rhetoric", or when journalists or researchers use the term to distinguish fact from fiction in public discourse: accordingly, "or reality" and "and reality" rank among the top Google search strings to accompany "rhetoric". The popular implication is that rhetoric is empty frippery at best, deliberately misleading at worst.

Equally, the word has different meanings to scholars of different disciplines. For some, "rhetoric" denotes the speech itself, an utterance; for others, it denotes more particularly eloquence or elegance in choice of language, and in this it is closer to the depreciative usage above. There is a certain irony in the realisation that researchers may be speaking in different languages when they speak about rhetoric. It is also further justification for going back to the source – to use a metaphorical framing that will be the focus of much of the subsequent discussion – and to interrogate rhetoric's evolution into a term that has multiple meanings and usages.

The *Oxford English Dictionary* reflects this apparent multiplicity, or perhaps ambiguity, of meaning. Its primary definition of the noun is:

> 1. a. The art of using language effectively so as to persuade or influence others, esp. the exploitation of figures of speech and other compositional techniques to this end; the study of principles and rules to be followed by a speaker or writer striving for eloquence, esp. as formulated by ancient Greek and Roman writers.

For scholars and students of Classics (Ancient Greek and Roman history and literature), rhetoric is precisely this. Indeed, the *OED*'s definition owes much to that of Aristotle, who likewise deemed rhetoric to be an art (*techne*), and "the faculty of discovering the possible means of persuasion in reference to any subject whatsoever" (*Rhetoric* 1.2.1); the Ancient Greek understanding of art as a system or method for making or doing is echoed in the modern definition of rhetoric as "the study of principles and rules".[1] While successive authorities differed and sometimes disagreed on what precisely those rules should be, their

DOI: 10.4324/9781003028062-1

utility was beyond dispute, and effectiveness as an orator was judged by established standards.

Alternative definitions that refer to English prose composition as a school exercise (*OED* 1.e.), "Eloquent, elegant, or ornate language, esp. speech or writing expressed in terms calculated to persuade. Frequently depreciative: language characterized by artificial, insincere, or ostentatious expression; inflated or empty verbiage. Also figurative" (2.c.), and "The language or discourse characteristically associated with a particular subject, concept, or set of ideas" (4.c.) document the term's broader applications. But it is the primary, original, definition with which this book is preoccupied. Indeed, it is the very codification of rhetoric as a system of rules that enables comparative analysis across contexts and centuries.

About this book

One of the chief aims of this book is to demonstrate the value of ancient rhetorical textbooks as keys for decoding persuasive representations of security issues, even when specialist knowledge is lacking to the reader or listener. While the author has some expertise in Roman literature, technology policy and law enforcement, it will be immediately clear to experts in US politics that she is not among their number – and that is precisely the point. Communication on security issues is ripe primary material for two related reasons to which we will return in subsequent chapters. As will become evident, security rhetoric demonstrates a degree of consistency across contexts: what emerges is something of a lateral shorthand that makes similar use of imagery, arrangement, and rhetorical devices such as metaphor and antithesis.[2] At the same time, comparative analysis of ancient and modern texts reveals remarkable longitudinal consistency in the application of these devices to communications concerning security.

The texts analysed have been selected for their contributions to public discourse on security issues: an emperor's account of his own achievements, another's visual messaging, a speech delivered in praise of yet another, and a satirical depiction of urban life (Chapter 1); government security strategy as both internal planning document and universal broadcast (Chapter 2); published government and media content on technology policy, specifically online safety (Chapter 3); depictions of cyber threats by a range of actors (Chapter 4); and finally, government and citizen communications on the COVID pandemic and threat from China (Chapter 5). The focus of the chapters is not so much on the substance of these utterances as on their presentation. Although the source material – and, hopefully, the proposed analytical approach – will be of interest to students and scholars of political science, law, linguistics, speech communication, media studies, and other fields, it is not the task of this book to investigate from the perspectives of these disciplines. Rather, Classical rhetorical theory serves as a tool for the identification of persuasive devices in modern security discourse. In a strict sense, it is a study in applied rhetoric.

Artifice in and of itself does not make for an inauthentic communication. Even as commentators have debated the relative oratorical accomplishments and stylistic differences of Presidents Obama and Trump, the routine description of public figures as "rousing" or "inspirational" speakers demonstrates our persistent willingness to acknowledge persuasive ability as a positive attribute. For all that, an ability to recognise common rhetorical and stylistic devices empowers an audience to consider the extent to which speakers consciously construct communications in order to elicit specific reactions.

This book does not provide a comprehensive introduction to or glossary of rhetorical terms. Key terms will be explained in the chapters where relevant. A number of reference guides are widely available, of which Richard Lanham's *A Handlist of Rhetorical Terms* and Christopher Kelen's *An Introduction to Rhetorical Terms* are arguably the most helpfully structured and accessible.[3] Readers seeking a more detailed textbook would do well to consult Edward Corbett and Robert Connors' *Classical Rhetoric for the Modern Student*, which includes useful taxonomies, lesson plans, exercises, and stylistic study sheets.[4]

An interdisciplinary approach necessarily yields a wealth of primary material and a plethora of relevant scholarship. Throughout this book, the reader is urged to get to grips with rhetorical treatises composed in Ancient Greek and Latin, and it would be a dereliction of my duty not to implore them to read the works of Aristotle, Cicero, and Quintilian (even though, at 12 books in length, the last of these is something of a commitment). While English translations are provided in all instances, the original language is also reproduced where the acoustic or visual effect is worthy of remark. Unless otherwise stated, text and translation are taken from the editions of the Loeb Classical Library, whose facing page translations enable those without knowledge of Greek or Latin to observe these effects *in situ.*

Modern scholarship on Classical Rhetoric is extensive. Its centrality to Greco-Roman education and civic engagement dictates its interrogation by researchers of every literary genre, from epic poetry to satire and the ancient novel, and every line of historical enquiry. Discussion of ancient security rhetoric in the first chapter of this book draws on and responds to this tradition. Aristotelian scholar George Kennedy's *Classical Rhetoric and Its Christian and Secular Tradition from Ancient to Modern Times* and *A New History of Classical Rhetoric* are thorough, practical surveys of Classical Rhetoric as a discrete discipline.[5] A number of edited volumes bring together essays by specialists in Classical rhetorical theory, oratorical practice, and literary criticism. Among them are *Roman Eloquence: Rhetoric in Society and Literature* (ed. William J. Dominik) and *A Companion to Roman Rhetoric* (eds William Dominik and Jon Hall), both of which provide an overview of the social functions and creative manifestations of rhetoric in the cityscape and empire of Chapter 1.[6]

Neither does this book hope to be a complete study of the history of rhetoric. On the contrary, it deliberately telescopes 2,000 years, neglecting Late Antiquity, the Middle Ages, the Renaissance, and the Enlightenment. James Herrick's *The History and Theory of Rhetoric* conscientiously charts this evolution with a focus on rhetoric's social function in public discourse:

> The audience is a vital element in rhetoric's capacity to test ideas. In seeking an audience's consent, we recognize that the audience members will exercise critical

> judgment. Some audiences test ideas carefully while others are careless about this responsibility. The better equipped an audience is to test ideas advanced for their consideration, and the more care that goes into that testing, the better check we have on the quality of ideas. This testing of ideas in public settings constitutes a distinct benefit to society. Thus, training in the art of rhetoric is just as important for audience members as it is for advocates.[7]

The conception of an understanding of rhetoric as a civic duty is assumed and taken forward in this book. Likewise, there is much in the subsequent chapters that aligns with Kenneth Burke's definition of rhetoric as symbolic inducement, specifically "the use of language as a symbolic means of inducing cooperation in beings that by nature respond to symbols".[8] The figure of Burke towers over contemporary rhetorical theory. His thesis that the words we choose act as a kind of filter, or "terministic screen", that directs an audience's attention towards *and away from* alternative interpretations has inspired a body of research on rhetorical framing, silence, and silencing, with which the discussion in this book engages.[9]

Interdisciplinary heritage

Classical studies teach the importance of intertextuality. The term as first used by Julia Kristeva in the last century denotes the idea that "any text is constructed as a mosaic of quotations; any text is the absorption and transformation of another".[10] But the notion that texts build on and respond to other texts – that they speak to each other within and across genres, through and across time, is central to the study of Ancient Greek and Latin literature. Detecting intertextual allusion and describing the process and possible impact of "creative imitation" (*imitatio* and *aemulatio*) are core activities of the Classics scholar.[11] Application of this investigative tactic in the chapters that follow reflects the training of the author: it also gives rise to a book that is inescapably interdisciplinary.

Classical authorities' codification of a system of rhetoric to aid both the production and understanding of oratory (and, in practice, literature) serves as a justification for the application of textual analysis to "non-literary" texts and audio-visual artefacts. This escape of literary criticism from the strictly literary sphere is mirrored by the work of a number of twentieth-century theorists, detailed discussion of whose works is a luxury not permitted to this book. Much modern rhetorical theory is indebted to Michel Foucault's theses on power and social control, especially as regards the questions of who can speak and in what contexts. Roland Barthes' work, meanwhile, is a landmark in the identification of both literary and non-literary forms as "narrative" suitable for structural analysis.[12] At a general level, this book subscribes to literary theory's impulse to subject texts and other artefacts to a close reading.

In the field of political science, Michael Dillon's contentions that "We are not simply the people who employ discourses of security, we are the people who are ensnared in and used by them", and that "there is never security without insecurity and the one always occurs in whatever form with the other" invites enquiry into the means by which state and non-state actors construct narratives of insecurity, and their motives for doing so.[13] Dillon's choice of the Classical Era as a hermeneutic frame of reference also provides a parallel for this book's undertaking. Dillon roots constructivism in the idea of politics as *techne*, "conceived in Platonic terms as something that must be constructed, instituted or founded; the product of craftsmanship"; also as *praxis*, "essentially conceived in Aristotelian terms to be a mode of action which takes place in a public world or public space – classically the *polis* – concerned not simply with all the questions that arise in respect of living together, but with enacting who we are both individually and collectively".[14] His work is instructive, not least for its call to look back further than Hobbes and the imposition of Westphalian Order for landmarks in security craft and action, to a preoccupation of metaphysics with security that is millennia old.[15] Moreover, its etymological focus has kindred aims:

> Government and rule are not answers to the riddle of the political, they themselves, in themselves, pose that riddle and force us to think about it in ways which in going through and beyond government and rule, are not determined by the particular means by which government and rule continuously bring it to our attention. Etymology makes a critical contribution to the process of responding to this riddle by teaching us, as Nietzsche says, "to read *well*, that is to read slowly, deeply, looking continuously behind and ahead, with reservations, with doors left open, with delicate eyes and fingers".[16]

Where Dillon's investigation centres on the term "(in)security" and its impact on political thought, this book examines the imagery and structures used to convey (in)security issues. It is an exploration of applied rhetoric, as opposed to rhetorical theory. It nonetheless shares with Dillon's thinking a recognition of security discourse's propensity to generate fear:

> It is evident, if we pause to think about security for a moment, that any discourse of security must always already, simultaneously and in a plurality of ways, be a discourse of danger too. For example, because security is engendered by fear (fundamentally aroused by the uncanny, uncertain, different, awesome and uncalculable), it must also teach us what to fear when the secure is being pursued. Any appeal to security must, therefore, also and simultaneously be a specification, no matter how inchoate, of the fear which engenders it. But because security is engendered by fear it also calls for counter-measures to deal with the danger which initiates fear, and for the neutralisation, elimination or constraint of that person, group, object or condition which engenders fear. Hence, while it teaches us what we are threatened by, it also seeks in turn to proscribe, sanction, punish, overcome – that is to say, in its turn endanger – that which it says threatens us.[17]

As we shall see at various points in this book, the urge to secure through fear generation and proscription is strong in modern security rhetoric, and the targets are not always the immediate source of the threat.

Mention of fear brings to mind the research of Frank Furedi, whose best-known works, *The Culture of Fear* and *The Politics of Fear*, consistently demonstrate the construction of insecurity narratives and their utility in twentieth- and twenty-first-century Western politics.[18] His charting of the emergence of self-perpetuating narratives rooted in a declining faith in humanity and increasing misanthropy aligns with this book's discussion of contemporary public discourse on safety and security issues that goes beyond (and is often anything but) unadorned presentation of fact based on robust evidence.

Furedi highlights the negative consequences of such discourse: "The culture of fear estranges people from one another. It also distracts people from facing up to the challenges confronting society."[19] In seeking to counter "the misanthropic dogma of our times" and "today's sad attempt to pathologise risk-taking", he draws attention to the fact that the ways in which security and safety risks are portrayed are not inevitable. Furedi's focus on the inflation of danger to children and from technology, and his drive to deconstruct modern moral panics and technophobia, is particularly relevant to Chapters 3 and 4 of this book.

The rhetorical counterpart of threat inflation is hyperbole, defined by Quintilian in his *Institutio Oratoria* ("Orator's Education") as "an appropriate exaggeration of the truth" (*decens veri superiectio*, 8.6.68).[20] Drawing attention to society's tendency to threat inflation, and in Furedi's words, "to regard a growing range of phenomena as threatening and dangerous",[21] is not to deny that atrocities such as child abuse and terrorism exist, nor to negate their impact. It does, however, encourage an objective, dispassionate assessment of policy and communications on such issues in the interest of delivering proportionate responses to security and safety problems. The forensic approach espoused in this book has a similar motivation.

Also relevant to the discussion of threat inflation is the Copenhagen School's theory of securitisation, the process first described by Barry Buzan, Ole Wæver, and Jaap de Wilde, through which non-political concerns are politicised and constructed as urgent security issues requiring emergency responses.[22] Conspicuous in twenty-first-century security strategising, the inclusion of non-military issues in security messaging is by no means an entirely modern phenomenon. As will become evident in the chapters that follow, a process which expands the scope of security also aligns with a rhetorical tendency to depict problems as bigger, more pressing, and more threatening.

In the study of mass media security communications, mention must be made of Noam Chomsky. His influential 1988 work with Edward Herman, *Manufacturing Consent*, famously challenged the presumption in democracies "that the media are independent and committed to discovering and reporting the truth, and that they do not merely reflect the world as powerful groups wish it to be perceived".[23] Drawing case studies from US mass media coverage of a range of security and foreign policy events – including the American invasion of Vietnam, the Russian invasion of Afghanistan, and the genocide in Cambodia – Herman and Chomsky identified a propaganda model that suggested "that the 'societal purpose' of the media is to inculcate and defend the economic, social, and political agenda of privileged groups that dominate the domestic society and the state".[24]

This book makes no such claim for univocal media acquiescence. It does, however, identify rhetorical similarities between media and government representations of safety and security issues in the twenty-first century. While the motivations of these similarities are sadly outside the scope of the current research, the rhetorical evidence presented in Chapter 3 points rather to a bi-directional, perhaps dialogic, exertion of rhetorical influence. Likewise, Herman's and Chomsky's identification of several instances of alleged media suppression and exclusion provides a precedent for this book's inclusion of what appears to be the rhetoric of omission (and its sister, silence) in the public discourse between governments and technology companies.

Chomsky's 2003 "Wars of Terror" and the 2015 edition of his *Culture of Terrorism* are of particular relevance to Chapter 2's discussion of President George W. Bush's counter-terrorism policy (the so-called Bush Doctrine).[25] At a more general level, Chomsky's observations on the recycling of security rhetoric and his motivation for calling out its frames and techniques align with the arguments and objectives of this book:

> To repeat the obvious, we basically have two choices. Either history is bunk, including current history, and we can march forward with confidence that the global enforcer will drive evil from the world much as the President's speech writers declare, plagiarizing ancient epics and children's tales. Or we can subject the doctrines of the proclaimed grand new era to scrutiny, drawing rational conclusions, perhaps gaining some sense of the emerging reality. If there is a third way, I do not see it.[26]

While the chapters that follow will emphasise greater continuity in rhetorical practice than is evident in Chomsky's designation of a new era, they share his ambition to intensify citizen scrutiny in the interest of policy development that reflects reality. George Lakoff's work on metaphor is also instructive in this regard. His arresting statement that "metaphors can kill" underscores a twofold thesis of the cognitive aspect of politics: first, that "Framing matters. Frames once entrenched are hard to dispel"; second, that "Awareness matters. Being able to articulate what is going on can change what is going on - at least in the long run."[27] The output of both scholars indicates that knowledge of rhetorical devices and techniques can empower the citizen. This book builds on this proposition, contending moreover that it is the duty of citizens to engage with security policy and communications by scrutinising their rhetoric.

Chapter summary

The chapters that follow examine the rhetoric of security communications in a number of different contexts, with a view to identifying longitudinal and horizontal patterns and connections. Chapter 1 outlines the principle features of Classical rhetorical theory, including prescriptions on types of oratory, speech structure, and figures of speech. While frequent reference is made to Aristotle, Cicero, Quintilian, and others, Quintilian features most prominently by virtue of having produced the most comprehensive and systematic ancient textbook. Four samples of Roman security communication are then subjected to scrutiny: the Emperor Augustus' record of his own security and foreign policy achievements; the Emperor Nero's issue of security-themed coinage; the Younger Pliny's eulogy to the Emperor Trajan; and the satirist Juvenal's depiction of life in the city of Rome. The US National Security Strategy is the focus of Chapter 2, specifically the presidential prefaces that introduce and commend the seven strategies issued in the twenty-first century to date. Using the Classical authorities as a key, the rhetorical and stylistic features of each of the prefaces are discussed in turn. From Clinton's millennial strategy to Trump's 2017 security theatre, comparative analysis seeks to identify similarities and divergence in the rhetorical approaches of the different presidents, to consider the impact of these, and to highlight possible points of contact with the ancient security communications discussed in the previous chapter.

Chapter 3 is an exploration of constructions of ideological Others, in this case the UK government's depiction of US technology companies in the context of security and safety issues. Characterisation of the companies in the 2014 parliamentary debate on the death of Lee Rigby is analysed in detail and compared to media coverage. Tabloid representations of online safety issues are then compared to the ministerial preface and problem statement in the 2019 legislative proposal known as the Online Harms White Paper, with a view to testing possible rhetorical commonality. The rhetoric of the other party is also examined, with a focus on the silence and silencing of technology companies. Continuing with the theme of technology, the discussion in Chapter 4 centres on cybersecurity and insecurity. Particular attention is paid to the use of metaphor and hyperbole in communication by government, industry, and criminal actors, with examples drawn from official law enforcement material, vendor advertisements, and scam emails and pop-ups. Probing the mode of cyber threat inflation, it seeks alternative representations with which to engage the public.

Chapter 5 serves as both Epilogue and Conclusion. Against the backdrop of the COVID-19 pandemic, short-form rhetoric on social media has given dissenters and conspiracy theorists alike a global audience. Their utterances and those of government figures seeking compliance with public health measures are scrutinised as instances of human security emergency communication. An intensification of the so-called "tech war" between the US and China concurrent with the pandemic provides an opportunity to examine a number of US government communications on a foreign technology threat. The book concludes with brief speculation on the future of short-form social media and synthetic rhetoric generated by artificial intelligence (AI), a consideration of the current study's limitations, and identification of avenues for further research.

Notes

1 Aristotle. *Art of Rhetoric*. Translated by J. H. Freese. Revised by Gisela Striker. Loeb Classical Library, 193. Cambridge, MA: Harvard University Press, 2020. Aristotle uses the Greek term *methodos* to describe a system arranged according to the principles of art (*techne*) at *Rhetoric* 1.1.11.
2 While outside the scope of this book, a comparative rhetorical assessment of security discourse in different (especially non-Western) cultures is worthy of investigation.
3 Richard A. Lanham (1991) *A Handlist of Rhetorical Terms* (2nd edn), Berkeley: University of California Press; Christopher Kelen (2007) *An Introduction to Rhetorical Terms*, Tirril: Humanities-Ebooks.
4 Edward P. J. Corbett and Robert J. Connors (1999) *Classical Rhetoric for the Modern Student* (4th edn), New York; Oxford: Oxford University Press.
5 George A. Kennedy (1980) *Classical Rhetoric and Its Christian and Secular Tradition from Ancient to Modern Times*, Chapel Hill: University of North Carolina Press; (1994) *A New History of Classical Rhetoric*, Princeton, NJ: Princeton University Press.
6 William J. Dominik, ed. (1997) *Roman Eloquence: Rhetoric in Society and Literature*, London; New York: Routledge; William Dominik and Jon Hall, eds (2007) *A Companion to Roman Rhetoric*, Blackwell Companions to the Ancient World, Malden, MA; Oxford: Blackwell.
7 James A. Herrick (2018) *The History and Theory of Rhetoric: an introduction* (6th edn), Abingdon; New York: Routledge, p. 17.
8 Kenneth Burke (1969) *A Rhetoric of Motives*, Berkeley: University of California Press, p. 43.
9 Kenneth Burke (1966) *Language as Symbolic Action*, Berkeley: University of California Press, p. 45 (original emphasis): "Even if any given terminology is a *reflection* of reality, by its very nature as a terminology it must be a *selection* of reality; and to this extent must function also as a *deflection* of reality."
10 Julia Kristeva (1980) *Desire in Language: A Semiotic Approach to Literature and Art*. Edited by Leon S. Roudiez and translated by Thomas Gora, Alice Jardine, and Leon S. Roudiez. New York: Columbia University Press.
11 For the definition, see David West and Tony Woodman, eds (1979) *Creative Imitation in Latin Literature*, Cambridge: Cambridge University Press.
12 Roland Barthes and Lionel Duisit (1975) "An Introduction to the Structural Analysis of Narrative", *New Literary History* 6.2: 237–272.
13 Michael Dillon (1996) *Politics of Security: Towards a Political Philosophy of Continental Thought*, London; New York: Routledge, pp. 16, 19.
14 Ibid., p. 54.
15 Ibid., p. 77.
16 Ibid., p. 116, quoting J. Sallis (1991) *Crossings: Nietzsche and the Space of Tragedy*, Chicago: Chicago University Press, p. 10.
17 Ibid., p. 121.
18 Frank Furedi (2005) *Politics of Fear: Beyond Left and Right*, London; New York: Continuum (2006); *Culture of Fear Revisited: Risk-taking and the Morality of Low Expectation*, London; New York: Continuum.
19 Furedi (2006) p. xx.
20 Quintilian. *The Orator's Education*. Edited and translated by Donald A. Russell. Loeb Classical Library, Cambridge, MA: Harvard University Press, 2002, pp. 124–127 and 494.
21 Ibid., p. xvii.
22 Barry Buzan, Ole Wæver, and Jaap de Wilde (1998) *Security: A New Framework for Analysis*, Boulder, CO: Lynne Rienner.
23 Edward S. Herman and Noam Chomsky (1994) *Manufacturing Consent: The Political Economy of the Mass Media* (2nd edn), London: Vintage, p. xi.
24 Ibid., p. 298.

25 Noam Chomsky (2003) "Wars of Terror", *New Political Science* 25.1: 113–127; (2015) *Culture of Terrorism* (2nd edn), London: Pluto Press.
26 Chomsky (2003) p. 118.
27 George Lakoff (2003) "Metaphor and War, Again", *Alternet* 18 March 2003, www.alternet.org/2003/03/metaphor_and_war_again/; reprinted by the author on the UC Berkeley website, https://escholarship.org/uc/item/32b962zb#author(UC Berkeley Previously Published Works).

1 The Classical heritage of modern (in)security rhetoric

The Classical rhetorical tradition

For scholars of the cultures of Ancient Greece and Rome, rhetoric is a formalised system for constructing speeches, for the training of public speakers, and a core feature of the elite youth's preparation for public life. Authorities on rhetoric and oratory, the practical application of rhetorical theory, produced text books on the subjects. Not all of these works have survived into the modern era. Of those extant, the most notable and extensive are Aristotle's *Rhetoric* (fourth century BCE), Cicero's *De Inventione, De Oratore, Brutus* and *Orator* (first century BCE), and Quintilian's *Institutio Oratoria* (first century CE). From Cicero, we also have extensive evidence of what it was like to *be* a celebrated orator in practice, including large numbers of his speeches. Cicero builds on Aristotle's definition of rhetoric as *techne*, emphasising its role in political discourse (*De Inventione* 1.5):[1]

> There is a scientific system of politics which includes many important departments. One of these departments - a large and important one - is eloquence based on the rules of art, which they call rhetoric. For I do not agree with those who think that political science has no need of eloquence, and I violently disagree with those who think that it is wholly comprehended in the power and skill of the rhetorician. Therefore we will classify oratorical ability as a part of political science. The function of eloquence seems to be to speak in a manner suited to persuade an audience, the end is to persuade by speech.

Noting that the commonest definition is "the power of persuading" (*vim persuadendi, Inst.Or.*2.15.3), Quintilian also records some variations from Aristotle. Cornelius Celsus, for example, is recorded as stating that the aim of rhetoric is "to speak persuasively on disputable public matters", clearly emphasising the role of rhetoric and oratory in politics and other forms of citizen deliberation (2.15.22). Rhetoric comes to be the tool used by Ancient Greek and Roman societies to judge whether a speech is "good" or "bad": to question the validity of its argumentation, the appropriateness of its language and figures of speech, and the effectiveness of its delivery. As such, it is closely associated with the study of logic and literature.

DOI: 10.4324/9781003028062-2

Rhetoric's relationship with the truth has always been problematic. Its stated aim of persuasion aligns it with a suspicion of manipulative quality. As far back as the fourth century BCE, Plato has Socrates brand rhetoric as "a pursuit that is not a matter of art, but showing a shrewd, gallant spirit which has a natural bent for clever dealing with mankind, and I sum up its substance in the name flattery [*kokaleia*]" (*Gorgias* 463B).[2] Quintilian records the definitions of Critolaus (second century BCE) and an otherwise unknown Athenaeus, respectively that rhetoric is a "knack of speaking", or the "art of deceiving" (*Inst.Or.*2.15.23).

The perception of rhetoric as a tool for manipulation has persisted to the twenty-first century. Its ancient aims of imposing standards, and both naming and promoting the use of common methods of speech construction and figures of speech, may themselves be taken to associate rhetoric with the artificial and the insincere. For the young elite Roman, however, rhetorical training was the equivalent of modern higher education. Having passed through the hands of the *ludi magister* (primary or elementary school teacher) and the *grammaticus* (secondary school teacher of language and literature), at around age 15, Roman boys progressed to study under the *rhetor*, the master of rhetoric.

By the second century CE, rhetorical education was so established at Rome that the satirist Juvenal – whose first and third satires will be the focus of close reading later in this chapter – bemoans the lot of the teacher as follows (*Satires* 7.150–161):[3]

> Do you teach rhetoric? Vettius must have a heart of steel, when his crowded class slays "The Cruel Tyrant." You know how it is: what they've just read sitting down each in turn will repeat standing up, chanting the same things in the same lines. All that rehashed cabbage kills the poor teachers. Everyone wants to know the arguments and the types of cases and the crucial points and the shots that will be fired from the other side, but no one is prepared to pay. "You ask me to pay? But what have I learned?" "I suppose it's the fault of the teacher, then, that our Arcadian teenager feels nothing throb in the left side of his breast when he fills my poor head every five days with his 'Hannibal the Terrible'?"

The teaching of rhetoric is identified as one of the chief exports of Greco-Roman culture: "Nowadays the whole world has its Greek and Roman Athens. Eloquent Gaul has been teaching the lawyers of Britain. Thule is already talking about hiring a professor of rhetoric" (*Satires* 15.110–112). Variously identified as Iceland, Norway, the Shetland Islands, and the Arctic Circle, Thule is the semi-mythical designation for the place furthest away in the Roman imagination. For the satiric observer of Roman culture, rhetorical education is so pervasive that even places of doubtful existence are after it.

The most comprehensive extant textbook on Classical rhetoric is Quintilian's *Institutio Oratoria*, which translates as *The Orator's Education*. In 12 books, it covers subjects as diverse as the preferred education for Roman boys (Books 1 & 2), the different types of oratory (Book 3), parts of speech (Books 4–6), arrangement (Book 7), style (Books 8 & 9), practice through imitation (Book 10), and memory and delivery (Books 11 & 12). The systematic presentation of the material and its thorough treatment make it perhaps the most useful ancient comparator for modern rhetorical usage.

John Quincy Adams certainly appears to have thought so. Earlier in his career, the sixth president of the United States served as Boylston Professor of Rhetoric and Oratory at his *alma mater*, Harvard University. His 26 lectures, first published in 1810, betray an obvious admiration for Cicero.[4] But the sheer size of the extant work and the systematic approach to the different branches of rhetoric, sections of a speech, parts and figures of speech, not to mention lectures on memory and delivery, owe much to Quintilian. His debt to the two Roman orators is demonstrated by the fact that they are the only individuals to whom he dedicated lectures (the fifth to Cicero, the sixth to Quintilian). One could argue that while the spirit of Adams' teaching is Ciceronian, its arrangement is Quintilian's. From his inaugural oration and throughout the lecture course, Adams regularly cited "Aristotle, Cicero and Quintilian" as his preferred authorities on matters of rhetoric and oratory.

There is already a notable body of research tracing the influence of Classical thought and culture on the Founding Fathers of the United States: it is of course no coincidence that the upper chamber of the United States Congress is known as the Senate, after the governing body of Rome.[5] While Classical authors are the dominant authorities on rhetoric in this book, reference in subsequent sections of this chapter to relevant prescriptions in Adams' lectures serves to illustrate the persistence of Classical rhetorical theory in the educational canon of Western elites.

Key features of Classical rhetorical theory

Classical rhetorical theory divides oratory into three types, according to their settings and functions ("the three kinds of hearers", Aristotle, *Rhetoric*.1.3.1):[6]

> The deliberative kind is either hortatory or dissuasive; for both those who give advice in private and those who speak in the assembly invariably either exhort or dissuade. The forensic kind is either accusatory or defensive; for litigants must necessarily either accuse or defend. The epideictic kind has for its subject praise or blame.

Deliberative oratory is most closely aligned with policy-making, and has the future as its focus (*Rhetoric* 1.3.4). Forensic oratory, now most often seen in law courts, enquires into past actions. Epideictic or demonstrative oratory concerns the present condition but, as Aristotle notes, "It is not uncommon, however, for epideictic speakers to avail themselves of other times, of the past by way of recalling it, or of the future by way of anticipating it."

The categorisation of oratory into three types reflects the needs of public life in Ancient Greece. It remained largely unchanged in Ancient Rome, where the pleading of legal cases was a common activity for elite men, where members of the senatorial class were expected to contribute to policy and governance, and where leading citizens could be called upon publicly to pay tribute to or condemn the actions of others. Both Cicero (*De Inventione* 1.5.7, 2.4.12) and Quintilian (*Inst. Or.* 3.3.14) endorse this threefold categorisation. In the early nineteenth century, Adams translates Aristotle's categories as follows:

> Now of the three learned professions, which more especially demand the preparatory discipline of a learned education, there are two, whose most important occupations consist in the act of public speaking. And who can doubt, but that in the sacred desk, or at the bar, the man, who speaks well, will enjoy a larger share of reputation, and be more useful to his fellow creatures, than the divine or the lawyer of equal learning and integrity, but unblest with the talent of oratory? ... But besides these two professions, of which oratory may be called the vital principle, a free republic, like that, in which an indulgent providence has cast our lot, bestows importance upon the powers of eloquence, to every class and description of citizens.[7]

Classical rhetoricians likewise set out the activities, or "parts", into which the practice of rhetoric should be divided. Thus Cicero, at *De Inventione* 1.7:

> Invention [*inventio*] is the discovery of valid or seemingly valid arguments to render one's cause plausible. Arrangement [*dispositio*] is the distribution of arguments thus discovered in the proper order. Expression [*elocutio*] is the fitting of the proper language to the invented matter. Memory [*memoria*] is the firm mental grasp of matter and words. Delivery [*pronuntiatio*] is the control of voice and body in a manner suitable to the dignity of the subject matter and the style.

In his Harvard lecture course, Adams deploys these same divisions (Lecture 7). With regard to argumentation, Classical rhetoricians emphasise the close links between rhetoric and logic. At least as far back as Aristotle (*Rhetoric* 1.2.3), rhetorical theory outlines three kinds of proofs:

> Now the proofs furnished by the speech are of three kinds. The first depends upon the moral character [*ethos*] of the speaker, the second upon putting the hearer into a certain frame of mind [*pathos*], the third upon the speech [*logos*] itself, in so far as it proves or seems to prove.

Having focused on logical proofs and arguments early in his lecture course, Adams expounds on both ethical and emotional proofs in his sixteenth lecture on "Excitation and Management of the Passions". Noting that "the Christian morality has commanded us to suppress the angry and turbulent passions in ourselves, and forbids us to stimulate them in others", he concedes that "there are still, however, occasions, in every class of public speaking, when the orator may obtain his end by operating upon the passions of his hearers". He nevertheless urges caution in its use: "It is however an instrument, which requires the management of a skilful hand, and which, to retain its efficacy, must be very rarely employed." As we shall see in later chapters, modern security communications make free use of appeals to our emotions.

The division of a speech into different sections, each with its own function, is also an ancient innovation. For Aristotle, these are four in number: exordium, statement, proof, epilogue (*Rhetoric* 3.13.4). Cicero lists six in the *De Inventione*: exordium, narrative, partition, confirmation, refutation, peroration (1.14.19). Quintilian writes that "in every forensic cause there are five parts: of these, the Exordium wins the hearer's attention, the Narrative informs him, the Proof confirms our position, the Refutation demolishes our opponents', and the Peroration either refreshes the memory or arouses emotions" (*Inst.Or.* 8.Pr.12). Adams introduced early nineteenth-century Harvard students to each of the parts in turn, with lectures on the Exordium (17), Narration (18), Proposition and Partition (19), Confirmation, Ratiocination and Induction (20–21), Confutation (22), and Conclusion (24). In this respect also, analysis of modern communications may be aided by Classical signposting. Indeed, we may recognise in these divisions the prevailing hallmarks of a "good" deliberative speech in the Western tradition: a rousing opening, a vivid story, logical presentation of the main points – preferably with appeal to evidence, anticipation of objections, and a neat summary.

Classical rhetorical theory likewise elucidates the tropes and figures that may be used to support or embellish the content of a speech. For Quintilian (*Inst. Or.*8.3–6), these include use of vivid language for emphasis (*enargeia*), simile, amplification and diminution, pithy maxims (*sententiae*), metaphor, synecdoche and metonymy (both forms of substitution), epithets, allegory, irony, and hyperbole. Metaphor is defined as follows (8.6.9):

> In general terms, metaphor is a shortened form of simile; the difference is that in simile something is compared with the thing we wish to describe, while in metaphor one thing is substituted for the other. It is a comparison when I say that a man acted "like a lion," a metaphor when I say of a man "he is a lion."

Metaphor is "the commonest and by far most beautiful of the tropes" (*frequentissimus est tum longe pulcherrimus, Inst.Or.*8.6.4), Quintilian adding that "so long as it is correctly employed (*recte modo adscita*), it cannot be vulgar or mean or unpleasing" (8.6.5). In his estimation, incorrect employment includes excessive use, coarse or ugly imagery, and imagery that is too grand or unlike the subject (8.6.14–16). Its purpose is to "affect the emotions, put a clear mark on things, and place them before our eyes" (*tralatio permovendis animis plerumque et signandis rebus ac sub oculos subiciendis reperta est*, 8.6.19).

The visual focus echoes Cicero's assessment that

> a great impression is made by dwelling on a single point, and also by clear explanation and almost visual presentation of events as if practically going on – which are very effective both in stating a case and in explaining and amplifying

the statement, with the object of making the fact we amplify appear to the audience as important as eloquence is able to make it.

(*De Oratore* 3.53.202)[8]

John Quincy Adams devoted five of his lectures on rhetoric to figurative language: his designation of metaphor as "the most frequent and most beautiful of the tropes" (Lecture 33) is a direct translation of Quintilian, as is his distinction between metaphor and simile. In addition to rousing emotions, its value in public discourse is as a device that conveys unfamiliar concepts in familiar images, as Aristotle identified at *Rhetoric* 3.10.2.[9] Metaphor therefore both illustrates and seeks to promote a particular interpretative response.[10] As will become evident in the next chapter, it is a particular favourite of some of Adams' successors to the US presidency when communicating on security issues.

Rhetoric as preparation for public life

For Adams, at least, much of Classical rhetorical theory was still of relevance and utility to contemporary orators. What about today's budding public communicators? It may be no coincidence that Harvard still teaches a lecture course devoted to rhetoric.[11] In line with the practice of studying examples advocated by Cicero and Quintilian, it focuses on analysing the speeches of great men and women, and has as its objective not only understanding the theory (rhetoric), but also training students to write and deliver speeches in practice (oratory).

The modern Harvard course exhibits other Classical features. It divides oratory into three types: judicial, deliberative, and epideictic. It introduces students to the Classical division of oratorical activity into invention, arrangement, style, memory, and delivery. It highlights the three modes of appeal, *logos, ethos*, and *pathos*. It encourages students to recognise the same tropes and schemes (figures) used in Ancient Greece and Rome. It breaks speeches down into five parts: *exordium, narratio, confirmatio, refutatio*, and *peroratio*.

Western elites continue to receive instruction in rhetorical principles that are overwhelmingly Classical in origin. At the time of writing (late 2020), the UK has a Prime Minister who read Classics at Oxford, and who professes to have a particular fondness for the fifth century BCE orator Pericles.[12] As recent media coverage has highlighted, a Classical education would have been compulsory for all the boys who were to become Prime Minister until the appointment of David Lloyd George in 1916. Until the nineteenth century, all UK students reading for a liberal arts degree studied both logic and rhetoric.

In 1920 the University of Oxford introduced the degree of Philosophy, Politics and Economics (PPE) as a more 'modern' alternative to Greats (*Literae Humaniores*), the traditional Classics degree. PPE is remarkable for its role in the education of many of the UK's ruling elite, including Prime Ministers, a host of cabinet ministers, party leaders, and political journalists, not to mention world leaders such as Bill Clinton, Benazir Bhutto, and Aung San Suu Kyi.[13] To this day, all first year PPE students are required to study the logic of argument, while Plato and Aristotle are on the curriculum as options for the second and third years.

Among the intellectual skills the course seeks to develop are the ability to

> recognise the logical structure of an argument, and assess its validity, to assess critically the arguments presented by others, and by oneself, and to identify methodological errors, rhetorical devices, unexamined conventional wisdom, unnoticed assumptions, vagueness and superficiality; construct and articulate sound arguments with clarity and precision; engage in debate with others, to formulate and consider the best arguments for different views and to identify the weakest elements of the most persuasive views.[14]

The *de facto* course of choice for the UK government is grounded in the principles of Classical rhetorical theory as outlined by Aristotle, Cicero, and Quintilian. Moreover, the Oxford tutorial system for humanities and social science students is a kind of oratorical performance. Students read out their essays to their tutors, who then raise questions and objections, in an arrangement not dissimilar to the presentation of narrative (*narratio*), proof (*confirmatio*), and counter-argument (*refutatio*) in Classical forensic oratory.

At least in the UK and US, twenty-first-century political elites are trained to present information in a way that conforms with Classical rhetorical theory, and to recognise others' deployment of these constructions. The system elaborated by Aristotle, Cicero, and Quintilian is therefore both the craft itself (*techne*) and a tool for deciphering the skill and persuasive aims of public discourse. Turning specifically to discourse with issues of (in)security at its centre, it is likewise possible to discern commonality of imagery, devices, and effects down the ages.

Augustan security rhetoric – bigger, further, great again

Just as Western rhetorical theory and oratorical practice have their origins in Athens and Rome, so too we may find ancient parallels for public communication on issues of safety and security. Among these are *The Deeds of the Divine Augustus* (*Res Gestae Divi Augusti*), an account of the first emperor's achievements published after his death in 14 CE. The *Res Gestae* takes the form of a eulogy (*elogium*) customarily delivered at a funeral. Although it was written down – and indeed published all over the empire as monumental inscriptions – the words are a direct first-person address to Roman citizens. Crucially, they reflect how Augustus wanted Roman citizens to remember him, and we may reasonably conclude that he deliberately chose to include some matters, and exclude others. Security, specifically foreign policy, occupies 20 of the 35 chapters. Among the highlights of his reign, the emperor celebrates the closure of the doors to the temple of Janus Quirinus (*RGDA* 13):[15]

> It was the will of our ancestors that the gateway of Janus Quirinus should be shut when victories had secured peace by land and sea throughout the whole

> empire of the Roman people; from the foundation of the city down to my birth, tradition records that it was shut only twice, but while I was the leading citizen the senate resolved that it should be shut on three occasions.

As the emperor explains, the doors to the temple of Janus Quirinus were closed only when there was peace across the empire. Here we see a recurring feature of the account of Augustus' achievements in this text, namely the assertion that he was bigger and better, and went further than his predecessors. In fact, the name conferred on the emperor in 27 BCE reflects this preoccupation. Augustus is derived from the verb *augere*, meaning to grow or increase. It may be no coincidence, then, that the emperor uses this word to describe his extension of empire (26):

> I extended [*auxi*] the territory of all those provinces of the Roman people on whose borders lay peoples not subject to our government. I brought peace to the Gallic and Spanish provinces as well as to Germany, throughout the area bordering on the Ocean from Cadiz to the mouth of the Elbe. I secured the pacification of the Alps from the district nearest the Adriatic to the Tuscan sea, yet without waging an unjust war on any people. My fleet sailed through the Ocean eastwards from the mouth of the Rhine to the territory of the Cimbri, a country which no Roman had visited before either by land or sea, and the Cimbri, Charydes, Semnones and other German peoples of that region sent ambassadors and sought my friendship and that of the Roman people.

The emperor wants citizens and posterity to know that his foreign policy actions were bigger, more extensive, and unprecedented: hence the land of the Cimbri is pointedly "a country which no Roman had visited before either by land or sea" (*quo neque terra neque mari quisquam Romanus ante id tempus adit*). The territory of the Pannonians (modern Austria and Hungary) is likewise described as that "which no army of the Roman people had ever penetrated before my principate" (30). Embassies from India are listed as "a thing never seen before in the camp of any general of the Romans" (31).

At the same time, we see the language of restoration. In military terms, this is seen in the recovery of provinces previously lost (27):

> I recovered [*reciperavi*] all the provinces beyond the Adriatic Sea towards the east, together with Cyrene, the greater part of them being then occupied by kings. I had previously recovered Sicily and Sardinia which had been seized in the slave war.

Also in the recovery of lost military standards (29):

> By victories over enemies I recovered [*recepi*] in Spain and in Gaul, and from the Dalmatians several standards lost by other commanders. I compelled the Parthians to restore to me [*reddere*] the spoils and standards of three Roman

armies and to ask as suppliants for the friendship of the Roman people. Those standards I deposited in the innermost shrine of the Temple of Mars Avenger.

We see the recurrent use of the language of safe return in chapters 11 and 12 of the *RGDA*:

> The Senate consecrated the altar of Fortuna Redux before the temples of Honour and Virtue at the Porta Capena in honour of my return, and it ordered that the *pontifices* and Vestal virgins should make an annual sacrifice there on the anniversary of my return to the city from Syria in the consulship of Quintus Lucretius and Marcus Vinucius, and it named the day the Augustalia from my *cognomen*.
>
> In accordance with the will of the senate some of the praetors and tribunes of the plebs with the consul Quintus Lucretius and the leading men were sent to Campania to meet me, an honour that up to the present day has been decreed to no one besides myself. On my return from Spain and Gaul in the consulship of Tiberius Nero and Publius Quintilius after successfully arranging affairs in those provinces, the senate resolved that an altar of the Augustan Peace should be consecrated next to the Campus Martius in honour of my return, and ordered that the magistrates and priests and Vestal virgins should perform an annual sacrifice there.

In the Latin, the effect of the *re*-prefix is more pronounced, emphasising return and restoration (emphasis added):

> Aram Fortunae ***Red***ucis ante aedes Honoris et Virtutis ad portam Capenam pro ***red***itu meo senatus consacravit, in qua pontifices et virgines Vestales anniversarium sacrificium facere iussit eo die quo, consulibus Q. Lucretio et M. Vinicio, in urbem ex Syria ***red***ieram, et diem Augustalia ex cognomine nostro appellavit.
>
> Ex senatus auctoritate pars praetorum et tribunorum plebi cum consule Q. Lucretio et principibus viris obviam mihi missa est in Campaniam, qui honos ad hoc tempus nemini praeter me est decretus. Cum ex Hispania Galliaque, rebus in iis provincis prospere gestis, Romam ***redi***, Ti. Nerone P. Quintilio consulibus, aram Pacis Augustae senatus pro ***red***itu meo consacrandam censuit ad campum Martium, in qua magistratus et sacerdotes virginesque Vestales anniversarium sacrificium facere iussit.

The consecration of the new altar to Fortune Restored [*Fortuna Redux*] is included here as a highlight for Augustus. Without wanting to stretch a comparison to modern political discourse too far, he is seeking to demonstrate that he has made Rome secure, peaceful, great again. As the personality who brought an end to the civil wars of the first century BCE, Augustus could feel justified in making that claim. He was by no means the last of the emperors to do so.

Nero – coinage as security messaging, security as performance

In the Ancient World, the issue of coinage was a form of public address. Roman emperors minted coins that very often featured a portrait of themselves on one side (the obverse) and a symbolic representation of a deity or anthropomorphised virtue on the other (the reverse). We may read the visual messages on these coins as rhetorical: just as the *Res Gestae* of Augustus, they present the emperor directly to citizens as he would like to be seen.[16] The coinage of the Emperor Nero (54–68 CE) is considered among the highest quality in aesthetic terms, with the emperor himself believed to have had a direct hand in choosing its themes.[17]

In the years 64 and 65 CE, Rome witnessed two events that posed significant threats to its national (urban and imperial) security. The first was a fire at Rome, during which the biographer Suetonius reports that Nero performed his poem on the fall of Troy: this is the likely origin of the saying that Nero "fiddled while Rome burned".[18] The second key security event was the failure of the Pisonian conspiracy to depose and murder the emperor. Nero chooses these two years of marked insecurity for the empire to issue coinage featuring security (*Securitas*) personified as a woman seated and at ease, and the temple of Janus Quirinus with doors closed.

While not the earliest appearance of *Securitas* personified on the coinage that survives, Nero's issues are considered to be the first consistent campaign to communicate the notion of security in this format.[19] For both the coins struck at Rome and at Lyon, numismatists see in the text *Securitas Augusti* and the depiction of the personified *Securitas* allusions to the personal safety of the emperor and the security of his reign, also to material security in the form of the *securitas annonae*, the corn supply.[20] Theorists engaged in tracking the securitisation of non-military concerns may be interested to note that food securitisation is by no means an entirely modern phenomenon.

Based on what we know of the historical events surrounding the issue of this coinage, it is reasonable to assert that Nero is attempting to persuade his citizens of a certain level of safety and security, to reassure them that security has been preserved, or at least restored. Later variants of this type issued by Galba, Otho, and Vitellius during the civil war of 69 CE, the "year of the four emperors" that followed Nero's murder, suggest a similar motivation. Galba, Nero's immediate successor, changes the legend from *Securitas Augusti*, with a focus on the emperor's personal security, to *Securitas P[opuli] R[omani]*, with a focus on the security of the Roman people.[21] The new message is that the new emperor acts for the benefit of all, not just his own. His successor Otho issues coins with the same slogan. Coinage issued in the name of Otho's successor Vitellius bears the legend *Securitas Imp. German.* – "the security of the emperor by will of the armies of the German provinces" – in reference to the support he received from the military.

As Tacitus recalls in his *Histories* (1.3), this time was one of profound insecurity for the citizens of Rome:[22]

> Yet this age was not so barren of virtue that it did not display noble examples. Mothers accompanied their children in flight; wives followed their husbands into exile; relatives displayed courage, sons-in-law firmness, slaves a fidelity which defied even torture. Eminent men met the last necessity with fortitude, rivalling in their end the glorious deaths of antiquity. Besides the manifold misfortunes that befell mankind, there were prodigies in the sky and on the earth, warnings given by thunderbolts, and prophecies of the future, both joyful and gloomy, uncertain and clear. For never was it more fully proved by awful disasters of the Roman people or by indubitable signs that the gods care not for our safety [*securitatem nostram*], but for our punishment.

In the years 66 to 68 CE, *salus* (safety, or perhaps well-being) emerges as a coin type and legend. This also is seen as linked to Nero's personal safety, particularly his recovery from the Pisonian conspiracy, not least because Tacitus records Nero's dedication of a temple to Salus at this time (*Annals* 15.74).[23] During the subsequent civil war, legends on coinage not attributable to an individual emperor or general align Safety with Freedom [*Salus et Libertas*] and again mark a shift from the personal safety of the emperor to the safety of humankind [*Salus Generis Humani*]. This latter type is issued also in the name of Galba.[24]

Given their context, these highly aspirational proclamations of, or appeals to, security and safety accentuate the very present insecurity and lack of public safety.[25] We are reminded of Dillon's etymological analysis of security as a negative concept, as the state of being free from care in Latin (*securus*), and an absence of unsteadiness (*asphaleia*) in Greek.[26] Since the aim of Roman coinage of the 60s CE appears to be to persuade citizens that they are safe and secure, we may reasonably conclude that a good number of them – the elite and governing family included – did not feel so. We may even feel there is reason to suspect that it is precisely at times of insecurity that governments are prompted to make assurances of security.

Pliny (Trajan): security restored as distancing device

Following Vespasian's successful claim to power in 69 CE, his Flavian dynasty ruled for nearly 30 years. Vespasian's sons Titus (79–81 CE) and Domitian (81–96 CE) ruled after him. In the subsequent historical and literary tradition, the latter has come to be known along with Nero as one of the "bad" emperors. Following his murder, his memory was condemned (*damnatio memoriae*). This process expunged all traces of Domitian's name and achievements from public records, with an effect converse to that of Augustus' *Res Gestae*. Prominent Romans subjected to *damnatio memoriae* lost the right to any kind of control over their own posterity, and the opportunity to persuade the public posthumously.

New regimes have a tendency to distance themselves from old regimes. The elderly emperor Nerva succumbed to ill health just two years after his appointment by those who had conspired to depose Domitian. He had adopted Trajan as his son and successor a year previously (97 CE), thereby ensuring a comparatively smooth transition of power for the period. Pliny the Younger was among those to serve in his government. In addition to an extraordinary collection of letters between the emperor and Pliny that are important sources for our understanding of government machinery at the turn of the second century CE, Pliny also left us an expanded version of the speech he delivered to give thanks to the emperor on his appointment as consul in 100 CE, under the title *Panegyricus.*

As in the case of the *Res Gestae*, the *Panegyricus* takes its origin from funeral orations, and in the sense that it is written by someone other than the subject it is more typical of the genre. From the perspective of Classical rhetorical theory, panegyric sits firmly within Aristotle's definition of epideictic or demonstrative oratory, namely to deliver praise or blame. In fact, Pliny's speech performs both of these functions. Throughout, Domitian's blameworthy qualities and actions are set against Trajan's praiseworthy record. Specifically, the fear, tyranny, and servitude characteristic of the past are contrasted with the security, safety, and freedom of the present. Pliny refers to Trajan's adoption by Nerva as "the basis of no servitude for us, but of security [*securitas*], happiness [or perhaps safety, *salus*], and freedom [*libertas*]" (*Panegyricus* 8.1). At this point, "every disturbance died away at once" (8.5).

The entire speech may be identified as an extended exercise in antithesis, between then and now (44.5):[27]

> No one could imagine it easy for any comer to repeat a situation where no one need purchase security by disgrace, where everyone's life is safe and safe with honour, where foresight and prudence no longer prompt men to spend a lifetime keeping out of sight.

The historical and rhetorical other, the damned Domitian, stands for fear and tyranny. He is repeatedly rejected and contrasted with Trajan:

> Away, then, with expressions formerly prompted by fear: I will have none of them … Nowhere should we flatter him as a divinity and a god; we are talking of a fellow-citizen, not a tyrant, one who is our father not our over-lord.
>
> (2.2–3)

Tyranny as emblematic of "bad" government harks back to the schools of rhetoric, where The Cruel Tyrant was a stock topic of declamation satirised by Juvenal (*Satires* 7.151 above).[28] Antithetical arrangement, meanwhile, is an established figure of Classical rhetorical theory. What modern audiences would hear as antithetical is divided into two ancient devices. The first, *antítheton*, denotes something of a narrower application, according to Quintilian (*Inst.Or.*9.3.81ff.): "The antithesis may be between single words, as in the passage quoted above, 'Lust prevailed over shame, rashness over fear'; between pairs of words as in 'not a matter of my talent, but of your aid'; or between sentence and sentence, as in 'Let it dominate in the assemblies, but collapse in the courts.'" A broader application, *alloiosis*, literally "othering", "points out the differences between persons, things, and actions" (*Inst.*

*Or.*9.3.91). In the *Panegyricus* it serves as a distancing mechanism, the sharp contrast widening the space between Domitian's record and that of Trajan. Antithesis also serves to simplify complex information: as S. R. Slings puts it, it is a "chunking device", used "to ensure that the information packaged in a clause or sentence does not become so dense as to obstruct its successful processing by a listener".[29]

Pliny goes on to characterise the entire age in terms of security: "Such is our prince's goodness of heart, such the security of our times [*securitas temporum*], that he believes us worthy of princely possessions and we have no fears about seeming so" (*Panegyricus* 50.7). In yet another antithetical construction, material security is contrasted with the material collapse of earlier times: "The walls and roofs in the city have stopped shuddering as they did at the passage of huge blocks of stone; our houses stand safe and secure, and the temples are no longer threatened with collapse" (51.1). The restoration of good order and public safety is also tied to the personal safety of the emperor.[30] Pliny's closing *exordium* gives pride of place to issues of safety and security. He calls on the gods as follows (94.2–3):

> We are not burdening you with vows - we do not pray for peace, concord, and serenity [*securitatem*], nor for wealth and honours: our desire is simple, all-embracing, and unanimous: the safety of our prince [*salus principis*]. This is no new concern we ask of you, for it was you who took him under your protection [*tutelam*] when you snatched him from the jaws of that monster of rapacity; for at the time when all the peaks were tottering to their fall, no one could have stood high above them all and remained untouched except by your intervention.

The gods protect the emperor, so that the emperor can protect his citizens. It is an early form of social contract, conditional on the good conduct of the emperor (67.3–5):

> We were accustomed to offering vows to ensure the eternity of the empire and the safety of the emperors, or, rather, the safety of the emperors and thereby the eternity of the empire. But in the case of our present emperor, it is worth noting the wording of these vows, and the clause "if he has ruled the State well and in the interests of all." Such vows are indeed worthy of being always renewed and always discharged. At your instigation, Caesar, the State has struck a bargain with the gods that they shall preserve your health and safety as long as you do the same for everyone else; otherwise they are to turn their attention from protecting your life, and to abandon you to such vows as are taken in secret.

Earlier in the speech, Pliny reports that when Trajan entered the city of Rome in 99 CE, the sick had dragged themselves out of bed in the belief that they could be healed (*quasi ad salutem sanitatemque prorepere*, 22.3). The emperor is therefore depicted as personally, as well as nationally, restorative: "everyone's prayers were for your safety alone, since each man knew they would be answered for himself and his children if they were granted for you" (23.5); "So prompt is your power, Caesar, so prepared and ready for all alike your goodness of heart [*bonitas*], that if any of your subjects suffers misfortune he has only to tell you to find help and security in you" (30.5). Trajan is a good man, in contrast to Domitian the madman (*demens*, 33.4) and fearful monster (*immanissima belua*, 48.3), who "licked up the blood of his murdered relatives". Metaphor and hyperbole in the depiction of the past serve to heighten the collective sense of relief towards the regime of the present.

Liberty has been restored (*redditae libertatis*, 58.3). This, too, is dependent on the emperor, and contrasts with the dominance of fear in the Domitianic era (66.4):

> You bid us be free, and we shall be free; you tell us to express ourselves openly, and we shall do so, for our previous hesitation was due to no cowardice or natural inertia, but to fear and apprehension, and the lamentable caution born of our perils which bade us turn eyes and ears and minds from our country, from that republic which was utterly destroyed.

The alignment of fear with peril here sets up a further opposition between danger and security, and echoes a scene imagined earlier in the speech (48.1):

> And you yourself - awaiting and receiving everyone in person - devote a large part of every day to so many cares of State, while preserving the unhurried atmosphere of a life of leisure. So we gather round you, no longer pale and terrified, slow of step as if in peril of our lives [*periculum capitis*], but carefree [*securi*] and happy, coming when it suits us.

In this context, we see *securitas* in its range of meanings: freedom from care, freedom from fear, and a leisurely attitude that is mirrored by the emperor despite his attendance to the business of government (*inter tot imperii curas*).

In the final words of the speech, Pliny says of himself that "in bad times I was one of those who lived with grief and fear, and can be counted among the serene [*securos*] and happy now that better days have come" (95.4). Bad versus good, fearful versus secure: security has become an explicitly rhetorical tool in imperial ideology. The terror and tyranny of the past is a constant presence. In a social and political context where the listeners had lived in fear for their lives, the deployment of fear as counterpoint here plays on personal experience to heighten emotion, and in turn works to heighten the feeling of relief at the rule of a "good prince" (*bonus princeps*, 26.5, 27.1):

> Above all, you are a prince whose reign makes it both pleasure and profit to rear children. No father now need fear more for his son than the hazards of human frailty - among fatal illnesses he need not count his emperor's wrath. There is indeed great encouragement to have children in the promise of allowances [*in spem alimentorum*] and donations [*in spem congiariorum*], but greater still when there is hope of security and freedom from fear [*in spem libertatis, in spem securitatis*].

The repetition of *spem*, "hope", completes the emotional transformation, converting traumatised survivors into engaged and productive citizens once more. For the translator of the *Panegyricus* and Pliny's letters, Betty Radice, the depiction of the emperor in this speech is "skilful propaganda, a subtle blend of fact and 'wishful thinking', a tactful way of telling Trajan what his grateful subjects would have him be".[31] Coinage of the period indicates also that Security, Liberty Restored and Good Fortune were motifs with which the emperor wanted to be seen to be associated.[32] To this degree, then, Pliny is not merely giving the customary thanks to Trajan, but speaking on his behalf, presenting his manifesto.[33]

The insecurity of everyday life: Juvenal and urban danger

A rather different narrative from a near contemporary of Pliny challenges the panegyrical representation of the Roman empire at the turn of the second century CE as free from fear and danger. Juvenal's third satire begins:

> Quamvis digressu veteris confusus amici
> laudo tamen, vacuis quod sedem figere Cumis
> destinet atque unum civem donare Sibyllae.
> ianua Baiarum est et gratum litus amoeni
> secessus. ego vel Prochytam praepono Suburae;
> nam quid tam miserum, tam solum vidimus, ut non
> deterius credas horrere incendia, lapsus
> tectorum adsiduos ac mille pericula saevae
> Vrbis et Augusto recitantes mense poetas?

> Although I'm distressed at the departure of my old friend, all the same I approve of his decision to establish his home at empty Cumae and to donate a single fellow-citizen to the Sibyl. It's the gateway to Baiae, a lovely coast, delightfully secluded. Personally, I would prefer even Prochyta to the Subura. After all, have you seen any place so dismal and lonely that you wouldn't consider it worse to live in dread of fires, and buildings collapsing continually, and the thousand other dangers of savage Rome - and poets reciting in the month of August?

The savage city of Rome (*saevae Vrbis*, 8f.) presents a thousand dangers (*mille pericula*, 8) in addition to material collapse and ruin. The imagery used figuratively by Pliny to refer to the integrity and security of the empire, is here actual and has apparently prompted a resident to abandon the city.

In these opening lines, we see the use of several rhetorical features that have come to be associated with Juvenal's satire. There is antithesis in the contrast of city and country life, made more pointed by the depiction of Cumae as empty (*vacuis*, 2) and the coast as secluded (*secessus*, 5). The figure turns on the speaker's claim that they would prefer a small island in the Bay of Naples (Prochyta, now Procida, 5) to the busiest street in Rome (the Subura, 5). Second person singular direct address to the audience (*credas*, 7) and a lengthy rhetorical question draw each individual listener/reader into both the scene and the predicament. Hyperbole is deployed not only by means of the speaker's identification of a thousand dangers, but also of material collapse at Rome as continuous (*adsiduos*). The repetition of *tam* (6) builds a sense of urgency, while *horrere* (more literally to bristle, to tremble or to quake, 7[34]) builds fear. The question and imagery build ... but to an anti-climax. The bathetic closing representation of sweltering summer poetry recitals where we would expect to see the least tolerable of Rome's inconveniences dispels the tension, reminding us that this is not the loftiest of speeches. This is satire. But of what, and of whom?

Comparatively little is known about Juvenal outside of the *Satires*, his only extant work. He is identified as having been active in the reigns of Trajan and Hadrian. Writing in hexameters, the traditional meter of Roman verse satire, Juvenal's work is known for its "grand style" and its extensively rhetorical quality.[35] E. J. Kenney goes so far as to say that the rhetoric of Rome's declamation schools was Juvenal's idiom.[36] The rhetorical devices deployed in the 16 *Satires* that survive are instantly recognisable as those itemised by Cicero and Quintilian, and it has been suggested that he was a student of the latter.[37] Juvenal is a master of the pithy slogan (*sententia*), so much so that several of his maxims are still in use today. When we snidely quip that all the mob cares about is bread and circuses, and counsel that all we should wish for is a healthy mind in a healthy body, these are direct translations of phrases in Juvenal's tenth satire: *panem et circenses* (10.81); *mens sana in corpore sano* (10.356). When those of us who conduct research on security and privacy issues caution "But who will guard the guards themselves?", this too is a quotation from Juvenal, in this case from his sixth satire (*sed quis custodiet ipsos custodes*, 6.O31f.).

Scrutinising poetry for evidence of security rhetoric may at first seem something of a strange undertaking. But while these are not the words of a government or other official, Juvenal's *Satires* constitute public discourse in a number of important respects. First, poetry was performed, recited by the poet to select and suitably cultured audiences. As John Henderson has observed,[38] Juvenal signals this performance by opening his work in the recitation hall itself (*Satire* 1.1–6):

> Semper ego auditor tantum? numquamne reponam
> vexatus totiens rauci Theseide Cordi?
> inpune ergo mihi recitaverit ille togatas,
> hic elegos? inpune diem consumpserit ingens
> Telephus aut summi plena iam margine libri
> scriptus et in tergo necdum finitus Orestes?

> Shall I always be stuck in the audience? Never retaliate for being tortured so often by hoarse Cordus' Song of Theseus? Let them get away with it, then? - this one reciting to me his Roman comedies and that one his love elegies? Let them get away with wasting my whole day on an enormous Telephus, or an Orestes written on the back when the margin at the end of the book is already full - and still not finished?

Second, there is evidence that Romans read aloud, even to themselves. As such, poetry retained an aspect of performance long after its first publication. This performative quality is intensified by the influence on Juvenal's work of rhetorical instruction, and specifically the declamation schools of the late first century CE. Last, Juvenal's subject matter is contemporary morality. Social commentary necessarily has a public dimension in a way that, for instance, love poetry does not (or not always).[39] Keeping in mind at all times that the satirist's voice and the voices of others who speak in these poems are distinct from the historical Juvenal, we can state that the *Satires* represent the city and empire of Rome to some degree. In the words of Anderson, "If, then, we think of Juvenal's *Satires* as poetic equivalents of epideictic oratory, which aim at *vituperatio urbis* [censure of the city, or perhaps urban censure], we are likely to reach a closer approximation of his literary effect."[40]

Like Pliny, Juvenal's speaker looks back to Domitian's reign as a truly negative *exemplum* of tyrannical rule, most notably in his fourth satire, which depicts in a mock-epic style the responses of Domitian's court to the landing of a monstrously large fish. In his first satire, he sets out his programme for writing, and for choosing satire over other genres (1.45–61):

> quid referam quanta siccum iecur ardeat ira,
> cum populum gregibus comitum premit hic spoliator
> pupilli prostantis et hic damnatus inani
> iudicio? quid enim salvis infamia nummis?
> exul ab octava Marius bibit et fruitur dis
> iratis, at tu victrix, provincia, ploras.
> haec ego non credam Venusina digna lucerna?
> haec ego non agitem? sed quid magis? Heracleas
> aut Diomedeas aut mugitum labyrinthi
> et mare percussum puero fabrumque volantem,
> cum leno accipiat moechi bona, si capiendi
> ius nullum uxori, doctus spectare lacunar,
> doctus et ad calicem vigilanti stertere naso;
> cum fas esse putet curam sperare cohortis
> qui bona donavit praesepibus et caret omni
> maiorum censu, dum pervolat axe citato
> Flaminiam puer Automedon?

Why should I describe the immense rage burning in my fevered guts, when the people are intimidated by the herds that follow someone who's defrauded his ward and reduced him to prostitution, and someone else who's been found guilty in a meaningless verdict? After all, what's disgrace, if their money is safe? Marius in exile starts his boozing in the afternoon and savours the anger of the gods, while you, Province, the winner of the case, are in tears. These outrages - can't I think they merit the Venusian lamp? These outrages - can't I have a go at them? What would be better, then? - stories of Heracles or Diomedes or the bellowing in the labyrinth and the sea hit by a boy and the flying workman? - when a pimping husband accepts his wife's lover's gifts, if she's not entitled to inherit, an expert at watching the ceiling, an expert, too, at snoring over his goblet with a wide-awake nose? - when someone who's lavished his wealth on the stables, who's gone through his entire family fortune, thinks he's entitled to aspire to the command of a cohort, all the while racing his chariot along the Flaminian Way at top speed, a boy Automedon?

The speaker reveals himself to be an angry urban moralist. He states his motivation plainly at 1.79: *facit indignatio versum*; literally, "indignation makes the verse". As Henderson and others have noted, this indignant attitude was a stock feature of Roman rhetorical and declamatory training.[41] But we do not need to take his word for it. We can hear his anger in his style. Multiple rhetorical questions pile on multiple illustrative *exempla* to express both the volume of the outrages confronted and the speaker's frustrated desperation at them.[42] They are also direct appeals to the audience to engage with each outrage individually and in their totality. Repetition of *haec ego* at the beginnings of lines 51 and 52 is the verbal equivalent of lectern thumping for emphasis, drawing the listener-reader's attention to contemporary vice, and heightening the antithesis with the mythological subject matter of epic poetry. Disdainfully metonymic representations of the latter add to the antithetical effect: the story of Theseus and the Minotaur is summarised as "the bellowing [or 'mooing'] in the labyrinth" (53), that of Daedalus and Icarus as "the sea hit by a boy and the flying workman" (54).

In contrast to Greek myth, the canvas for Juvenal's poetry is the city streets of Rome. In line 60f. the scene is the main road North out of the city. Just a couple of lines later, we find the speaker himself at street level (1.63–8):

nonne licet medio ceras implere capaces
quadrivio, cum iam sexta cervice feratur
hinc atque inde patens ac nuda paene cathedra
et multum referens de Maecenate supino
signator falsi, qui se lautum atque beatum
exiguis tabulis et gemma fecerit uda?

Surely I'm allowed to fill a roomy notebook while standing at the crossroads, when an accessory to fraud is carried past on as many as six necks already, exposed to view on this side and that, in his almost naked litter, strongly recalling the languid Maecenas, someone who's turned himself into a wealthy toff with a brief document and a moistened signet ring?

Street level is also where we find the speaker of the majority of the third satire. After setting the scene in the first 20 lines of the poem, the satirist's voice gives way to that of his friend Umbricius. It is Umbricius, whose name means something like "Shady", and conjures ancient associations with notions of pastoral leisure and freedom from care – security in its most literal meaning – but also of the ghosts (*umbrae*) of Romans and Roman-ness past.[43] Since the early twentieth century, Latinists have sought meaning in Juvenal's tasking of this monologue to a character distinct from his authorial voice. So Braund notes that "this distinction … encourages an objective scrutiny of Umbricius and his motives", and asks: "perhaps the city is not as entirely bad as Umbricius depicts it if the speaker can bear to remain behind?"[44]

Whatever the import of the distinction between "Juvenal" and Umbricius, there is some consistency in their subject matter and style of presentation. The references made by the authorial voice to fires, material collapse, and the dangers of Rome prefigure Umbricius' more detailed descriptions. Three episodes highlight the dangers for Romans, particularly those of modest means. In the first, Umbricius constructs a narrative of destruction by fire around a number of antitheses (3.190–214):

> Quis timet aut timuit gelida Praeneste ruinam
> aut positis nemorosa inter iuga Volsiniis aut
> simplicibus Gabiis aut proni Tiburis arce?
> nos Vrbem colimus tenui tibicine fultam
> magna parte sui; nam sic labentibus obstat
> vilicus et, veteris rimae cum texit hiatum,
> **securos** pendente iubet dormire ruina.
> vivendum est illic, ubi nulla incendia, nulli
> nocte metus. iam poscit aquam, iam frivola transfert
> Vcalegon, tabulata tibi iam tertia fumant:
> tu nescis; nam si gradibus trepidatur ab imis,
> ultimus ardebit quem tegula sola tuetur
> a pluvia, molles ubi reddunt ova columbae.
> lectus erat Cordo Procula minor, urceoli sex
> ornamentum abaci, nec non et parvulus infra
> centaurus recubans ab eodem marmore Chiron,
> iamque vetus Graecos servabat cista libellos
> et divina opici rodebant carmina mures.
> nil habuit Cordus, quis enim negat? et tamen illud
> perdidit infelix totum nihil. ultimus autem
> aerumnae cumulus, quod nudum et frusta rogantem
> nemo cibo, nemo hospitio tectoque iuvabit.
> si magna Assaraci cecidit domus, horrida mater,
> pullati proceres, differt vadimonia praetor.
> tum gemimus casus Vrbis, tunc odimus ignem.

> Has anyone now or in the past dreaded collapsing buildings at cool Praeneste or at Volsinii among its wooded hills or at simple Gabii or on the hilltop of sloping Tibur? We inhabit a Rome for the most part supported by thin props. After all, that's how the agent blocks the buildings from falling down. Once he's covered a gaping ancient crack, he tells us to not to worry, as we sleep in

> a building on the point of collapse. The ideal place to live is without fires and panics in the night. Ucalegon is already shouting "Fire!" He's already moving out his odds and ends, and the third floor where you live is already smoking. But you don't know anything about it. After all, if the alarm is raised at the bottom of the stairs, the person protected from the rain by only a little roof tile - where the gentle doves produce their eggs - will be the last to burn. Cordus' possessions were: a bed too small for Procula, six small jugs to decorate his sideboard, and, underneath, a little centaur, Chiron, made from the same "marble," and a box, by now ancient, which kept his little Greek books safe - and the philistine mice were gnawing the immortal poems. Cordus had nothing, who'd disagree? And yet the wretched man lost that entire "nothing." But the crowning point of his misery is that no one will help him with food or hospitality or shelter when he's naked and begging for scraps. If the grand mansion of Assaracus has been destroyed, then his mother is in mourning and the nobles are in black and the praetor adjourns his hearings. That's when we lament the disasters of Rome and that's when we detest its fires.

Familiar rhetorical devices are at work here. Questions encourage listener-readers to consider their potential responses, to engage directly with the scene and its themes. The listener-reader is not only addressed directly, but in this episode becomes a character at risk: "the third floor where *you* live is already smoking. But *you* don't know anything about it" (*tibi … tu*, 199f.). Repetition hammers home the antitheses. The ideal place to live is where there are *no* fires, *no* fears at night (*nulla incendia, nulli nocte metus*, 197f.). Repetition of the Latin word for "nothing", *nihil* – or *nil* in its contracted form – frames a paradoxical and hyperbolical image of theft of even that nothing, which in turn serves to heighten our impression of Cordus' misfortune. There is recurrent extremity of experience in the repetition of *ultimus*, denoting both the apartment at the top of the stairs that will be the last to burn (201), and the peak of poor Cordus' misery (209). Negation is repeated for emphasis again at 211. No one (*nemo*) will help Cordus with food, no one with shelter. A further opposition is established with *tum* and *tunc* in 214 in relation the destruction of Assaracus' mansion: it's *then* we complain about disasters; it's *then* we hate fire (you, too).

Throughout this section of the poem, the language of fear is a constant presence. Umbricius encourages us to think of out-of-town locations like Praeneste as places where inhabitants need have no fear of collapse (*quis timet aut timuit*, 190), where there is no nightly panic (*nocte metus*, 198). By implication, fear is the correct response to material insecurity at Rome. When the landlord tells residents not to worry – literally, "he bids us sleep free from care in a hanging ruin" (*securos*, 196) – it is clear that this is a false sense of security. *Securitas* in the sense of freedom from care is called out expressly to be challenged by the prevalence and enormity of urban danger: in the Latin, the opposing *securos* and *ruina* frame both the clause and the line. Juvenal/Umbricius borrows the name Ucalegon from Virgil's description of the fall of Troy in his epic poem the *Aeneid*: along with other echoes of epic poetry in these lines, this echo triggers a sensation of catastrophic destruction.[45]

After a characteristically hyperbolical treatment of noise at night that includes the memorable maxims (*sententiae*) "Here at Rome very many invalids die from insomnia" (*Plurimus hic aeger moritur vigilando*, 232) and "You have to be very rich to get sleep in Rome" (*magnis opibus dormitur in Vrbe*, 235), Umbricius moves to his second set piece, a street scene filled with pedestrian and vehicular traffic (239–248):

si vocat officium, turba cedente vehetur
dives et ingenti curret super ora Liburna
atque obiter leget aut scribet vel dormiet intus
(namque facit somnum clausa lectica fenestra),
ante tamen veniet: nobis properantibus obstat
unda prior, magno populus premit agmine lumbos
qui sequitur; ferit hic cubito, ferit assere duro
alter, at hic tignum capiti incutit, ille metretam.
pinguia crura luto, planta mox undique magna
calcor, et in digito clavus mihi militis haeret.

If duty calls, the crowd gives way as the rich man is conveyed, racing along above their faces in his huge Liburnian galley, reading or writing on the way or sleeping inside (you know how a litter with its window closed brings on drowsiness). Yet he'll get there first. As I hurry along, the wave ahead gets in the way and the great massed ranks of people behind me crush my kidneys. One pokes me with his elbow, another with a hard pole. This guy bashes my head with a beam, that guy with a wine cask. My legs are caked with mud. Soon I'm trampled by mighty feet from every side and a soldier's hobnail sticks into my toe.

The description of the rich man's litter as a warship maintains the hyperbolical style. The crowd is accordingly a wave (*unda*, 244), but also a column of infantry (*magno ... agmine*). With the language of pitched battle, and the graphic image of a nail from a soldier's boot piercing the protagonist's toe, making one's way through the streets of Rome is likened to defending oneself against military onslaught.[46] A few lines later, the dominant images are of precarity, threat and oblivion in more than one sense (254–267):

scinduntur tunicae sartae modo, longa coruscat
serraco veniente abies, atque altera pinum
plaustra vehunt; nutant alte populoque minantur.
nam si procubuit qui saxa Ligustica portat
axis et eversum fudit super agmina montem,
quid superest de corporibus? quis membra, quis ossa
invenit? obtritum vulgo perit omne cadaver
more animae. domus interea **secura** patellas

iam lavat et bucca foculum excitat et sonat unctis
striglibus et pleno componit lintea guto.
haec inter pueros varie properantur, at ille
iam sedet in ripa taetrumque novicius horret
porthmea nec sperat caenosi gurgitis alnum
infelix nec habet quem porrigat ore trientem.

Tunics just recently mended are ripped. A long fir log judders as its waggon gets closer and another cart trundles a whole pine tree. They wobble threateningly way above the crowds. After all, if the axle that's transporting rocks from Liguria collapses and spills an upturned mountain on top of the masses, what will be left of the bodies? Who will be able to find any limbs or bones? Every corpse, crushed indiscriminately, will disappear, exactly like its soul. Meanwhile the household is oblivious. By this time they are washing the dishes and puffing at the embers with full cheeks, clattering the oily strigils, filling the oil flasks, and arranging the towels. The slave boys bustle around on these different tasks, but their master is already a newcomer sitting on the bank, shuddering at the hideous ferryman. The wretched man has no hopes of a bark across the muddy torrent, because he doesn't have a coin in his mouth to offer.

With further echoes of the language and motifs of epic poetry, once more of the fall of Troy in the second book of the *Aeneid*, also of an incident of death by crushing in Statius' more recent *Thebaid*, Umbricius describes the pulverisation of the victim of a traffic accident.[47] Again, the dominant device is hyperbole: the victim is not "just" crushed to death; every trace of him is extinguished. Antithesis once more heightens a contrast, this time between the horrific street scene and routine domesticity. While the scene indoors echoes the dramatic irony of preparations in Book 22 of Homer's *Iliad* for the bath of the dead Hector, use of the term *secura* for the ignorance of the household harks back to the Roman residents who were erroneously reassured earlier in the poem (196).

Following this episode, Umbricius asks us to "consider the various other dangers of the night" (*respice nunc alia ac diversa pericula noctis*, 268). He presents his examples in a characteristically expansive fashion (269–275):

quod spatium tectis sublimibus unde cerebrum
testa ferit, quotiens rimosa et curta fenestris
vasa cadant, quanto percussum pondere signent
et laedant silicem. possis ignavus haberi
et subiti casus improvidus, ad cenam si
intestatus eas: adeo tot fata, quot illa
nocte patent vigiles te praetereunte fenestrae.

What a long way it is from the high roofs for a tile to hit your skull! How often cracked and leaky pots tumble down from the windows! What a smash when they strike the pavement, marking and damaging it! You could be

> thought careless and unaware of what can suddenly befall if you go out to dinner without having made your will. As you pass by at night, there are precisely as many causes of death as there are open windows watching you.

The scale and frequency of danger is emphasised by the qu-antifying words here (*quod ... quotiens ... quanto ... quot*). Hyperbole is again in use in the assertion of the need to make a will before going out to dinner, and in the quantification of threats to life as the total of all the open windows in the city. Where the apartment block tenants and the household of the crushing victim earlier in the street scene are described as *securi* because they are unaware of impending or occurring disaster, here failure to provide for one's death is taken as a mark of carelessness and ignorance. By implication, the Roman who is prepared for daily and nightly life in the city lives in a constant state of alert to myriad dangers, and is prepared in advance, however sudden (*subiti*, 273) they may be. The contrasting alertness of the windows above (*vigiles ... fenestrae*, 275) does nothing to compensate for this fear, but rather contributes to the feeling of insecurity.[48]

The night-time scene reaches a satiric climax with the description of a mugging that draws heavily on epic imagery. The insomniac assailant is likened to Achilles in Book 24 of *The Iliad*, perhaps also to his son Pyrrhus, when he dispatches the elderly King Priam of Troy in Book 2 of *The Aeneid.* [49] These and multiple other echoes of epic poetic representations of heroic combat inflate the mugging threat and once more bring at least a distorted kind of war to the city's streets. Umbricius in the temporary role of moralising satirist gifted to him by the author seeks to convince us of both the magnitude and frequency of dangers at Rome.

Whether we believe him or not, Umbricius' overall strategy is one of threat inflation. This is not the rosy picture of freedom and security painted by Pliny. Despite authorial distance from the most graphic depictions in *Satire 3*, and the inclusion of bathetic material that goes some way to relieving the tension, the lasting impression – for a modern audience, at least – is that the Rome of Juvenal's time was a pretty dangerous place. In the second century CE, rhetorical features such as hyperbole, antithesis, repetition, and the involvement of individual listener-readers through direct address and questioning, are deployed to generate fear, and to heighten a sense of insecurity.

In fact, Juvenal's *Satires* are suffused with the notions of threat and precarity. Moralising satire seeks to uphold standards in the face of perceived onslaughts. The *Satires* abound not only with hyperbolical depictions of threats to life, but also threats to "our" (pure bred, Roman, male) way of life. While women, gay people, and immigrants are singled out for special treatment – *Satire* 3 is as much about the Greek "invasion" of Rome as about the perils of living in the city – moral degeneracy is the focus of much of Juvenal's work. In customarily amplificatory tone, the first, programmatic, satire sets out the author's position (1.147–149):

> Nil erit ulterius quod nostris moribus addat
> posteritas, eadem facient cupientque minores,
> omne in praecipiti vitium stetit.

> Posterity will have nothing to add to our ways: our descendants will do and desire exactly the same. All depravity is standing on the brink of the chasm.

Even the later, less vituperative, satires argue for the precarity of human existence. They emphasise the fickleness of good fortune, with shipwrecks, political downfall, loss of wealth, loss of youthful vigour all set to strike us down as suddenly as a flying chamber pot on an ill-lit street.

Where Pliny states in the *Panegyricus* that things are so much better now, Juvenal's speaker claims that things can't get any worse. Since the last century, commentators have sought to resolve the speaker's claim in the closing lines of the first satire, "I'll see what I can get away with saying against the people whose ashes are covered by the Flaminian and the Latin roads" (*experiar quid concedatur in illos/ quorum Flaminia tegitur cinis atque Latina*, 1.170f.), interpreting this statement as a climb down from satirising contemporary events and public figures. While Juvenalian satire does indeed fall short in respect of *ad hominem* attacks on externally identifiable contemporaries, and while some of the events depicted are clearly historical – *Satire* 4's dramatisation of the emperor Domitian's court among them – I would argue that at times we as listener-readers certainly *feel* like the dangerous city depicted in *Satire* 3 is immediate, and not that of a dim and distant past, or even a previous regime.

Analysis of the texts discussed above reveals the devices and tropes of which ancient (in)security rhetoric made use. Augustus' deployment of the imagery of expansion and novelty is accompanied by the construction of a personal cult of restoration, on which Nero draws to reassure himself as much as his people at a time of great personal, urban, and national insecurity. Pliny makes liberal use of antithesis to contrast the bad old days with the Trajanic restoration. Like Pliny, Juvenal's speaker Umbricius characterises insecurity as physical destruction and danger. That which is metaphorical for Pliny becomes concrete collapse and routine obliteration in Juvenal's third satire, a study in urban threat inflation that has frequent recourse to hyperbole. Where Pliny amplifies the fear of the past in order to heighten the sense of relief at the present, Juvenal's speaker seeks to leave his audience in a heightened state of alert. Augustus', Nero's and Pliny's rhetoric is that of security achieved and restored; in Juvenal we find instead the rhetoric of its absence.

The persistence of elements of Classical rhetorical theory in the education of Western political elites propels us to consider the extent to which these ancient security constructs are discernible in modern public discourse. In the next chapter, we will examine how elements such as the imagery of restoration, sensitisation to amplified dangers, and the construction of both simplifying contrasts and ideological others manifest in twenty-first century national security strategies.

Notes

1 Cicero (1949) *On Invention. The Best Kind of Orator. Topics.* Translated by H. M. Hubbell. Loeb Classical Library 386. Cambridge, MA: Harvard University Press.
2 Plato. *Lysis. Symposium. Gorgias.* Translated by W. R. M. Lamb. Loeb Classical Library 166. Cambridge, MA: Harvard University Press, 1925.

3 Juvenal, Persius. *Juvenal and Persius.* Edited and translated by Susanna Morton Braund. Loeb Classical Library 91. Cambridge, MA: Harvard University Press, 2004.
4 John Quincy Adams (1810) *Lectures on Rhetoric and Oratory Delivered to the Classes of Senior and Junior Sophisters in Harvard University Vols. I & II.* Cambridge, MA: Hilliard and Metcalf.
5 See, for example, the contributions to Michael Meckler's 2006 edited volume *Classical Antiquity and the Politics of America From George Washington to George W. Bush* (Waco: Baylor University Press), which include analysis of "Classical Education in Colonial America" (William J. Ziobro) and "Classical Antiquity and Early Conceptions of the United States Senate" (Carl J. Richard).
6 Aristotle, *Rhetoric*, 2020.
7 John Quincy Adams (1810) *Lectures on Rhetoric and Oratory Delivered to the classes of Senior and Junior Sophisters in Harvard University Vol. I.*, Cambridge, MA: Hilliard and Metcalf.
8 E. W. Sutton and H. Rackham trans. (1942) *Cicero, On the Orator: Books 1-2*, Loeb Classical Library 348, Cambridge, MA: Harvard University Press.
9 "Now we do not know the meaning of strange words, and proper terms we know already. It is metaphor, therefore, that above all produces this effect; for when Homer calls old age stubble, he teaches and informs us through genus; for both have lost their bloom."
10 Cf. Jeffery Scott Mio (1997) "Metaphor and Politics", *Metaphor and Symbol* 12.2: 113–133. "It is this notion of limited information-processing abilities and the need for simplification that leads me to conclude that metaphor and other forms of symbolic representation can be most useful in the political arena. Metaphor seems uniquely designed to address the information-processing capacity problems discussed by the political cognition theory advocates." Also Elena Negrea-Busuioc's assertion that "More often than not, politicians seek to exploit the highly persuasive power of metaphors in order to promote and impose preferred interpretations of these ideas in accordance to their own or their parties' political interests." Elena Negrea-Busuioc (2017) "Leading the War at Home and Winning the Race Abroad: Metaphors Used by President Obama to Frame the Fight Against Climate Change", in F. Ervas, E. Gola, and M. G. Rossi eds (2017) *Metaphor in Communication, Science and Education*, Berlin: De Gruyter.
11 Harvard University (n.d.) "Rhetoric: The Art of Persuasive Writing and Public Speaking", https://online-learning.harvard.edu/course/rhetoric-art-persuasive-writing-and-public-speaking?delta=1
12 Peter Jones (2019) "Pericles for PM: Boris Should Forget Augustus and Stay Focused on His Hero", *The Spectator*, www.spectator.co.uk/article/pericles-for-pm-boris-should-forget-augustus-and-stay-focused-on-his-hero
13 Jon Kelly (2010) "Why Does PPE Rule Britain?", *BBC News* 30/08/2010, www.bbc.co.uk/news/magazine-11136511; cf. Andy Beckett (2017). "PPE: The Oxford Degree That Runs Britain", *The Guardian* 23/02/2017, www.theguardian.com/education/2017/feb/23/ppe-oxford-university-degree-that-rules-britain
14 University of Oxford (2019) *Student Handbook: PPE Prelims 2019–2020*, www.ppe.ox.ac.uk/files/ppehandbookprelims2019-20v1pdf
15 P. A. Brunt and J. M. Moore (1967) *Res Gestae Divi Augusti: The Achievements of the Divine Augustus with an Introduction and Commentary*, Oxford: Oxford University Press.
16 Olivier Hekster, Erika Manders, and Daniëlle Slootjes (2014) "Making History with Coins: Nero from a Numismatic Perspective". *Journal of Interdisciplinary History* XLV.1: 25–37.
17 Miriam Griffin (2013) *Nero: The End of a Dynasty* (2nd edn), Abingdon: Routledge, pp. 120ff.
18 For the role of the emperor in urban security including protection from fire, see Virginia Margaret Closs (2013) *While Rome Burned: Fire, Leadership, and Urban Disaster in the Roman Cultural Imagination.* PhD diss. University of Pennsylvania.

19 Harold Mattingly and Edward Allen Sydenham (1923) *The Roman Imperial Coinage. Vol. 1, Augustus to Vitellius*, London: Spink & Son, p. 220.
20 Mattingly and Sydenham (1923) p. 179f.; cf. Cecilia Ricci (2018) *Security in Roman Times. Rome, Italy and the Emperors*, London: Routledge, p. 48f.
21 Mattingly and Sydenham (1923) p. 196.
22 Clifford H. Moore trans. (1925) *Tacitus. Histories: Books 1–3*, Loeb Classical Library 111, Cambridge, MA: Harvard University Press.
23 Mattingly and Sydenham (1923) p. clxxv.
24 Ibid., pp. cxcvi, ccv.
25 Cf. Ricci's assertion that from the middle of the first century CE onwards, "the theme of *securitas* would be used at times when there is most fear for security, and in phases of affirmation of a new dynasty" (2018, p. 57).
26 Michael Dillon (1996) *Politics of Security: Towards a Political Philosophy of Continental Thought*, London: Routledge, pp. 113–128.
27 Betty Radice trans. (1969) *Pliny the Younger. Letters, Volume II: Books 8–10. Panegyricus*, Loeb Classical Library 59, Cambridge, MA: Harvard University Press.
28 Cf. Ricci (2018) p. 32.
29 S. R. Slings (1997) "Figures of Speech and their Lookalikes: Two Further Exercises in the Pragmatics of the Greek Sentence", in *Grammar as Interpretation: Greek Literature in its Linguistic Contexts.* Edited by Egbert J. Bakker. Leiden: Brill, pp. 169–214.
30 Hammond notes that Pliny echoes this sentiment in his letters to the emperor, for example at *Letters* 10.52: "to keep you in health and prosperity on behalf of the human race, whose security and happiness depends on your safety"; Mason Hammond (1938) "Pliny the Younger's Views on Government", *Harvard Studies in Classical Philology* 49: 115–140; see also *Letters* 10.102, "we have celebrated with due solemnity the day on which the security of the human race was happily transferred to your care". Cf. also Ricci (2018) p. 31: "the term [*securitas*] refers to both the safeguarding of the security of the public places of Rome, and to the subjective and objective *Securitas Principis*, in the sense of a sovereign who not only guarantees the security of his people, but at the same time can move freely because he knows he is being protected in public and private spaces."
31 Betty Radice (1968) "Pliny and the *Panegyricus*", *Greece and Rome* 15.2: 166–172, p. 168.
32 Harold Mattingly and Edward Allen Sydenham (1926) *The Roman Imperial Coinage. Vol. 2, Vespasian to Hadrian*, London: Spink & Son, at pp. lxvi n.2, xcvii n.2.
33 Cf. Ricci's description of Pliny as "the prophet of the 'new security'" (2018, p. 55).
34 P. G. W. Glare (1968–82) *Oxford Latin Dictionary*, Oxford: Clarendon Press, at "horreō".
35 Commentators since the nineteenth century have identified Juvenal's *Satires* variously as examples of stock rhetorical *theses* or diatribes, among them Ludwig Friedländer ((1895), *D. Junii Juvenalis Saturarum libri V.* Leipzig: S. Hirzel) and F. Gauger ((1936) *Zeitschilderung und Topik bei Juvenal*, diss. Griefswald). Josué De Decker ((1913), *Juvenalis Declamans: étude sur la rhétorique declamatoire dans les satires de Juvénal.* Gand: van Goethem & Cie) provides a more statistical treatment of the rhetorical devices used.
36 E. J. Kenney (1963) "Juvenal, Satirist or Rhetorician?", *Latomus* 22: 704–720, p. 707.
37 For example, by William S. Anderson (1982) *Essays on Roman Satire*, Princeton: Princeton University Press, p. 397.
38 John Henderson (1995) "Pump Up the Volume: Juvenal, Satires 1.1–21", *Proceedings of the Cambridge Philological Society* 41: 101–137, p. 103.
39 Cf. Anderson (1982) p. 428: "If the Satires continue, as the first eighty lines of Satire 1 have certainly done, to represent the irrepressible reactions of an honest Roman to the degeneration of his native city, then Juvenal has fulfilled his rhetorical duties, and simultaneously his moral duties - he has, indeed, chosen a theme of great moral interest - and his poetic function - he has, as we shall observe in greater detail later, integrated

the precepts of the rhetoricians with the requirements of his particular form of poetry"; see also Hooley (2007) *Roman Satire*, Malden, MA, Oxford: Wiley-Blackwell, p. 3: "satire becomes a public genre characterized by big dramatic effects setting out to please, contra Persius [Juvenal's satiric predecessor], a large audience".

40 Anderson (1982) p. 439; so also E. J. Kenney (1962) "The First Satire of Juvenal", *Proceedings of the Cambridge Philological Society* 8: 29–40, p. 40: "it is the age he is attacking; indeed it would be no great exaggeration to say that all Juvenal's satire boils down to one vast ramifying commonplace *de saeculo*".

41 Henderson (1995) p. 127f.; see also Anderson (1982) pp. 293–361: "Anger in Juvenal and Seneca"; pp. 396–486: "Juvenal and Quintilian". *Indignatio* as a rhetorical attitude appears in the earliest extant Latin work on rhetoric, the *Rhetorica ad Herennium* (4.15.22, 39.51), Cicero's *De Inventione* (1.53.100), and Quintilian's curriculum (*Inst. Or.*11.3.61).

42 Noting Juvenal's fondness for this device, De Decker produced a list of 86 locations in the text of the *Satires* where at least one rhetorical question is used ((1913): pp. 150ff.).

43 For more on this, see Susanna Morton Braund's commentary ((1996), *Juvenal Satires Book I*, Cambridge: Cambridge University Press, p. 232).

44 Braund (1996) p. 230.

45 *Aeneid* 2.311f. See Closs (2013) for imperial Roman writers' use of urban conflagration as a metaphor for political unrest.

46 For more on Juvenal's use of epic imagery in these lines, see Victoria Baines (2003) "Umbricius' 'Bellum Ciuile': Juvenal, Satire 3", *Greece and Rome* 50.2: 220–237; (2004) *Bella satirica: Rhetorical Engagement with Epic in Juvenal's Satires*, PhD diss., Nottingham.

47 Baines (2003) p. 223.

48 For the related theme of surveillance, particularly the reaction in the post-Domitianic era to the prominence of informers (*delatores*) under Domitian, see James Uden (2015) *The Invisible Satirist: Juvenal and Second-Century Rome*, Oxford: Oxford University Press; also Tom Geue (2017) *Juvenal and the Politics of Anonymity*, Cambridge: Cambridge University Press. Pliny celebrates Trajan's punishment of informers at *Panegyricus* 34f. Juvenal's speaker is driven by a traditional satiric impulse to expose the faults of others, but is warned by an unidentified interlocutor of the deadly consequences of naming contemporaries. While the *delatores* mentioned at *Satires* 3.116, 4.48, and 10.70 are from the reigns of Nero, Domitian and Tiberius respectively, the figure of the *delator* is also present in the first satire's catalogue of apparently contemporary Romans (1.33).

49 See Baines (2003) pp. 224ff. for a more detailed discussion of these allusions.

2 The rhetoric of the US National Security Strategy

On 18 December 2017, the Trump administration constructed an unprecedented media and social media moment for the publication of its inaugural National Security Strategy. The President's Twitter account shared a video of a speech in which he outlines the four pillars of the new National Security Strategy. The tweet introducing the video reads as follows [original emphasis]:

> With the strategy I announced today, we are declaring that AMERICA is in the game and AMERICA is determined to WIN!
> OUR FOUR PILLARS OF NATIONAL SECURITY STRATEGY:[1]

The caption on the embedded video reads [original emphasis]:

President Donald J. Trump | National Security Strategy

> Our rivals are tough, tenacious, & committed to the long term & so are we! To succeed, we must INTEGRATE every dimension of our NAT'L STRENGTH & we must COMPETE w/every instrument of our NAT'L POWER.

The video is professionally edited: title slides that mark the transition to each pillar. The speech is scripted, save for a handful of obviously ad lib comments: for example, "Our strategy breaks from the damaging defence sequester – *we're gonna get rid of that*" [emphasis added]. The President seeks to draw attention to the novelty of his strategy – "So for the first time ever, American strategy now includes a serious plan to defend our homeland"; "We will develop new ways to counter those who use new domains, such as cyber and social media, to attack our nation or threaten our society"; and, "For the first time, American strategy recognises that economic security is national security". At several points, President Trump pauses for applause from an unseen audience. The video cuts to a final slide with the text, "President Trump & Vice President Pence Return To The White House … MAKING AMERICA SAFE AND GREAT AGAIN!" [original emphasis], and closes with silent footage showing the two men's return.

The US National Security Strategy has become a popular media event. A 55-page strategy document originally intended to hold the President to public account has

DOI: 10.4324/9781003028062-3

been reduced to a soundbite totalling six minutes of video and 347 characters. By late 2020, this video had received 1.5 million views via Twitter alone. What this communication has lost in detail it has gained in audience, boosted by its circulation by broadcast and online media outlets including CNN and Time. How did a planning document become short form security theatre? A close reading of the presidential prefaces to the strategies issued in the twenty-first century will help us to track and understand this evolution.

The US National Security Strategy as public discourse

The etymology of the word "strategy" is overwhelmingly military. *Stratēgós* is the Classical Greek word for "general"; the Classical Greek antecedent of modern English "strategy", *stratēgía*, therefore means "generalship" or "the offices of a general". Its usage has broadened in the course of two and a half millennia. The *Oxford English Dictionary* (*OED*) notes the use of *strategia* to denote an administrative district in Classical Latin, *stratégie* for the same in sixteenth-century France, and traces a definition of the "art of planning for the moves of opposing parties more generally" back to at least the 1830s. Modern English usage retains something of a dual quality, as itemised by the *OED*:

> 4.a. The art or practice of planning or directing the larger movements or long-term objectives of a battle, military campaign, etc.
> b. The art or practice of planning the future direction or outcome of something; the formulation or implementation of a plan, scheme, or course of action, esp. of a long-term or ambitious nature. Also: policy or means of achieving objectives within a specified field, as political strategy, corporate strategy, etc.
> 5.a. A plan or scheme governing the larger movements or long-term objectives of a battle, military campaign, etc.
> b. A plan, scheme, or course of action designed to achieve a particular objective, esp. a long-term or overall aim.

The term is therefore military and civilian in equal measure. In the context of security, national security specifically, we may be drawn to consider how a term with hybrid meaning may be received differently by different audience constituents. To members of the military or defence apparatus, it may have professional connotations that conjure notions of campaigns and movements with specific objectives and orders; to civilians, it may signify rather a conscious choice, plan, or scheme in any context. For both meanings, use of the term in discourse, whether private or public, may have a reassuring effect: reference to a strategy implies that there is a plan. It may even be possible to identify speeches and texts in which such reference brings a plan into existence where hitherto there was none. While this may read as somewhat cynical, in Chapter 5 we will examine an instance in which a security structure is brought into existence by its naming in a US National Security Strategy.

"Strategy" is a word that appears to have enjoyed increasingly frequent use in the last century. Data drawn from Google Books indicates a proliferation of the term from 1950 onwards, in line with research interest in Cold War and subsequent diplomacy and the development of International Relations as an academic discipline.[2] The phrase "national security" is also subject to a similar trajectory: the only difference being that the latter starts to see increased use slightly earlier, following the First World War.[3]

Discussion of this latter phrase prompts the question of how we are to parse the title of the document commonly known as the *National Security Strategy of the United States of America*. Are we to understand that it is the national strategy for security [national+security+strategy] or the strategy for national security [(national security)+strategy]? Semantics matter here, as "national security" in modern parlance denotes a discrete sphere of operations and influence, that of defence and the intelligence services. As we shall see, twenty-first-century US presidents and their administrations apply their own interpretations of the scope of security. When a president includes the economy and trade (as in Trump's video address above), international development and even overseas contraception in a plan for security, are we to understand these as issues that are not only in the US national interest, but also the legitimate business of the US national security machinery?[4]

The objectives and audiences of the US National Security Strategy

The US National Security Strategy has its origins in the Goldwater-Nichols Department of Defense Reorganization Act of 4 October 1986. Its long title [emphasis added],

> To reorganize the Department of Defense and strengthen civilian authority in the Department of Defense, to improve the military advice provided to the President, the National Security Council, and the Secretary of Defense, to place clear responsibility on the commanders of the unified and specified combatant commands for the accomplishment of missions assigned to those commands and ensure that the authority of those commanders is fully commensurate with that responsibility, *to increase attention to the formulation of strategy and to contingency planning*, to provide for more efficient use of defense resources, to improve joint officer management policies, otherwise to enhance the effectiveness of military operations and improve the management and administration of the Department of Defense, and for other purposes

clearly announces that one of the aims of the Act was to compel the US government's defence functions to *have more of a plan*. Under Title VI ("Miscellaneous"), SEC. 603 amends the National Security Act of 1947 as follows:

> SEC. 104. (a)(1) The President shall transmit to Congress each year a comprehensive report on the national security strategy of the United States (hereinafter in this section referred to as a "national security strategy report").

(2) The national security strategy report for any year shall be transmitted on the date on which the President submits to Congress the budget for the next fiscal year under section 1105 of title 31, United States Code.

(b) Each national security strategy report shall set forth the national security strategy of the United States and shall include a comprehensive description and discussion of the following:

(1) The worldwide interests, goals, and objectives of the United States that are vital to the national security of the United States.

(2) The foreign policy, worldwide commitments, and national defense capabilities of the United States necessary to deter aggression and to implement the national security strategy of the United States.

(3) The proposed short-term and long-term uses of the political, economic, military, and other elements of the national power of the United States to protect or promote the interests and achieve the goals and objectives referred to in paragraph (1).

(4) The adequacy of the capabilities of the United States to carry out the national security strategy of the United States, including an evaluation of the balance among the capabilities of all elements of the national power of the United States to support the implementation of the national security strategy.

(5) Such other information as may be necessary to help inform Congress on matters relating to the national security strategy of the United States.

Ostensibly the aim of the report is to hold the President accountable for the budget requested for security and defence. From its outset, the strategy is concerned with the United States' interests worldwide. The scope to move beyond the strictly military sphere of operations and influence is also clearly signalled. The primary stated audience is the US Congress, elected members of the House of Representatives, and Senate. In the respect that Congress represents the people, the National Security Strategy report is therefore billed as an instrument of public accountability.

At the same time, strategy setting communicates to internal stakeholders – in this case security and defence actors within the US government. Snider's study on the formulation process for US National Security Strategies, based on his own experience preparing the 1988 report, emphasises the role of that process in creating "internal consensus on foreign and defence policies" in the executive branch. It also raises a further consideration on the strategy's construction, intimating that at the very least it is a consultative process resulting in a text that is to some degree negotiated.

To these constituencies, Snider adds foreign governments and "selected domestic audiences".[5] In the 25 years since the publication of Snider's paper, technology has had a profound and lasting impact on international diplomacy and public communication by political figures. It is now commonplace, expected even, for heads of state to react in the moment to world events on social media, and to share photographic or video evidence of diplomatic engagements. Around the world, political campaigns make extensive use of advertising on platforms such as Facebook and Twitter.

President Trump is the epitome and perhaps the most extreme example of this approach to public diplomacy and communication. The appearance of spontaneously writing his own Tweets – complete with spelling and typing errors – may create an impression of authenticity and transparency. But our study of rhetoric as a means of persuasion and of constructing communication, the examples from Ancient Rome that we have examined, and the quite considerable public relations machinery surrounding political figures today should alert us to the fact that political figures rarely engage in public speech without considering first how they would like to be seen.

The presidential voice has always been evident in the US National Security Strategy reports in the form of prefaces used by successive presidents to introduce and commend the work of their administrations. Without exclusive access to the internal workings of each administration, it is impossible to say with any accuracy to what degree these prefaces reflect the "true thoughts" of each president or the extent to which they have been drafted by staffers. Mindful of Snider's recollections that National Security Strategies were in his experience a product of consensus, we may be tempted to see evidence of a number of hands in the construction of the prefaces also. The following section uses Classical rhetorical theory as a toolkit to examine the techniques and devices used in these texts, to distil their key rhetorical features, and to test the hypothesis that distinctive voices can be discerned.

Rhetoric by numbers – comparative analysis

At the time of writing (late 2020), seven US National Security Strategies have been published to date in the twenty-first century: two under the Clinton administration, two under George W. Bush, two during Obama's presidency, and one under Donald Trump.[6] Even the most cursory consideration of these presidents prompts comparison of their speaking styles. While Obama has been lauded for his oratorical skill, opponents of Trump have characterised his communication style as infantile and unsophisticated. Bush Jr.'s malapropisms – including the now famous 2000 utterance "They misunderestimated me" – are now designated "Bushisms", this new coinage itself mimicking the President's penchant for neologism.[7] Clinton, meanwhile, is popularly associated with a more paternalistic, evangelising style.

Before embarking on analysis of the content of the prefaces to the US National Security Strategies (henceforth NSS), it is worth comparing their length and verbal complexity (see Table 2.1). Perhaps as we might have expected, Trump's 2017 preface contains almost exactly half the number of words of Obama's 2015 text. Clinton's prefaces are on the longer side; his 2001 preface is slightly shorter than its predecessor. This difference in length between first and second strategies is also reflected in Bush Jr.'s respective word totals, and we may posit that strategies

Table 2.1 Presidential Prefaces by Word and Paragraph Length

Year	*Author*	*Words*	*Characters (no spaces)*	*Characters (with spaces)*	*Paragraphs*	*Lines*	*Average Word Length (characters)*	*Average Paragraph Length (words)*
2000	*Clinton*	1243	6741	7978	14	108	5.4	89
2001	*Clinton*	1084	5592	6667	9	85	5.2	120
2002	*Bush Jr*	1265	6683	7930	11	89	5.3	115
2006	*Bush Jr*	897	4583	5460	20	89	5.1	45
2010	*Obama*	1355	6718	8061	12	108	5.0	113
2015	*Obama*	1365	7149	8493	14	98	5.2	98
2017	*Trump*	686	3697	4370	11	59	5.4	62

which serve rather as progress updates may require less of an introduction than those that set out an administration's security priorities and preoccupations for the first time. A steady downward trend in the length of Clinton's prefaces in the previous decade, from a whopping 2552 words in 1996, suggests there may be some truth to this notion.

The differences between Bush Jr.'s first and second prefaces do not end there, however. While the total word length decreases by 29 per cent, the number of paragraphs almost doubles. The result is far fewer words per paragraph (45), fewer than any other twenty-first-century president. We may therefore expect that when we come to examine the content and styles of these two prefaces, different effects and apparent purposes are discernible.

Of the presidents who have issued more than one NSS, Obama is arguably the most consistent statistically. He clocks up the two highest word counts in our sample, his 2015 preface challenging the hypothesis that prefaces to inaugural strategies are *necessarily* longer. There is also only a small amount of variation in the average length of the individual words used by each president, which perhaps goes some way to challenging some of our preconceptions about the eloquence of these four men.

Other measures of linguistic complexity may help us to assess the accessibility of presidential rhetoric in the NSS prefaces. Using a free readability tool such as Readable, we can evaluate the prefaces against a number of indexes (see Table 2.2).[8] Complex words are defined as comprising three or more syllables. It may come as something as a surprise that Obama's inaugural preface registers the lowest percentage of complex words, and that Trump's 2017 preface registers the highest. A lower proportion of complex words is not of itself evidence that a speaker or writer is "dumbing down". Likewise, a slightly higher percentage of complex words does not of itself indicate greater eloquence or sophistication. In the case of Trump's 2017 preface, this higher percentage may be a result of incorporating the requisite technical language of security into a much smaller number of words overall.

Table 2.2 Statistical Analysis of Presidential Prefaces by Readability Index

Year	*2000*	*2001*	*2002*	*2006*	*2010*	*2015*	*2017*
Author	*Clinton*	*Clinton*	*Bush Jr*	*Bush Jr*	*Obama*	*Obama*	*Trump*
Flesch-Kincaid Reading Ease	24.9	39	41.5	42.9	42.7	36	41.6
Gunning Fog Score	19.5	16.5	14.8	14.8	16.4	16.8	13.7
SMOG Index	14.9	12.2	11.2	11.1	12.1	12.7	11.4
Coleman-Liau Index	14.8	13.6	14.6	14.1	12.9	14.2	15
Automated Readability Index	19.2	14.2	12.5	12.5	14.7	14	12
No. of complex words	263	202	249	162	222	290	150
% of complex words	20.92%	18.53%	19.68%	18.41%	16.54%	21.18%	21.80%

The indexes listed each measure and score readability slightly differently. The higher the score for Flesch-Kincaid Reading Ease, the easier it is to read. As popularised by Rudolf Flesch, the minimum score for plain English is 60: accordingly, all the prefaces require the reading skill of a college student, with the exception of Clinton's 2000 preface, which requires the reading skill of a college graduate.[9] The Gunning Fog Index calibrates readability for most people at a score of around 12, and distinguishes between different years of college (university) education.[10] By this measure, a college freshman (first year university student) would find Trump's 2017 preface easy to read, but Clinton's 2000 preface would be beyond the reading level of the average college graduate.

The Simple Measure of Gobbledygook (SMOG) index score reflects the years of education required to understand a text. The Coleman-Liau and Automated Readability Index calculates readability based on the number of characters rather than syllables.[11] Trump's 2017 preface is assessed statistically to be the easiest to read by multiple indexes. At the other end of our sample, Clinton's 2000 preface is deemed the hardest to read by all measures except the percentage of complex words.

That the presidential prefaces to the National Security Strategies are to some degree specialist communications is illustrated by the requirement of a reading ability of US Grade 13 or above when averaged across all indexes. This equates to the first year of university. The distribution of simplified highlights via mass media, as in the case of Trump's video address and tweet, is thus a move to include a wider audience and reading ability: the readability tests applied to the prefaces above return lower corresponding grade levels and reading ages for Trump's tweet (grade 10, age 15–16) and video caption (grade 9, age 14–15).

Subjecting each of the prefaces in turn to a close reading permits the identification of some stylistic and rhetorical characteristics that are peculiar to individual presidents, and others that appear to indicate a consistent presidential shorthand for issues of security and foreign policy.

Clinton the sermoniser

Statistical analysis designates Clinton as one of the "wordier" twenty-first-century presidents on the issue of security. This is reflected in the rhetorical tropes and figures of which he is evidently fond. *Asyndeton* is the omission of conjunctions between clauses. There is an early example of this in the second paragraph of the 2000 preface [emphasis added]:

> Americans benefit when nations come together *to deter aggression and terrorism, to resolve conflicts, to prevent the spread of dangerous weapons, to promote democracy and human rights, to open markets and create financial stability, to raise living standards, to protect the environment – to face challenges that no nation can meet alone.* The United States remains the world's most powerful force for peace, prosperity and the universal values of democracy and freedom. Our nation's central challenge – and our responsibility – is to sustain that role by seizing the opportunities of this new global era for the benefit of our own people and people around the world.

In the assessment of one political speechwriter, in oral delivery this omission creates a sense of urgency and "a breathless effect, so it sounds as if the speaker is almost hyperventilating".[12] To some extent the impression of urgency would depend on the speaker's speed of delivery: while it is possible to deliver what is essentially a list of items more slowly, this has the risk of causing the listener to forget the thrust of the argument towards the end of the extended sentence. In a text such as this preface, the reader has the luxury of being able to reread the start of the sentence if the thread is lost. But it is arguably undesirable to force the reader to do that too often.

Classical rhetorical theory urges moderation in the use of tropes and figures.[13] By both ancient and modern standards, Clinton's use of asyndeton in his 2000 preface is remarkable, bordering on excessive. Three consecutive paragraphs in the second half of the text comprise 37 semi-colon separated clauses amounting to a total of 429 words, and over one-third of the entire text. The choice of presentation is to some extent encouraged by the content to be conveyed: in this section of the preface, the president commends the actions that have been taken, and outlines the work that still needs to be done. Given the stated global reach of the strategy, these activities are far-ranging. For a strategy that is primarily intended as a report card to the House of Representatives, this construction may be an appropriate form of presentation. In a public communication to citizens, however, an endless list of items including the peace processes in the Middle East, the Balkans and Northern Ireland, nuclear and ballistic weapons control in Russia, North Korea and Iran, regime change in Iraq, easing tensions between India and Pakistan, and Greece and Turkey, "supporting democratic transitions from Nigeria to Indonesia", and the small matter of "reversing global climate change", is little short of overwhelming.

Overuse of a rhetorical device that *should* make Clinton's words more staccato and urgent in fact overloads the text with information, and gives it a density that challenges the reader. In respect of the President's account of actions taken by his administration, the intention may have been to impress the reader with a bounty of security. Conversely, the piling up of security concerns and measures in this way may have a contrary effect of convincing the reader that security is an issue too complex and bewildering for the average citizen to understand. It is, in this respect, a hyperbolic use, albeit not engaged in the service of threat inflation.

The passage above exhibits other features that are characteristic of the rhetoric in Clinton's prefaces. The first is the use of *triads*, presenting three items or sense units in succession. The Rule of Three is one of the most popular and persistent modern survivals of Classical rhetoric. Whether applied to speech or text arrangement, the introduction of ideas, or structure within a sentence, presentation in threes (as here in this sentence) is such a regular feature of modern rhetoric – at least, its Anglo-Saxon branch – that audiences have come to expect it. According to one assessment, arrangement in threes aids in the creation of soundbites because it "leaves an impression of finality".[14] By this token, its application to security matters may have a reassuring effect, inasmuch as the "x, y and z" formula may also leave the impression that the speaker/writer's assessment is suitably comprehensive and methodical. In the security sphere, the listener/reader may want to hear and feel that all relevant outcomes and courses of action have been considered.

In addition to the early statement that "The United States remains the world's most powerful force for peace, prosperity and the universal values of democracy and freedom", the President presents three core objectives of the 2000 strategy: to enhance America's security; to bolster America's economic prosperity; to promote democracy and human rights abroad. He states that he has asked for additional budget "for readiness, modernization, and other high priority defense requirements". At one point, he delivers triads within triads (emphasis added):

> To be secure, **we must** not only have a strong military; **we must** also **continue** to lead in limiting the military threat to our country and the world. **We continue** to work vigilantly to curb the spread of nuclear, chemical and biological weapons and missiles to deliver them. **We are continuing** the START process to reduce Russian and American nuclear arsenals, while discussing modification of the Anti-Ballistic Missile Treaty to allow for development of a national missile defense against potential rogue state attacks. **And we** remain committed to obtaining Senate advice and consent to ratification of the Comprehensive Nuclear Test Ban Treaty (CTBT), and to bringing this crucial agreement into force.

This paragraph is an extended triad on the theme of continuation and commitment, the effect of which is reinforced by repetition. The first sentence presents something of an antithesis – at once building and limiting military power. Repetition of "we must" at the start of the second clause (*anaphora*) signals that both these activities are to be given equal consideration. This second clause is also the first of three sense units that repeat both the first-person plural "we" and "continue" (*conduplicatio*) and its inflected form "continuing" (*polyptoton*). The second sentence then includes its own triad in the form of a list – "nuclear, chemical and biological". Following the last of the three mentions of the first-person plural and continuation, the final sentence repeats the concept in slightly different language – "and we remain committed". When this sentence concludes, we realise that it is also the last in another triad of full sentences that begins with "We continue to work" in the second sentence.

In the format of a speech, this emphasis through repetition would have a rhythmic quality. We might imagine emphatic gestures accompanying these verbal equivalents of downward strikes. The devices deployed by the President here have a distinctly oral quality, further endorsing the notion that we should appreciate them as a direct address to an audience, rather than merely a text foreword. At the same time, the intricacy of their arrangement speaks both to the care taken to construct this text and to its level of accessibility to people who are not themselves formally schooled in rhetoric. Artifice threatens to distract from and obscure meaning.

Antithesis in the above passage lends a sense of completeness, also an impression of innovative thinking, of tackling the issue from more than one perspective. A similar structure appears later in the text (emphasis added):

> America must be willing to act alone when our interests demand it, **but** we should also support the institutions and arrangements through which other countries help us bear the burdens of leadership. That's why I am pleased that we reached agreement with Congress on a plan for paying our dues and debts to the United Nations. It is why we must do our part when others take the lead in building peace: whether Europeans in the Balkans, Asians in East Timor, or Africans in Sierra Leone. **Otherwise** we will be left with a choice in future crises between doing everything ourselves **or** doing nothing at all.

In fact, there are at least three antithetical arrangements here, and I would argue that they achieve different effects. While the first sentence accords with the impression of completeness of approach, the remainder of the paragraph seeks to sharpen the contrast between partnership in global affairs, endorsed by a demonstrative use of anaphora – "That's why … It is why" – and the alternative presented in the final sentence. We are left with a dilemma, a choice between two undesirable extremes, itself antithetical, and we may note that this threefold construction takes us from a realm of greater opportunity to progressively more constrained options. In this way, the President shows us the path we must avoid.

Clinton's 2000 preface is entitled "A National Security Strategy for a New Century". The language of novelty and innovation is prominent throughout. The President claims to be pursuing "a forward-looking national security strategy for the new century". He trumpets "the first long-term sustained increase in defense spending in over a decade". He sets forth the need to secure "new energy routes from the Caspian Sea that will allow newly independent states in the Caucasus to prosper", and for "launching a new global trade round". He advocates "seizing the opportunities of this new global era", and asserts that "America today has power and authority never seen before in the history of the world". While the passing of the millennium certainly could not have gone without mention, what we see in this text is a carefully crafted tension between past and future that situates the President and his audience on the threshold, looking back and looking forward. To some extent, the "report card" structure of the preface forces this, with its requirement simultaneously to review progress and outline activities outstanding. It is heightened by an opening appeal to the President's ancestors:

> Nearly 55 years ago, in his final inaugural address, President Franklin Delano Roosevelt reflected on the lessons of the first half of the 20th Century. "We have learned," he said, "that we cannot live alone at peace. We have learned that our own well being is dependent on the well being of other nations far away. We have learned to be citizens of the world, members of the human community."

There is an implicit appeal to emotion (*pathos*) here in the word "final", since Roosevelt was to die less than three months after delivering this speech. By quoting Roosevelt directly, Clinton invokes a recognised authority, a technique known in Classical rhetoric as *apomnemonysis.* He also reminds us that the United States' engagement in global affairs is precedented, as is its basis on an appeal to the character (*ethos*) of Americans as human beings, with sufficient humility to learn – here presented with emphatic use of *tricolon* with *anaphora.* His words are themselves an endorsement for taking stock of past events. Our sights are then immediately turned to the future: "Those words have more resonance than ever as we enter the 21st century." We may be forgiven for thinking that it is an exciting time to be alive, even when faced with complex security considerations.

Clinton's 2001 preface opens with a continuation of the theme of novelty and an appeal to ancestors:

> As we enter the new millennium, we are blessed to be citizens of a country enjoying record prosperity, with no deep divisions at home, no overriding external threats abroad, and history's most powerful military ready to defend our interests around the world. Americans of earlier eras may have hoped one day to live in a nation that could claim just one of these blessings. Probably few expected to experience them all; fewer still all at once.

Forebears are conjured again, this time to intensify the benefits of a life that is beyond their wildest dreams. Representation of modern America as marvellous is the twenty-first-century counterpart to Classical rhetoric's device of *thaumasmus*, a formulaic exclamation of wonder: accordingly, language with religious or faith-based overtones is more prominent than in 2000. The 2001 preface is also more forceful in its convictions (emphasis added):

> Our success is cause for pride in what we've done, and gratitude for what we have inherited. But the most important matter is what we now make of this moment. **Some may be tempted to believe** that open markets and societies will inevitably spread in an era of expanding global trade and communications, or assume that our wealth and power alone will protect us from the troubles of the outside world. But that approach falls for the **old myth** of an "outside" world, and ignores the defining features of our age: the rise of interdependence. More than ever, **prosperity and security in America depend on prosperity and security around the globe**. In this age, America can advance its interests and ideals only by leading efforts to meet common challenges. We must deploy America's financial, diplomatic and military resources to stand up for peace and security, promote global prosperity, and advance democracy and human rights around the world.

Alternative approaches are dismissed here by means of several devices. The President anticipates a counterargument in order to refute it, a device familiar in Classical rhetoric as *prolepsis*. The fallacy of that argument is prefigured by the language of weakness and error: "tempted", "assume", "fall for", "ignores". In effect, this is a straw man argument, whose presentation as "old myth" serves to strengthen our reception of the President's own contrasting assessment as scientific and factually compelling. The notion of interdependence is reinforced by a sentence in which repetition in close proximity (*diacope*) of "prosperity and security" bestows identical fortunes on the US and the wider world. While the penultimate sentence closes down any possibility of an alternative perspective, two sets of triads in the final sentence create the impression that the matter has been methodically and completely considered. Of the triads used freely elsewhere in the text, perhaps the most striking concerns an aspect of human security that is not necessarily a priority for all subsequent presidents: "Our leadership in the international fight against infectious diseases, especially HIV/AIDS, is critical to defeat a threat that kills massively, crosses frontiers and destabilizes whole regions."

As in the 2000 preface, Clinton gives voice to one of his predecessors (emphasis added):

> More than 50 years ago, Harry Truman said: "We are in a position now of making the world safe for democracy, if we don't crawl in a shell and act selfish and foolish." He believed that in the wake of our triumph in World War II, America had **the ability and a responsibility** to **shape world events, so that we would not be shaped by them**. Truman was right, and the historical forces he saw then have only intensified since the Cold War.

While it uses a similar formula, this appeal to an ancestor goes further than that to Roosevelt. In addition to direct quotation, Clinton presumes to have privileged access to Truman's thoughts and to speak for him (*ethopoeia*). The subsequent conclusion on the correctness of Truman's assessment is based not only on what we knew to be his position on the matter, but also Clinton's own interpretation of it. The effect is to commend to us both Truman and Clinton-as-Truman.

Lest we forget that this is a direct address for us to hear in our heads, the President associates concepts by similarity in sound (*homoioteleuton*, "like ending"), mimicking Truman's own use of the device in "selfish and foolish". The ring of "ability" and "responsibility" has the effect of suggesting an essential link between the two, while the reversed parallel structure (*chiasmus*) emphasises both the need for active engagement in global affairs, and the central notion of interdependence. A further repetitive turn of phrase in the closing paragraph – "But the actions of many nations often follow from the actions of one" – pushes home the core message of America's leading role in global affairs.

George W. Bush and inevitable war

The 2002 NSS has arguably enjoyed more academic and media attention than any other. It presents President Bush's rationale for the War on Terror, which has come to be known as the Bush Doctrine: a brief search of the Bodleian Library's holdings returns over 5,000 results containing the phrase, more than 40 books among them. In the years since its publication, prominent researchers and commentators alike have challenged its logic, and probed its neo-conservative influences.[15] At 1,265 words, the strategy's presidential preface is longer than either of those of Clinton. While its paragraphs are of a similar average length to Clinton's 2001 preface, it registers a higher Flesch-Kincaid Reading Ease score (41.5), with a smaller average number of words per sentence (19.17, compared with Clinton's 32.23 in 2000 and 24.22 in 2001). It opens with an extraordinary narrative scene setter, an appeal to historical precedent, and eight mentions of what will be a key concept in this text – "freedom", "liberty" and their cognates (emphasis added):

> The great struggles of the twentieth century between **liberty** and totalitarianism ended with a decisive victory for the forces of **freedom** - and a single sustainable model for national success: **freedom**, democracy, and **free** enterprise. In the twenty-first century, only nations that share a commitment to protecting basic human rights and guaranteeing political and economic **freedom** will be able to unleash the potential of their people and assure their future prosperity. People everywhere want to be able to speak **freely**; choose who will govern them; worship as they please; educate their children - male and female; own property; and enjoy the benefits of their labor. These values of **freedom** are right and true for every person, in every society—and the duty of protecting these values against their enemies is the common calling of **freedom-loving** people across the globe and across the ages.

There is a monumental quality to this opening. Its immediate imagery is martial: the invocation of twentieth-century history puts us in mind of war, hot and cold; words such as "struggle", "victory", "forces", and "enemies" have the effect of identifying military action with the appropriate response to infringements on human rights and freedoms. Military language applied to concepts not strictly military is a persistent feature in the preface. When later the President asserts, "To defeat this threat we must make use of every tool in our arsenal - military power, better homeland defenses, law enforcement, intelligence, and vigorous efforts to cut off terrorist financing", we may remark not only on the apparent clumsiness of the mixed metaphor, but also on the metaphorical inclusion of all the listed capabilities (of which military power is just one) as weaponry. By implication, everything is warfare now.

The certainty of the arguments advanced in the opening paragraph is striking. Highly general assertions that might otherwise be open to challenge are presented as universal truths. They bear more than a passing resemblance to Classical apothegms and maxims (*sententiae*) that schoolboy orators committed to memory for their introduction as logical proofs.[16] From the start, an effort is made to close down alternatives to the world view presented. Meanwhile, individual humans in hundreds of sovereign states are rendered indistinct "people", whose wishes are listed at high speed by means of asyndeton. Perhaps unwittingly, these people are dehumanised by the description of their potential being "unleashed", as if somehow animal.

This is deliberative oratory that, in contrast to Clinton's prefaces, do not let reader/listeners in on the deliberations. The President presumes to speak for all citizens of the world, and tells us how the world is, rather than how he has reached his conclusions. This effort is reinforced throughout through the construction of numerous binary oppositions and repeated use of keywords: liberty vs. totalitarianism, freedom vs. tyranny/terror/evil, chaos vs. order, and so on. Some terms are so heavily used that the preface reads almost as an attempt at indoctrination through verbal stimuli. For instance, cursory analysis reveals 25 occurrences of "free-", 15 of "terror-", 8 of "peace-". In contrast, "security" and its cognates receive only two mentions. Through repeated and consistent use of antithetical language, the President expounds on the binary opposition he articulated to Congress following the 9/11 terrorist attacks: "Either you are with us, or you are with the terrorists." There are no shades of grey, and no room for debate.

By grouping together bad actors and concepts, and creating associations between their perceived opposites, the President distils multiple antitheses into a single primordial opposition. Terrorism and tyranny are associated through collocation, as here in the second paragraph (emphasis added):

> In a world that is safe, people will be able to make their own lives better. We will defend the peace by fighting **terrorists and tyrants**. We will preserve the peace by building good relations among the great powers. We will extend the peace by encouraging free and open societies on every continent.

Close analysis of these lines betrays some of the most problematic features of the Bush Doctrine. The emphatic use of tricolon with anaphora – "We will defend/preserve/extend the peace", complete with a pleasing rhyme ending (*homoioteleuton*) in the first and last cola – appears to promote peace as the overriding objective. But the notion of defending the peace by fighting is paradoxical, the language oxymoronic, and cannot help but draw attention to the inherent illogicality of the strategy of pre-emptive war. This paradox arguably makes the linguistic gymnastics of the rest of the preface necessary. The assertion that safety will improve quality of life turns on its head Clintonian security logic, specifically the statement in the 2000 preface that "Every dollar we devote to preventing conflicts, promoting democracy, opening markets, and containing disease and hunger brings a sure return in security and longterm savings." Rhetorical and linguistic devices in Bush Jr's 2002 preface appear to betray the challenges inherent in presenting the War on Terror as not counterintuitive.

One way in which the President urges the need for action is by evoking danger. "Danger-" appears only three times in the Clinton prefaces, twice in relation to nuclear weapons. It makes six appearances in Bush's 2002 preface, the first in the very next paragraph:

> Defending our Nation against its enemies is the first and fundamental commitment of the Federal Government. Today, that task has changed dramatically. Enemies in the past needed great armies and great industrial capabilities to endanger America. Now, shadowy networks of individuals can bring great chaos and suffering to our shores for less than it costs to purchase a single tank. Terrorists are organized to penetrate open societies and to turn the power of modern technologies against us.

We see continued evidence of the association of terrorism with warfare, an antithesis that presents one as the easy, entry-level version of the other, and graphic imagery that heightens the listener's sense of insecurity: dramatic change is unsettling; terrorism threatens both the cosmic order ("great chaos") and individuals. Its impact on society is depicted as a physical violation ("penetrate"). Not for the last time in twenty-first century security rhetoric, bad actors are portrayed as figures in darkness, with technology as their weapon: the association of technology with terrorism and danger is restated later in the text.[17] It is difficult to avoid the conclusion that hyperbole is here used as an appeal to the emotion of fear, and as a justification for war.

Just as the opening lines of the preface abounded with freedom, so later we find lines in which "terror-" dominates (emphasis added):

> The war against **terror**ists of global reach is a global enterprise of uncertain duration. America will help nations that need our assistance in combating **terror**. And America will hold to account nations that are compromised by **terror**, including those who harbor **terror**ists - because the allies of **terror** are the enemies of civilization. The United States and countries cooperating with us must not allow the **terror**ists to develop new home bases. Together, we will seek to deny them sanctuary at every turn.

Stylistically, we may feel that this level of repetition is somewhat unsophisticated. It certainly reminds the reader of the strategy's focus. In fact, we have to wait a full 900 words for mention of a security threat other than terrorism (drug cartels).

Frequent repetition also endorses the preface's function as an oral performance of sorts. The sound of "terror" (in the President's distinctive pronunciation) serves as an auditory hook, as does use of alliteration elsewhere in the text. The President appears to be particularly fond of multiple "f" and "d" sounds, perhaps because of their associations with his core agenda of freedom and democracy – "first and fundamental commitment of the Federal Government", clauses contrasting "defend" and "defeat", "democracy, development, free markets, and free trade"; also "p" sounds – for example, the "peaceful pursuit of prosperity".

In case his audience were still tempted to consider an alternative course of action, the President impresses on the reader once again by means of antithesis:

> And, as a matter of common sense and self-defense, America will act against such emerging threats before they are fully formed. We cannot defend America and our friends by hoping for the best. So we must be prepared to defeat our enemies' plans, using the best intelligence and proceeding with deliberation. History will judge harshly those who saw this coming danger but failed to act. In the new world we have entered, the only path to peace and security is the path of action.

The catchy assonance of "common sense and self-defense" jars somewhat with the gravity of the proposed strategy of pre-emptive war. The alternative is constructed as the weakest of straw men: a choice between proactivity and "hoping for the best" is no choice at all. Moving on to appeal to the audience's duty to posterity, both novelty and imagery reminiscent of biblical teaching (path metaphor) are applied to signal the only correct choice.[18]

As the word "sanctuary" in the earlier passage also illustrates, religious and quasi-religious language is a consistent feature of this preface. This is perhaps unsurprising for a president who elsewhere referred to the War on Terror as a crusade, and it aligns with the certainty of conviction evident in the arguments put forward. In the third to last paragraph of the text, the President states that "the United States is guided by the conviction that all nations have important responsibilities". The preface closes with the sentence, "The United States welcomes our responsibility to lead in this great mission". The domestic and global audience is encouraged to conclude that there is no more righteous choice than to support this divinely inspired endeavour.[19]

George W. Bush's 2006 preface is almost a third shorter than his previous effort, and is the second shortest in our sample. The most marked change is in the length of the President's paragraphs, from an average of 115 words to just 45. Single-sentence paragraphs with anaphora of "We have" and close variants dominate the first half, rendering the tone of the preface overwhelmingly as that of a report card. As a result, this preface boasts the largest number of paragraphs (20) in our sample. It is arguably the most accessible by standard readability measures: it scores highest (42.9) for Flesch-Kincaid Reading Ease, joint lowest for Gunning Fog, lowest on the SMOG Index, lowest on the Coleman-Liau Index, and registers the second lowest percentage of complex words (18.41 per cent). Its opening lines declare a state of emergency:

> My fellow Americans,
>
> America is at war. This is a wartime national security strategy required by the grave challenge we face - the rise of terrorism fuelled by an aggressive ideology of hatred and murder, fully revealed to the American people on September 11, 2001. This strategy reflects our most solemn obligation: to protect the security of the American people.

The formulaic direct address is most commonly heard in formal speeches or broadcasts from the Oval Office. The reader is primed for news of great importance and severity. The subsequent declaration of war, however, is not news. It is delivered a full three years after Bush declared in a televised address on 19 March 2003: "My fellow citizens, at this hour, American and coalition forces are in the early stages of military operations to disarm Iraq, to free its people, and to defend the world from grave danger." While not making mention specifically to being "at war", several references to these operations as "conflict" would have left his audience in no doubt. On 1 May of the same year, Bush declared "Mission Accomplished" on board the USS Abraham Lincoln. Why would the American public and global audience require a reminder that the country was still at war? We may need to look to the domestic political exigencies of the time. Having won a close-run election against John Kerry in 2004, Bush's second term was dogged with criticism of his decision to go to war. His second-term National Security Strategy was an opportunity to reiterate the ongoing danger, restate his record and justify his actions.

To this end, we are immediately presented with the threat in terms similar to that of the 2003 address – the challenge now is "grave" as was the danger then – and of the language of the 2002 preface. The religious overtones of "most solemn obligation" testify to the President's moral rectitude, while the characterisation of terrorist ideology as aggressive, and the strategy's somewhat pleonastic (or perhaps deliberately vague) aim to "protect the security" of the American people, again depicts the war as defensive. Putting the American people at the climax of the paragraph, with no opening mention of liberating other nations, is arguably a pointed move to reframe the war as a largely domestic security matter and worthy priority. In contrast to the 2002 preface in which "security" and its cognates appear only twice, in this later, shorter text it registers six times, three of these in the first two paragraphs and five of them in relation to domestic American issues.

The two short paragraphs that follow include devices and language reminiscent of the 2002 preface: these include logically questionable generalisations ("because free nations tend toward peace, the advance of liberty will make America more secure"), association of tyranny with despair, tyranny and freedom as binary opposites, and freedom and the War on Terror as "inseparable". Having reminded the reader of the relevant ideological and rhetorical framework for the war, the President embarks on six single-sentence paragraphs that serve as a progress report of sorts. While some of the language used is consistent with the 2002 preface – "enemy", "defeated", "dangerous", "hope" among them – we see a new focus in this section on language that depicts the US as team player and assistant rather than leader (emphasis added):

> We have kept on the offensive against terrorist networks, leaving our enemy weakened, but not yet defeated.
>
> We have **joined with** the Afghan people to bring down the Taliban regime - the protectors of the al-Qaida network - and **aided** a new, democratic government to rise in its place.
>
> We have **focused the attention** of the world on the proliferation of dangerous weapons - although great **challenges** in this area remain.
>
> We have **stood for** the spread of democracy in the broader Middle East - meeting **challenges** yet seeing progress few would have predicted or expected.
>
> We have **cultivated** stable and **cooperative** relations with all the major powers of the world.
>
> We have dramatically expanded our efforts to **encourage** economic development and the hope it brings - and focused these efforts on the promotion of reform and achievement of results.

These lines are light on detail, but full of an image of the US' *contribution* rather than its leadership. When leadership is broached in the next sentence, the US is first among equals and the justification elaborate: "We led an international coalition to topple the dictator of Iraq, who had brutalized his own people, terrorized his region, defied the international community, and sought and used weapons of mass destruction." The text also emphasises in retrospect how difficult these tasks have been. "Challenge" and its inflected forms appear a full nine times in the preface, compared with just three in 2002.

While structurally and logically more straightforward than its predecessor, this preface is notable for more extensive use of graphic imagery and emotive language. Mention of "toppling" Saddam Hussein is a highly visual metaphor that recalls the destruction of the Firdos Square statue in 2003. While reference to casualties is expected in a review of any conflict, the description in this preface is a concerted appeal to our emotions (*pathos*) (emphasis added):

> We have also found that the defense of freedom brings us **loss** and **sorrow**, because freedom has determined enemies. We have always known that the war on terror would require great **sacrifice** - and in this war, we have **said farewell** to some **very good** men and women. The terrorists have used **dramatic acts of murder** - from the streets of Fallujah to the subways of London - in an attempt to undermine our will. The struggle against this enemy - an enemy that **targets the innocent without conscience or hesitation** - has been difficult.

The President here sets the tone for his audience's reaction, effectively instructing us how to feel. The word "sacrifice", often used metaphorically in modern English, here has a literal quality in respect of the service personnel killed. The euphemistic "said farewell" lends an air of sentimentality even as it works to soften the focus. In stark contrast is the cinematic sweep across Europe and the Middle East to zoom in on scenes of "dramatic acts of murder". Our sensation is heightened to absorb a key appeal to *ethos*: while US casualties were of "very good" character, their enemy was entirely devoid of conscience. This is still a battle of good and evil.

In the next four paragraphs the President revisits the path metaphor of his 2002 preface:

> America now faces a choice between the path of fear and the path of confidence. The path of fear - isolationism and protectionism, retreat and retrenchment - appeals to those who find our challenges too great and fail to see our opportunities. Yet history teaches that every time American leaders have taken this path, the challenges have only increased and the missed opportunities have left future generations less secure.

The metaphor commends forward movement, regardless of the choice made. This is not the identical choice of paths as in the earlier text, where the President stated that "the only path to peace and security is the path of action". But we are perhaps to assume that the path of action and the path of confidence are one and the same, given that their respective opposites are inaction and/or withdrawal. Continuation on this path is associated by implication with security and with fewer challenges: with these keywords, the President promises that his strategy will bring an easier and more domestically focused time ahead, even without withdrawing troops.

The reader hoping to have an input into the deliberations is once more disappointed. That choice has already been made:

> This Administration has chosen the path of confidence. We choose leadership over isolationism, and the pursuit of free and fair trade and open markets over protectionism. We choose to deal with challenges now rather than leaving them for future generations. We fight our enemies abroad instead of waiting for them to arrive in our country. We seek to shape the world, not merely be shaped by it; to influence events for the better instead of being at their mercy.
>
> The path we have chosen is consistent with the great tradition of American foreign policy. Like the policies of Harry Truman and Ronald Reagan, our approach is idealistic about our national goals, and realistic about the means to achieve them.

Consistent with the 2002 preface, a number of antitheses serve to demonstrate the undesirability of the alternative. Strikingly, we hear an echo of Clinton's 2001 preface, when he paraphrases President Truman's decision "to shape world events, so that we would not be shaped by them". Uncannily, Truman is then evoked in the briefest of appeals to presidential heritage. Again we note a lack of explanatory detail, this time regarding Truman's and Reagan's policies, and may wonder whether non-specialist readers would be left behind by this gloss. What follows suggests that the Clintonian ring may not be entirely coincidental.

In the two closing paragraphs, the President finally introduces the two pillars of his strategy. He uses 167 words to do so, comprising just 19 per cent of the preface:

> The first pillar is promoting freedom, justice, and human dignity - working to end tyranny, to promote effective democracies, and to extend prosperity through free and fair trade and wise development policies. Free governments are accountable to their people, govern their territory effectively, and pursue economic and political policies that benefit their citizens. Free governments do not oppress their people or attack other free nations. Peace and international stability are most reliably built on a foundation of freedom.
>
> The second pillar of our strategy is confronting the challenges of our time by leading a growing community of democracies. Many of the problems we face - from the threat of pandemic disease, to proliferation of weapons of mass destruction, to terrorism, to human trafficking, to natural disasters - reach across borders. Effective multinational efforts are essential to solve these problems. Yet history has shown that only when we do our part will others do theirs. America must continue to lead.

The keywords may be consistent with the 2002 Bush Doctrine and the War on Terror – frequent repetition of "free" and its forms, for instance. But terrorism is now just one of a number of threats, and there is a greater focus on human and environmental security. Commentators have noted that the 2006 National Security Strategy marked something of a reversion to Clinton's foreign policy.[20] But far from signalling a change of tack, the bulk of the President's preface has emphasised consistency with the 2002 strategy, even employing the same imagery and rhetorical devices as the earlier preface to give the impression of continuation. Rhetoric has pulled us in one direction, while the policy is headed in another. Whether motivated by a desire to save face, wishful thinking in the face of realpolitik, or the need to be distinct from Democrat policies, it is difficult to avoid the conclusion that this is stylistic sleight of hand.

Obama the craftsman

President Obama's two prefaces are the longest in our sample, at 1,355 and 1,365 words respectively. Despite this, the 2010 preface scores comparatively highly on Flesch-Kincaid Reading Ease (42.7 to Bush's 42.9 in 2006, and Clinton's 24.9 and 39.0 in 2000 and 2001). Strikingly, this preface registers the lowest percentage (16.54) of complex words in the sample. While Obama may be wordy, the words themselves are relatively simple.

The 2010 preface is very different to its predecessor. There are unavoidable mentions of "war", seven to be precise, but the general tone is far from martial. Gone are the "Bushist" references to "enemies", replaced by just one mention of "adversaries". This is to be a more balanced appreciation of national security, driven by multiple extended antitheses in which positive statements lead, and drawing heavily on the language of movement and change, novelty and restoration. The opening lines are very different to Bush's 2006 declaration of war (emphasis added):

> Time and again in our Nation's history, Americans have risen to meet - and to shape - moments of **transition**. This must be one of those moments. We live in a time of **sweeping change**. The success of free nations, open markets, and social progress in recent decades has **accelerated** globalization on an **unprecedented** scale. This has opened the doors of opportunity around the globe, extended democracy to hundreds of millions of people, and made peace possible among the major powers. Yet globalization has also intensified the dangers we face - from international terrorism and the spread of deadly technologies, to economic **upheaval** and a **changing** climate.

The now formulaic appeal to history and heritage here provides reassurance to citizens rather than justification for a course of action. The idea of shaping is here cited as part of the well-worn response to world events, suggesting that the President has taken note of its use by previous incumbents. Frequency of "globe" and "globalization", and the inclusion of climate change, signal something of a return to the Clintonian focus on interdependency and wider human security. The reference to danger here is one of just two in the text. We may note also the phrase "deadly technologies", and hear in it an echo of Bush Jr's collocation of technology with danger and terrorism.

We see a fondness for alliteration in "millions of people", "made peace possible", and "major powers". Elsewhere in the text, Obama employs both alliteration and assonance with evident relish: "*dis*rupt, *dis*mantle, and *de*feat *al*-Qa'ida and its *af*filiates"; "from *n*ations, *nonstate* actors, and failed *states* - we will *m*aintain the *m*ilitary *s*uperiority that has *s*ecured our country"; "advocate for and advance"; "every race and region"; "space and support for those who resist repression", and so on. This is a text designed to delight our mind's ear.

"Sweeping change" and "opened the doors" are early evidence of Obama's well-documented fondness for metaphor.[21] In this preface, we see pointed use of repeated metaphors related to textile manufacture, building and seafaring – workers' imagery of production and forward movement. Among them, the President states that security depends in part on intelligence and law enforcement that can "unravel plots" and "work seamlessly with other countries"; he states that America "stitched together a community of free nations and institutions to endure a Cold War"; US military superiority has "underpinned global security" for decades; the strategy commended "rebuilds the foundation of American strength and influence"; the Armed Forces "will always be a cornerstone of our security"; "we must see the horizon" beyond the current wars; America "has not succeeded by stepping outside the currents of international cooperation" but "by steering those currents in the direction of liberty and justice". A later reference to "the strength I drew from workers rebuilding their lives in Illinois" suggests that the preface has been crafted to speak directly to these workers to some degree.

Construction metaphors also serve a dominant theme of national renewal, as does the final clause of the preface, "America is ready to lead once more" – itself perhaps a response to or correction of the final sentence of Bush Jr's preceding preface, "America must continue to lead". We have seen renewal and restoration in security matters before: a full 2,000 years before, in the Rome of Nero and of Trajan. The choice of these metaphors may also be a conscious evocation of times and citizens past, the Americans who sailed to, built, and wove the social fabric of the country. The appearance of the word "foundation" five times in the text – once pointedly in relation to "our forefathers" – puts the reader in mind of the nation's origins, while America's status as a nation "whose people trace their roots to every country on the face of the Earth" is adduced as justification for global leadership.

This preface contains more instances of the term "security" and its forms than are apparent in its predecessors. A total of nine references serve to remind the reader of the focus of the strategy presented. While in one sense this has a limiting effect, at the same time security is remodelled as something that is no longer an entirely national matter, but is a joint enterprise with other countries:

> This is part of a broad, multinational effort that is right and just, and we will be unwavering in our commitment to the security of our people, allies, and partners. Moreover, as we face multiple threats - from nations, nonstate actors, and failed states - we will maintain the military superiority that has secured our country, and underpinned global security, for decades.

This aligns with positive representations of common efforts: "international", "multinational", "collective", "cooperation", "commitment", "share", and "community" itself; and negative depictions of the overextension of power and acting alone.

Depiction of America as poised on the brink of a wondrous future recalls Clinton's millennial preface and the Classical device of *thaumasmus*. Endorsed by frequent use of the language of novelty, innovation is branded "a foundation of American power". The President urges us to "pursue science and research that enables discovery, and unlocks wonders as unforeseen to us today as the surface of the moon and the microchip were a century ago". Later in the text, he recalls "the awe I felt as a child watching a space capsule pulled out of the Pacific". Allusion to the Space Race through a first-person anecdote generates excitement for American greatness by means of soft power; elsewhere in the text, repetition of the phrase "strength and influence" advances this point.

Personal recollection encourages the reader to identify with the President, to see him as one of us:

> As a citizen, Senator, and President, I have always believed that America's greatest asset is its people - from the awe I felt as a child watching a space capsule pulled out of the Pacific, to the strength I drew from workers rebuilding their lives in Illinois, to the respect that I have for the generation of Americans who serve our country today. That is why I also believe that we

> must foster even deeper connections among Americans and peoples around the globe. Our long-term security will come not from our ability to instill fear in other peoples, but through our capacity to speak to their hopes. And that work will best be done through the power of the decency and dignity of the American people - our troops and diplomats, but also our private sector, nongovernmental organizations, and citizens. All of us have a role to play.

The striking double triad construction in the first sentence arranges examples according to Obama's various roles in society, from the most humble to the highest status. The President's humility in the leading position here mirrors the strategy's greater emphasis on humility in global leadership. In this paragraph and throughout the preface there is a consistent appeal to *ethos*, here with emphasis on "the decency and dignity of the American people"; elsewhere through repeated mentions of "right", "just" and their cognates.

This is in many respects an anti-fear text; in addition to heeding the President's cautionary words about instilling fear above, we may note that there is only one reference to terrorism. There is aspiration in the positive depiction of innovation, and a clear effort to avoid demonising people from other countries. This is also a profoundly humane and humanising text. In fact, the President subjects both the nation and the passing of time to personification: "The burdens of a young century cannot fall on American shoulders alone - indeed, our adversaries would like to see America sap our strength by overextending our power."

All the imagery here points to human embodiment, an infant twenty-first century weighing down a nation comprised entirely of its people, acting as one body. It may be no coincidence that, in contrast to other presidential prefaces, the text contains not a single mention of the official governmental or administrative designation of "United States"; rather, we see only "America" the people, the collective idea. The country's independence is subsequently depicted as a new life:

> From the birth of our liberty, America has had a faith in the future - a belief that where we're going is better than where we've been, even when the path ahead is uncertain. To fulfill that promise, generations of Americans have built upon the foundation of our forefathers - finding opportunity, fighting injustice, and forging a more perfect Union. We have also created webs of commerce, supported an international architecture of laws and institutions, and spilled American blood in foreign lands - not to build an empire, but to shape a world in which more individuals and nations could determine their own destiny, and live with the peace and dignity that they deserve.

"Faith", "belief", and "destiny" all bestow a spiritual quality to American progress, while the uncertain path ahead echoes the paths of action and confidence in Bush Jr's prefaces. In line with a more humble approach, empire building is explicitly rejected. In the process of anticipating a counterargument (*prolepsis*), the President associates spirituality with ethical policy: "And we reject the notion that lasting security and prosperity can be found by turning away from universal rights - democracy does not merely represent our better angels, it stands in opposition to aggression and injustice."

This preface demands the ethical involvement of each and every citizen to an extent unseen in its predecessors. We are to understand not only that we are a part of the deliberations, but also a part of the delivery: "All of us have a role to play." We may challenge one another not to be inspired and reassured by this rhetoric. But we may also marvel at a strategy whose substance is more consistent with the policies of the previous administration than the preface's rhetorical features would suggest.[22]

At 1,365 words, Obama's 2015 preface is the longest in the sample. It scores less for Flesch-Kincaid Reading Ease than his previous effort (36.0, compared to 42.7 for 2010), and higher on the Gunning Fog, SMOG, and Coleman-Liau Indexes. The number of sentences has increased from 51 to 60 since 2010, even though the 2015 preface is only ten words longer. While the sentences in the 2015 preface are shorter than in 2010, both the number and percentage of complex words has increased (from 222 to 290, and 16.54 per cent to 21.18 per cent respectively).

Numerous features of this text are consistent with its predecessor. The focus on renewal, restoration, and innovation persists: "We have renewed our alliances from Europe to Asia"; "our rebalance to Asia and the Pacific is yielding deeper ties with a more diverse set of allies and partners". Immigration is identified as a source of that renewal: "We continue to attract immigrants from every corner of the world who renew our country with their energy and entrepreneurial talents."

There is a continued fondness for alliteration and assonance, creating pace when itemising progress in international relations: "we remain alert to China's *m*ilitary *m*odernization and *r*eject any *r*ole for intimidation in *r*esolving territorial disputes"; "we are deepening our investment in *A*frica, *acc*elerating *acc*ess to energy, health, and food security in a *r*apidly *r*ising *r*egion"; "*our o*pening to Cuba will *en*hance our *en*gagement in *our o*wn hemisphere, where there are enormous opportunities to consolidate gains in *p*ursuit of *p*eace, *p*rosperity, democracy, and energy security".

The construction and textile metaphors also persist: "The entrepreneurial spirit of our workers and businesses *undergirds* our economic edge"; "*Underpinning* it all, we are upholding our enduring commitment to the advancement of democracy and human rights"; and, reappearances of the word "foundation/s" in relation to national security and national power. Metaphor heightens the impression of strength and growth in one paragraph in particular (emphasis added):

> We are **building** on our own energy security - and the **ground-breaking** commitment we made with China to reduce greenhouse gas emissions - to **cement** an international consensus on arresting climate change. We are shaping global standards for cybersecurity and **building** international capacity to disrupt and investigate cyber threats. We are playing a leading role in defining the international community's post-2015 agenda for eliminating extreme poverty and promoting sustainable development while prioritizing women and youth.

In the final paragraph, the President commends his strategy as follows: "I believe this is an achievable agenda, especially if we proceed with confidence and if we restore the bipartisan center that has been a *pillar of strength* for American foreign policy in decades past."

Complex language and assumed knowledge, here of the stance of the "bipartisan center", mark this preface as less accessible than Obama's previous effort. In other respects also, this is very much a security professional's preface. Security is no longer an issue that can be met by inspiration and aspiration alone. It requires specialist knowledge, production of evidence, and a rigorous application of logic argument. Use of complex or specialist words such as "geostrategic", "lockstep", and "entrepreneurship", aligns with the President's assertion that this is a "complex world", in which "many of the security problems we face do not lend themselves to quick and easy fixes". References without further explanation to sequestration and to the Prague Agenda assumes knowledge of the federal military budget and nuclear non-proliferation commitments. While it is not impossible that these are moves intended to flatter citizens by including them in a circle of those in the know, they risk alienating a non-specialist readership. In effect, this preface is less concerned with ensuring that it is accessible to all.

At the same time, there is a much clearer emphasis on logical argument and proof. Statistics are adduced as evidence of job creation, the withdrawal of troops from Iraq and Afghanistan, and the importance of the Asia Pacific region to global trade. The requirement for America to lead is presented as an "undeniable truth", and we see the return of the Clintonian "that is why" to demonstrate the President's reasoning for leading international coalitions, and working to "ensure that America has the capabilities we need to respond to threats abroad".

Whether consciously or otherwise, repeated use of "strong" and its forms (nine times), "opportunity" (six times), "threat" (four), "risk" (three) and "challenge" (six) not only reinforces the impression that this is a balanced, logical assessment, but also mimics the work of the strategic security analyst. SWOT analysis – so called after its evaluation in turn of Strengths, Weaknesses, Opportunities and Threats of a particular issue or proposed course of action – is one of the core tools used by security analysts. In combination with liberal use of considered antitheses, emphasis on rules-based international engagement, and appeals to logic (*logos*) and evidence, the impression is that Obama in the role of analyst has conducted this assessment himself, using recognised tools of the security profession. He is not just endorsing the strategy; he is owning its reasoning and procedure.

The President further signals that we are to understand this National Security Strategy as one driven by creative use of brain power (emphasis added):

> The United States will always defend our interests and uphold our commitments to allies and partners. But, we have to make hard choices among many competing priorities, and we must always resist the over-reach that comes when we make decisions based upon fear. Moreover, we must recognize that a **smart** national security strategy does not rely solely on military power. Indeed, in the long-term, our efforts to work with other countries to counter

> the ideology and root causes of violent extremism will be more important than our capacity to remove terrorists from the battlefield.
>
> The challenges we face require strategic patience and persistence. They require us to take our responsibilities seriously and make the **smart** investments in the foundations of our national power.

As these lines illustrate, Obama is keen to reframe security as much more than a military issue. Indeed, the very first sentence of the preface sets a scene of general insecurity: "Today, the United States is stronger and better positioned to seize the opportunities of a still new century and safeguard our interests against the risks of an insecure world."

Economic security is the President's first priority in this preface. Of the 17 mentions of "security" and its forms, more than any other text in our sample, just three refer specifically to domains regularly associated with defence and armament (nuclear materials and cybersecurity). For the remainder, in additional to general references to national security and "global security", use of the term designates the economy, food, health, and energy *as* security issues. When the President claims "Globally, we have moved beyond the large ground wars in Iraq and Afghanistan that defined so much of American foreign policy over the past decade" – a sentence that echoes his own words in 2010, "Yet as we fight the wars in front of us, we must see the horizon beyond them" – we may remark that the linguistic cues in the text also encourage us to accept a wider ranging approach to national security.

The challenges are outlined earlier in the preface (emphasis added):

> Now, **at this pivotal moment**, we continue to face **serious challenges** to our national security, even as we are working to shape the opportunities of tomorrow. **Violent** extremism and an **evolving terrorist threat raise** a **persistent** risk of attacks on America and our allies. **Escalating challenges** to cybersecurity, aggression by Russia, the **accelerating** impacts of climate change, and the outbreak of infectious diseases all **give rise** to **anxieties** about global security. We must be clear-eyed about these and other **challenges** and recognize the United States has a **unique** capability to mobilize and lead the international community to meet them.

Adjectives of speed, growth and gravity, and verbs of emergence serve to reinforce the need for action right now. While not obvious examples of hyperbole on their own, together they serve to engender a sense of urgency, and to heighten the anxiety to which the President refers. It is our task to see through this mist, and it is not the first time that Obama has used the metaphor "clear-eyed" in this very context: in the 2010 preface he asserted, "We are clear-eyed about the challenge of mobilizing collective action".

While Obama to some extent succumbs to the rhetoric of insecurity in the above passage and the opening of the preface, his presentation of change also in a positive light when associated with innovation and entrepreneurship, particularly of young people, indicates that we need not be fearful of all future developments.

Indeed, as in his earlier preface, the President explicitly rejects fear as a driver for foreign policy. Building on his condemnation of over-reach prompted by fear, he opens the final section of the preface with the words: "Finally, I believe that America leads best when we draw upon our hopes rather than our fears. To succeed, we must draw upon the power of our example - that means viewing our commitment to our values and the rule of law as a strength, and not an inconvenience." It is an appeal to reader emotion (*pathos*) and national ethics (*ethos*) that stresses the importance of doing the right thing in the right way.

Unlike Clinton and Bush Jr, Obama does not invoke former presidents by name. We may nevertheless hear in his coupling of belief with the rejection of fear echoes of Franklin D. Roosevelt's first inauguration speech, in which he declared: "So, first of all, let me assert my firm belief that the only thing we have to fear is fear itself". A sentence earlier in the preface likewise evokes the challenges of the 1930s: "Since the Great Recession, we have created nearly 11 million new jobs during the longest private sector job growth in our history." The designation of the 2007–9 recession as the Great Recession inevitably invites comparison with the Great Depression. In fact, the phrase had been used before, to designate the recessions of 1974–5, 1979 and almost every recession since.[23] As late as 2007, media outlets around the world also referred to the Great Depression of the 1930s as the Great Recession.[24] While the phrase has been in popular usage since then in reference to the 2007–9 recession, its use by Obama in the context of national economic security arguably invites comparison with the trials of that earlier Depression. This and linguistic echoes of Roosevelt intimate cause for cautious optimism and a precedent for emergence from adversity.

Trump – security as personal cult

At just 686 words, Trump's is the shortest preface in our sample. Indeed, it is exactly half the length of Obama's 2015 text. Despite this, it registers a very similar Flesch-Kincaid Reading Ease score (41.6) to those of George W. Bush and Obama's 2010 preface. While its Gunning Fog and SMOG scores are comparatively low (13.7 and 11.4 respectively), it registers the highest percentage of complex words (21.8 per cent) and therefore the highest Coleman-Liau score (15.0) in our sample. It also contains the lowest average number of words per sentence (17.64), just over half of Clinton's in 2000. Trump's sentences may be short, but his words are long.

As did Bush Jr's 2006 preface, this text opens as a broadcast to all citizens (emphasis added):

> My fellow Americans:
>
> The American people elected **me** to make America great again. **I** promised that **my** Administration would put the safety, interests, and well-being of our citizens first. **I** pledged that we would revitalize the American economy, rebuild our military, defend our borders, protect our sovereignty, and advance our values.

> During **my** first year in office, **you** have witnessed **my** America First foreign policy in action. We are prioritizing the interests of our citizens and protecting our sovereign rights as a nation. **America is leading again** on the world stage. We are not hiding from the challenges we face. We are confronting them head-on and pursuing opportunities to promote the security and prosperity of all Americans.

It is immediately evident that the President's personal record is of primary concern. At the same time, the use of the second person "you" clearly marks this preface as a direct address. It is all the more remarkable for being the only use of the second person in our sample.

Much of the language and style is familiar from previous prefaces: challenges, opportunities, values, rights, leadership, interests, and so on; arrangement of ideas into triads, and specifically *tricolon with anaphora* of "we are". But there are evident differences in their context and application. These opening paragraphs present a mission apparently accomplished. In response to calls by predecessors (Clinton and Obama among them) that "America must lead", Trump's answer is that "America *is* leading again". In accordance with the America First policy, rights are now sovereign rather than human, national rather than global. For followers of US foreign policy, it will come as no surprise that "sovereignty" appears only in this text in the sample, and this preface contains the only references to the nation's borders.

The now customary presidential security rhetoric of restoration and renewal takes on additional significance when attached to the slogan "Make America Great Again". In this respect, Trump's entire campaign spoke to restoration. Accordingly, the negative "We are not hiding from the challenges we face" implies a failure of predecessors, specifically Obama, to tackle security issues decisively. In case we had forgotten the character of these challenges, we are reminded in colourful terms (emphasis added):

> The United States faces an **extraordinarily dangerous world**, filled with a **wide range** of **threats** that have **intensified** in recent years. When I came into office, rogue regimes were developing nuclear weapons and missiles to **threaten the entire planet**. Radical Islamist terror groups were flourishing. Terrorists had taken control of **vast swaths** of the Middle East. Rival powers were **aggressively undermining** American interests around the globe. At home, **porous borders** and **un**enforced immigration laws had created **a host of vulnerabilities**. Criminal cartels were bringing drugs and **danger into our communities. Un**fair trade practices had **weakened** our economy and exported our jobs overseas. **Un**fair burden-sharing with our allies and **in**adequate investment in our own defense had invited **danger** from those who wish us **harm. Too many** Americans had **lost** trust in our government, faith in our future, and confidence in our values.

While Obama and others had written of growing threats, Trump turns the current security landscape into a scene from a disaster movie. It is a landscape of profound insecurity, danger, loss, and lack. Threats are described in language that is so intensive and expansive as to be hyperbolical: "extraordinarily", "wide", "entire", "vast", "host", "too many". Previous countermeasures, meanwhile, are depicted as deficient or otherwise negative: "porous", "unenforced", "unfair", "inadequate", and so on. Obama's positive representation of immigration is pointedly rejected. The President paints the situation he inherited in the worst possible light, in order to announce (emphasis added):

> Nearly one year later, although serious challenges remain, we are charting a new and very different course.
>
> We are rallying the world against the **rogue regime** in North Korea and **confronting** the **danger** posed by the dictatorship in Iran, which those determined to pursue a flawed nuclear deal had neglected. We have renewed our friendships in the Middle East and partnered with regional leaders to help drive out terrorists and extremists, cut off their financing, and discredit their wicked ideology. We crushed Islamic State of Iraq and Syria (ISIS) terrorists on the battlefields of Syria and Iraq, and will continue **pursuing** them until they are destroyed. America's allies are now contributing more to our common defense, strengthening even our strongest alliances. We have also continued to make clear that the United States will no longer tolerate economic aggression or **unfair** trading practices.

Verbal echoes of the previous paragraphs draw attention to the internal structure of this part of the preface. Each threat highlighted is immediately answered with a solution already delivered: "rogue regimes" are being dealt with, Middle East peace restored, and there is greater balance in international affairs. The call-and-response structure persists in the lines subsequent (emphasis added):

> At home, we have **restored confidence** in America's purpose. We have **recommitted** ourselves to our founding principles and to the values that have made our families, **communities**, and society so successful. Jobs are **coming back** and our economy is growing. We are making historic **investments** in the United States military. We are **enforcing our borders**, building **trade** relationships based on **fairness** and reciprocity, and defending America's sovereignty without apology.

The solutions to lost confidence, drug dealing in communities, a weakened economy, inadequate investment in the military, porous borders, and unfair trade (again) are reported to already be in action. The President continues to press the theme of renewal and restoration:

> The whole world is lifted by America's renewal and the reemergence of American leadership. After one year, the world knows that America is prosperous, America is secure, and America is strong. We will bring about the better future we seek for our people and the world, by confronting the

> challenges and dangers posed by those who seek to destabilize the world and threaten America's people and interests.

By his own reckoning, Trump is the President who made America secure again. We may be tempted to see ancient parallels in the apparent simplicity of Nero's pronouncements of security restored, eulogistic representations of Trajan's reign, and Augustus' first-person performance assessment. At the same time, hyperbolical accentuation of the dangers of the world, particularly in relation to an earlier state of insecurity, has an analogy in ancient literature, not least Juvenal's satiric representations of contemporary life in Rome and Pliny's panegyric. The President reminds us that he owns this restoration (emphasis added):

> **My** Administration's National Security Strategy lays out a strategic **vision** for **pr**otecting the American **p**eople and **pr**eserving our way of life, **pr**omoting our **prosperity, pr**eserving **p**eace through strength, and **a**dvancing **A**merican influence in the world. We will **pursue** this **beautiful vision** - a world of strong, sovereign, and independent nations, each with its own cultures and dreams, thriving side- by-side in **prosperity**, freedom, and **peace** - throughout the upcoming year.
>
> In **pursuit** of that future, we will look at the world with **clear eyes** and fresh thinking. We will **promote** a balance of power that favors the United States, our allies, and our partners. We will never lose **sight** of our values and their capacity to inspire, uplift, and renew.
>
> Most of all, we will serve the American people and uphold their right to a government that prioritizes their security, their **prosperity**, and their interests. This National Security Strategy puts America First.

The notion of "America First" frames the text. The more closely one scrutinises this preface, the more evident it becomes that Trump does not conform to traditional Western notions of rhetorical or stylistic sophistication. There is alliteration and repetition here. But rather than pointed repetition for emphasis, words such as prosperity, pursue, promote, preserve, and peace do not appear to be as carefully arranged as in some earlier prefaces. This impression is perhaps to some extent heightened by the logical simplicity of the mirrored structure: response to security issues item by item requires disproportionate repetition of ideas and language. But there is also a sense in which, despite that structure, the comparatively small vocabulary of this text contributes to a sense of disorder. This and the repetition of the reporting timeframe with apparent inconsistency – "During my first year in office", "nearly one year later", then "after one year" – and further reference to "throughout the upcoming year" within such a brief text, suggest that the preface may not have enjoyed the polish of proof reading or extensive editing.

Imagery is more graphic and perhaps naïve than in some other texts in our sample. Terrorist ideology is "wicked", Trump's strategic vision "beautiful", and sovereign nations have "dreams". Where Obama had used metaphor consistently and lyrically to reassure, Trump uses the device aggressively - confronting "head-on", "crushing" ISIS, "lifting" the world. Whether consciously or otherwise, the phrase "with clear eyes" recalls Obama's use of "clear-eyed" in both his prefaces. Its collocation with "fresh thinking" is arguably clumsy – in that it is not strictly possible to look with thought - but perhaps more authentic for that. The impression, then, may be of a preface that seeks to persuade through an absence of artifice. For all its brevity, it is certainly unorthodox.

Discussion – presidential code and (in)security intertext

Analysis of the language and style of the presidential prefaces to the twenty-first-century US National Security Strategies reveals much that is formulaic. The language of freedom and prosperity highlights consistency of national values and aims, while the language of threats, opportunities, and challenges serves as an illustration that the basic task of security assessment and planning is the same for all four presidents, however world events or domestic politics may evolve.

At the same time, distinct presidential voices have emerged, despite the fact that the strategies and their prefaces will most likely have received input from multiple contributors and undergone several revisions. These voices exhibit varying levels of rhetorical sophistication, at least according to current Western and Classical standards of oratory and argumentation. For some, the focus is on vocabulary, for others on imagery, still others on structure. For all, there is a clear pattern of persuasive technique, which in turn reminds us that these prefaces are very evidently public communications with multiple audiences.

We have seen presidents appeal to tradition and to posterity, summon ghosts, conjure graphic images, create oppositions to commend their choices, and deploy pleasing stylistic devices such as alliteration and assonance to delight the ear or hammer a point home. We have seen them appeal alternately to our emotions (*pathos*), our morals (*ethos*), and to reason (*logos*). We have identified that they engage in intertextual reference, at times apparently copying each other's homework, at others seemingly answering or reframing statements and tropes in earlier prefaces.[25] They speak to their staff, legislators, fellow citizens, foreign citizens, and even their predecessors through these texts, using rhetorical devices recognisable from Classical theory.

Close reading of the prefaces also reveals the lengths to which presidents have gone to establish their security landscape and policy as novel or unique. As well as echoing a tradition that looks back at least as far as Augustus' *Res Gestae*, this emphasis itself becomes something of a formula in the NSS. Applied in the context of renewal, in combination with the ideas of restoration and regeneration, this can have a reassuring effect. In combination with the tropes of danger and threat escalation, its effect is the opposite. To see how differently the similar threat levels and responses can be presented, we need look no further than Bush Jr's 2006 and Obama's 2010 prefaces. When both were published, the United States was at war in Iraq. Where the former is overwhelmingly militaristic in tone, the latter seeks to encourage Americans to embrace change and see beyond the current conflict.

Differing preoccupations point to these prefaces as loci of securitisation in action. Argumentation, structure, tropes, and figures combine to produce persuasive representations of threats and their preferred responses. Accordingly, Hasian, Lawson, and McFarlane assert that "The formation and maintenance of America's national security state needs to be viewed as a rhetorical accomplishment", and that "The rhetorical crafting of states of 'insecurity' is an inventional and performative accomplishment".[26]

When we are able to discern that in one preface (Trump 2017) a president uses hyperbole to accentuate danger with the effect of immediately increasing the reader's sensation of relief on seeing the measures he has introduced or planned, we may legitimately feel that we are subject to manipulation beyond bare presentation of the facts. We also recognise that threat inflation as a policy technique is at least 2,000 years old.

Notes

1 Donald J. Trump (2017) @realDonaldTrump tweet, https://twitter.com/realDonaldTrump/status/942904686125965312, accessed 04/06/20. The four pillars of the strategy are: protect the American people, the homeland, and the American way of life; promote American prosperity; preserve peace through strength; advance American influence.

2 Jean-Baptiste Michel, Yuan Kui Shen, Aviva Presser Aiden, Adrian Veres, Matthew K. Gray, The Google Books Team, Joseph P. Pickett, Dale Hoiberg, Dan Clancy, Peter Norvig, Jon Orwant, Steven Pinker, Martin A. Nowak, and Erez Lieberman Aiden (2010) "Quantitative Analysis of Culture Using Millions of Digitized Books", *Science*, Published Online Ahead of Print 12/16/2010; Google Books Ngram Viewer case insensitive search for "strategy" between 1800 and 2008 (English corpus 2012), https://books.google.com/ngrams/graph?content=strategy&case_insensitive=on&year_start=1800&year_end=2008&corpus=15&smoothing=7&share=&direct_url=t4%3B%2Cstrategy%3B%2Cc0%3B%2Cs0%3B%3Bstrategy%3B%2Cc0%3B%3BStrategy%3B%2Cc0%3B%3BSTRATEGY%3B%2Cc0#t4%3B%2Cstrategy%3B%2Cc0%3B%2Cs0%3B%3Bstrategy%3B%2Cc1%3B%3BStrategy%3B%2Cc1%3B%3BSTRATEGY%3B%2Cc1

3 Google Books Ngram Viewer case insensitive search for "national security" between 1800 and 2008 (English corpus 2012), https://books.google.com/ngrams/graph?content=national+security&case_insensitive=on&year_start=1800&year_end=2008&corpus=15&smoothing=7&share=&direct_url=t4%3B%2Cnational%20security%3B%2Cc0%3B%2Cs0%3B%3Bnational%20security%3B%2Cc0%3B%3BNational%20Security%3B%2Cc0%3B%3BNational%20security%3B%2Cc0%3B%3BNATIONAL%20SECURITY%3B%2Cc0

4 See Don M. Snider ((1995) *The National Security Strategy: Documenting Strategic Vision* (2nd edn), Strategic Studies Institute, U.S. Army War College) for the subsumption of foreign policy into security implied in the language of the Goldwater-Nichols Act.

5 Snider (1995) p. 5.

6 Clinton's 2000 strategy was published in December 1999. It is included in the sample because it was clearly presented as the strategy *for* 2000, as witnessed by its title, "A National Security Strategy for a New Century".

7 Time (n.d.) "Top 10 Bushisms: A fond look back at George W. Bush's less-than-articulate moments in Office", http://content.time.com/time/specials/packages/article/0,28804,1870938_1870943_1870945,00.html, accessed 06/07/20.

8 WebFX Readability Test Tool, www.webfx.com/tools/read-able/

9 Rudolf Flesch (1979) *How to Write Plain English: A Book for Lawyers and Consumers*, New York: Harper & Row, p. 25.

10 Robert Gunning (1952) *The Technique of Clear Writing*, New York: McGraw-Hill.

11 Meri Coleman and T. L. Liau (1975) "A Computer Readability Formula Designed for Machine Scoring", *Journal of Applied Psychology* 60.2: 283–284.

12 Simon Lancaster (2010) *Speechwriting: The Expert Guide*, London: Robert Hale, p. 63.

13 Quintilian, for example, encouraged moderation in the use of soundbites (*sententiae, Inst.Or.*5.25–34), in elocution (8.Pr.18) and in the use of all figures of speech (9.3.100–102).

14 Lancaster (2010) p. 396.

15 See, for example, M. P. Leffler and J. W. Legro eds (2008) *To Lead the World: American Strategy after the Bush Doctrine*, New York: Oxford University Press; Cary, especially the contributions by Niall Ferguson ("The Problem of Conjecture", pp. 227–249) and Francis Fukuyama ("Soft Talk, Big Stick", pp. 204–226).

16 The apothegms of Roman mime-writer Publilius Syrus became part of this curriculum in the first century AD. Surviving to the present day as the *Sententiae*, they contain such gems as "For the freeborn, debt is bitter slavery" (*Alienum aes homini ingenuo acerba est servitus*), "To accept a benefit is to sell one's freedom" (*Beneficium accipere libertatem est vendere*), "Prosperity must be sensibly sustained or it crushes you" (*Bona quae veniunt nisi sustineantur opprimunt*), and "Whenever you benefit the deserving, you put the world in your debt" (*Beneficium dignis ubi des omnes obliges*). J. Wight Duff and Arnold M. Duff trans. (1934) *Minor Latin Poets, Volume I: Publilius Syrus. Elegies on Maecenas. Grattius. Calpurnius Siculus. Laus Pisonis. Einsiedeln Eclogues. Aetna*, Loeb Classical Library 284, Cambridge, MA: Harvard University Press.

17 "The gravest danger our Nation faces lies at the crossroads of radicalism and technology."

18 George Lakoff identifies the President's use of "friends" and "friendship" at this time as evidence of the Nation as Person metaphor, which lends greater immediacy to the machinations of International Relations: "friends are supposed to be supportive and jump in and help us when we need help. Friends are supposed to be loyal". Lakoff (2003) *Metaphor and War, Again*, California: UC Berkeley.

19 Hartnett and Stengrin see the "deeply religious character" of the 2002 NSS as contributing to a portrayal of America's enemies "not as political actors but as ontologically damaged subhumans", thereby heightening the contrast between the opposing sides; Stephen John Hartnett and Laura Ann Stengrin (2006) "War Rhetorics: The National Security Strategy of the United States and President Bush's Globalization-through-Benevolent-Empire", *The South Atlantic Quarterly* 105.1:175–205, pp. 194, 198. Cf. Noam Chomsky's observation that "In this version of the traditional 'city on a hill' conception, formulated by the founder of realist IR theory, America has a 'transcendent purpose,' 'the establishment of equality in freedom,' and American politics is designed to achieve this 'national purpose,' however flawed it may be in execution"; (2003) "Wars of Terror", *New Political Science* 25.1: 113–127, p. 115. In the preface to the 2015 edition of his *Culture of Terrorism* (London: Pluto Press), Chomsky likewise refers to Bush's "messianic mission" (p. xii).

20 See, for example, Ivo H. Daalder (2006) "Statement on the 2006 National Security Strategy", Washington, DC: The Brookings Institution, www.brookings.edu/opinions/statement-on-the-2006-national-security-strategy/

21 Identified by, amongst others, George Lakoff (2013) *Obama Reframes Syria: Metaphor and War Revisited*, California: UC Berkeley, https://escholarship.org/uc/item/8xm8z9s6; Marta Degani (2015) *Framing the Rhetoric of a Leader: An Analysis of Obama's Election Campaign*, Basingstoke: Palgrave Macmillan; Elena Negrea-Busuioc (2017) "Leading the War at Home and Winning the Race Abroad: Metaphors Used by President Obama to Frame the Fight Against Climate Change", in F. Ervas, E. Gola, and M. G. Rossi eds (2017) *Metaphor in Communication, Science and Education*, De Gruyter: Berlin.

22 Noted, among others, by Peter Feaver (2010) "Obama's National Security Strategy: Real Change or Just 'Bush Lite'?" *Foreign Policy* 27/05/2020, https://foreignpolicy.com/2010/05/27/obamas-national-security-strategy-real-change-or-just-bush-lite/; Christine Gray (2011) "President Obama's 2010 United States National Security Strategy and International Law on the Use of Force", *Chinese Journal of International Law* 10.1: 35–53.

23 For example, "The Wary Consumer", *Newsweek* 07/04/1975: "The American consumer is the principal actor in the ongoing drama of The Great Recession"; "Life After 40", *Forbes* 01/12/1975: "One of the oddities of the Great Recession is that it has apparently been a boon to an unlikely segment of the population - unemployed executives over 40"; "Survival Notes", *Forbes* 26/11/1979: "Until last month, The Great Recession of 1979 was largely a media hoax perpetrated by the Carter Administration."

24 For example, "Between the Lines: Central Problems Still Remain Despite Better Financial Organisation", *The Scotsman* 22/08/2007: "the financial system is better organised than it was at the time of the last global economic catastrophe, the Great Recession of the 1930s".

25 Cf. also Chomsky's assertion in the preface to the 2015 edition of *Culture of Terrorism* (London: Pluto Press, at xvii) that George W. Bush's declaration of the War on Terror was a redeclaration of Reagan's earlier policy.

26 Marouf Hasian Jr, Sean Lawson, and Megan D. McFarlane (2015) *The Rhetorical Invention of America's National Security State*, Lanham: Lexington, pp. 5, 15. See also p. 9f.: "As an apparatus, it produces and is, in part, produced by rhetorics of security and insecurity. It not only produces 'security', both symbolically and materially, but also insecurity via rhetorics of securitization, a particular form of problematization focused on the identification of threats and exigencies to which the technologies, tactics, procedures, and strategies of the national security state are seemingly a necessary response."

3 The war on Big Tech

Construction of internet companies as ideological others

A tradition of technophobia

Suspicion of technology has a long history in the popular imagination. As others have documented comprehensively, each globally disruptive communication technology has been met with a degree of apprehension and active resistance. Longitudinal study of technologies such as telegraphy, telephony, and now the internet has enabled researchers to determine just how disruptive – and accelerative – these have been. Policy makers know from experience that new technology has the potential to bring about change, and change is unsettling.[1]

Twenty-first-century policy makers have been brought up on the same diet of popular science fiction as their follow citizens, one of the central plot lines of which is what happens when technology fails, goes wrong, or supersedes the intelligence and power of humans.[2] As David S. Wall has demonstrated, "the reporting of dystopic narratives about life in networked worlds shapes public reactions to technological change. Reactions which heighten the culture of fear about cybercrime, which in turn, shapes public expectations of online risk, the formation of law and the subsequent interpretation of justice."[3] For Wall, the news media have an active role in perpetuating fear of online environments:

> News reporting tends to simultaneously feed the public's lust for "shocking" information, but also feeds off it – the relationship is dynamic rather than causal. This endless demand for sensationalism sustains the confusion of rhetoric with reality to create, what Baudrillard described as "le vertige de la realité" or "dizzying whirl of reality". By blurring predictions about "what could happen" with "what is actually happening" the message is given by various media that novel events are far more prevalent than they really are. Once a "signal event", such as a novel form of cybercrime, captures media attention and heightens existing public anxiety then other news sources will feed off the original news story and spread virally across cyberspace. In such manner, relatively minor events can have significant impacts upon public beliefs compared with their actual consequences, especially when they result in panics and moral panics.[4]

DOI: 10.4324/9781003028062-4

As will become evident in the discussion that follows, rhetorical analysis of public discourse on the misuse of technology and online harm permits the identification of a commonality of approach in policy-making and mass media coverage, especially in the use of emotive language and appeals.

Politicians and civil servants in many countries also experienced the Cold War first- or second-hand in their formative years, with its politically sanctioned demonisation of foreign actors and tendency to escalation and brinkmanship. International relations in the twenty-first century retain much of that flavour, with a strong focus on shows of strength towards, and getting a good deal from, other sovereign states. At the state level, there is a tradition of bringing big business and other non-state actors to heel. Governments are tasked with maintaining order, which very often means maintaining the *status quo*, or oversight of gradual, measurable progress. In the last 500 years, foreign trade, banking, oil and gas, transport, and other sectors have all been subject to domestic and international regulatory measures. In the last century, communications have increasingly been in regulatory focus. Until the advent of the World Wide Web, this has largely been a domestic matter.

Conversely, Big Tech, as embodied by providers such as Microsoft, Google, Facebook, and Apple, is i) often foreign, ii) a non-state actor, iii) massively wealthy, and iv) intellectually elitist by default. For all these reasons, it is deemed to be outside of the effective control of the government. But sovereign governments, especially elected ones, are tasked with protecting their citizens. In the field of online safety, this translates specifically to the unenviable objective of attempting to impose national authority on an entity over whom they logically and legally have none. The problem is epitomised by the popular observation that if Facebook were a country, it would be the world's largest in terms of population (2.7 billion monthly active users, as of 30/06/2020[5]).

Societies have defined themselves against other people for thousands of years. Constructing an "other" is both a cohesive and a polarising act. Classical Greek literature portrayed non-Greeks as barbarians (*barbaroi*), distinguished by their alien language and savagery.[6] Necessary in times of war to engender cohesion and commonality of identity and purpose, the urge to identify outsiders as such is a defensive measure that strengthens (or is perceived to strengthen) the security of the community. This urge has of course also given rise to numerous persecutions in the name of security and community protection, and to no small degree fuels the xenophobia and other intolerances of contemporary societies.

In the twenty-first-century sovereign state, the "other" is most often another state, or a non-state actor ideologically opposed to the dominant societal order. Separatists and domestic or international terrorists are often in this constituency; depending on the regime, criminals and criminal groups, people of other faiths, and political and human rights activists may also be so identified.[7] As we saw in the last chapter, George W. Bush's use of constraining antitheses and blurring of the distinctions between undesirable actors reinforced the notion of a "clash of civilisations".[8] Foreign regimes are not the only subjects of this construction. In 2019, media outlets began to describe President Trump's response to social media platforms' censorship of some of his posts as his "war on Big Tech".[9] While this is perhaps the most overt recent characterisation of hostility between governments and global technology companies, the rhetorical depiction of tech companies as hostile actors has a longer and more complex history.

Them and us: drawing the battle lines

On 25 November 2014, the UK House of Commons Intelligence and Security Committee (ISC) published its report into the murder of Fusilier Lee Rigby. Rigby had been attacked and killed on 22 May 2013 by two men. At the scene, one of the men claimed that the murder was an act of vengeance for Muslim deaths at the hands of British soldiers.[10] Both suspects were British nationals who had converted to Islam. On 19 December 2013, they were convicted of Rigby's murder, and subsequently sentenced to life imprisonment.

In the debate in the House of Commons, the then Prime Minister David Cameron led with the finding that the ISC did "not consider that, given what the [intelligence] Agencies knew at the time, they were in a position to prevent the murder of Fusilier Lee Rigby".[11] The Prime Minister went on to describe these agencies as "Britain's silent heroes, and the whole country owes them an enormous debt of gratitude". He reminded the House of the "extreme pressure that our agencies are under", and characterised the prioritisation of the "many and various potential threats to our security" as "incredibly difficult".

This depiction stands in clear contrast to that of internet companies. Reporting the ISC's finding that the role of one company "could have been decisive", the Prime Minister honed in on a "crucial online exchange" in which one of the suspects expressed a desire to kill a soldier, and about which the ISC concluded "this is the single issue which – had it been known at the time – might have enabled MI5 to prevent the attack".[12]

The entirety of Cameron's speech merits a close reading. It is replete with the language of expectations placed on companies, "serious concerns" over their actions, and of the unacceptability of terrorist communications being out of the reach of the authorities. Two statements in the debate require specific mention here, not least because they came to be the focus of media coverage that day. The first is a statement by the Prime Minister himself in relation to the companies: "Their networks are being used to plot murder and mayhem. It is their social responsibility to act on this, and we expect them to live up to that responsibility."[13]

The general sentiment here is beyond question; the logic is not. In the first place, it is something of a stretch from the ISC's finding in a specific case that disclosure of a message could have prevented a murder to a general assertion that networks are being used to plot murder.[14] Lee Rigby's murder was in fact not planned in the message mentioned, but the belief that online communication tools are being routinely used to plan terrorist attacks and expansive but ill-defined "mayhem" is what we are encouraged to adopt. To some degree, Rigby's murder serves as the modern rhetorical equivalent of the Classical *exemplum*, a real or fictional example intended to demonstrate an argument. Moreover, the language of responsibility has a curious dual effect. The thrust of the statement is that the internet companies are not living up to their responsibilities, that is, they are *ir*responsible. At the same time, the networks' collocation with and alleged facilitation of murder mark them as responsible, in the sense of culpable for the crimes.

That both these readings are possible is endorsed by subsequent media coverage and an exchange later in the debate. Former Labour Home Secretary and Foreign Secretary Jack Straw's intervention follows that of the Prime Minister in its antithetical structure, starting with the government agencies' performance:

> These agencies, and the police, have people who are very highly skilled and who are working very long hours – but, with the best will in the world, they are human. There will be some cases where the terrorists escape detection and there will therefore be terrorist outrages, as there have been in terrorist campaigns.

Drawing attention to the humanity of the agencies and the stresses faced by the people who work in them elicits our sympathy, just as did the Prime Minister's earlier emphasis of their calibre, heroic status, and difficult tasks. Internet companies are not afforded the same courtesy:

> Lastly, may I press the Prime Minister again on the issue of the United States-based internet companies and ask him to take it up with the US at the highest level? Is there not a cultural problem among the leadership of some of these companies, which have a distorted "libertarian" ideology and believe that somehow that allows them to be wholly detached from responsibility to Governments and to the peoples whom we democratically represent in this country and abroad?[15]

In contrast to the humans of the UK intelligence agencies, senior executives of internet companies are depicted as shadowy, non-specified, "leadership" figures. Echoing the Prime Minister's words earlier in the debate, they are irresponsible. But they are also problematic, possessed of a distorted ideology and apart from democracy. In the context of a debate on terrorism, which has elsewhere sought to attribute to internet companies responsibility for the failure to prevent a terrorist murder, this intervention effectively characterises internet companies as hostile non-state actors, not unlike terrorists.

The Prime Minister responds to Mr Straw's intervention by saying: "I agree with everything that the right hon. Gentleman has said", and takes another opportunity to restate the antithesis, contrasting the work of the intelligence agencies with lack of cooperation from the internet companies. In a move reminiscent of US government communications on the War on Terror, Cameron and Straw construct a binary opposition between good and evil, which has the effect of closing down nuanced, more thoughtful appreciations of, for example, company liability for communications of which they have no prior knowledge, and existing legal prohibitions against disclosure of communications content across jurisdictions. By depicting government agency MI5 as saintly and heroic fellow citizens, and by associating internet companies with terrorists, the "them and us" construction turns Big Tech into the inhuman, uncivilised, malevolent outsider. Unlike George W. Bush's ultimatum, "Either you are with us, or you are with the terrorists", this characterisation does not give the companies the opportunity to choose sides.

What happens next provides a further clue to the artifice of the House of Commons exchange. Under the headline, "Facebook 'could have prevented Lee Rigby murder'; Facebook has been named as the internet company which failed to pass on crucial information that could have stopped the murder of Fusilier Lee Rigby", *The Telegraph* newspaper reported in its edition the next morning: "Facebook failed to pass on information that could have prevented the murder of Fusilier Lee Rigby and is a 'safe haven for terrorists', a report has concluded."[16]

But the company involved had not been identified in the report or the debate the day before. Indeed, when the Prime Minister was asked to do so, he replied that he did

> not think that saying which company it was would be right, because I do not want to give a running commentary on which companies are better than others at analysing this problem and reporting it to the Government, for what I would have thought were quite obvious reasons about the signal that that would send to people who want to do us harm.

Interventions in the debate by ISC members Dr Julian Lewis MP and Fiona McTaggart MP draw attention to alleged leaks to the media, McTaggart stating:

> As a new member of the Intelligence and Security Committee, I was not able to hear all the evidence that led to the conclusions in the report, but I have observed the extensive leaks about its conclusions. Those leaks concern me deeply, because I think that they undermine the impact of the report, and they seem to have been designed to lead people to a particular conclusion.[17]

Dr Lewis, meanwhile, describes "a serious leak at an early stage from the redacted draft of the report, which was reported in a Sunday paper". On 14 November, *The Telegraph* had published an article with the headline: "Online clues may have signalled plans of Lee Rigby killers report expected to reveal; But crucial online activities of Lee Rigby killer Michael Adebolajo was [sic] not flagged to MI5 until after the murder".[18] It revealed the expected findings of the ISC's report over a week before its publication.

While it is impossible to test the validity of McTaggart's assessment above based on publicly available textual evidence, the article's headline focus on online activity, the self-fulfilling statement that "The issue will reignite the debate over the role of Internet companies in tackling extremists and terrorists who exploit their systems and whether appropriate safeguards are in place to spot them", and the recital of then GCHQ Director Robert Hannigan's description of US technology companies earlier that month as "the command and control networks of choice" for terrorists, align with the rhetorical trajectory of the 25 November debate as set out by the Prime Minister: namely, that one internet company was responsible for the failure to prevent Lee Rigby's murder.[19]

By the end of the day (in time to be included in the morning editions on the 26th), the UK media knew that the company in question was Facebook. The identity had not been revealed in the ISC's report, nor in any public communication by the government. So it is reasonable to infer that this, too, was a leak. Of the media outlets that followed the government's lead in attributing to Facebook at least partial responsibility for the murder, perhaps the headline most free from ambiguity was in *The Sun* on 26 November:

> BLOOD ON THEIR HANDS
>
> EXCLUSIVE by MIKE SULLIVAN
>
> LEE Rigby's family last night said Facebook had "blood on their hands" - after it emerged the US web giant could have foiled his killers.
>
> It never flagged up one of them crowing of a lust to "murder a soldier", a probe by MPs revealed yesterday.
>
> Facebook has still not divulged details from five more accounts the brute held - 18 months after Lee, 25, was butchered.
>
> Full Story - Pages 4 and 5

With the UK's largest paid-for newspaper circulation, *The Sun* has almost unmatched national reach, and a tendency to sensationalise, as the use of graphic, emotionally charged vocabulary such as "crowing", "lust", "brute" and "butchered" in the text above illustrate.[20] Whether the headline metaphor above was *The Sun*'s confection, or whether the paper indeed quoted the family's words verbatim, this highly graphic image depicts Facebook as one of the murderers.

One further item in *The Telegraph*'s coverage of the 25 November debate merits detailed consideration. The article reads:

> David Cameron accused internet companies of failing to assist in the fight against terrorism, warning that they had a "moral duty" to act because "their networks are being used to plot murder and mayhem".
>
> He claimed that the heads of global web firms had a "distorted libertarian ideology" that made them "wholly detached from responsibility to governments and to the peoples that we democratically represent".

In the second paragraph, *The Telegraph* puts in the Prime Minister's mouth words that Hansard, the official record of the UK Parliament, attributes to opposition politician Jack Straw. The effect is to give government endorsement to the belief that tech companies are ideologically opposed to democracy, much like the terrorists who use their platforms. One may speculate about the forensics of the matter: whether this was the result merely of sloppy journalism on the part of *The Telegraph*, whether the newspaper consciously misattributed these words, or even whether these words had originally been drafted for the Prime Minister to deliver. Regardless of the precise route, textual analysis of these communications has revealed that certain mainstream media outlets and the government appear to have been pressing the same rhetorical points.

Pathos and ethos, not logos: in defence of evidence-based policy-making

We have already seen an example of one tabloid newspaper's use of sensational language, designed to trigger an emotional response in its readership (*pathos*) in relation to a national security issue. We have seen how the US National Security Strategies have deliberated and proposed policy from a moral standpoint, and how UK politicians constructed an ethical antithesis in relation to US technology companies (*ethos*). When it comes to developing new national legislation, one would expect a strong basis in evidence (*logos*). A close reading of one text at the core of current plans to regulate in the online safety space suggests that may not always be the case.

The UK government makes use of two key documents to set forth policy proposals: in Parliament's words, Green Papers "set out for discussion, proposals which are still at a formative stage"; White Papers "are issued by the Government as statements of policy, and often set out proposals for legislative changes, which may be debated before a Bill is introduced".[21]

Following the publication of a Green Paper on Internet Safety in 2017, and a response to that Green Paper in 2018, in April 2019 the government issued a White Paper on Online Harms, endorsed and introduced jointly by the then Home Secretary Sajid Javid, and the then Minister for Digital, Culture, Media and Sport, Jeremy Wright.[22] According to Parliament's definition above, the entirety of this nearly 100-page document should be read as a statement of the government's proposed policy on the issue. Fortunately, its structure highlights two sections that allow for a more efficient rhetorical analysis: the aforementioned joint ministerial foreword (3ff.), and the Executive Summary (5ff.), containing a brief statement of the problem, and outlining the proposed response. The first of these is clearly intended as a public address to its readership; the second may be taken to be representative of the government's position and rationale (*logos*) for regulatory action. The ministerial foreword reads as follows (emphasis added):

> The internet is an integral part of everyday life for so many people. Nearly nine in ten UK adults and 99% of 12 to 15 year olds are online. **As the internet continues to grow and transform our lives, often for the better, we should not ignore the very real harms which people face online every day**.
>
> In the wrong hands the internet can be used to spread terrorist and other illegal or harmful content, **undermine** civil discourse, and abuse or bully other people. Online harms are widespread and can have serious consequences.
>
> Two thirds of adults in the UK are **concerned** about content online, and close to half say they have seen hateful content in the past year. The **tragic**

recent events in New Zealand show just how quickly **horrific** terrorist and extremist content can spread online.

We cannot allow these harmful behaviours and content to **undermine** the significant benefits that the digital revolution can offer. While some companies have taken steps to improve safety on their platforms, **progress has been too slow and inconsistent overall**. If we **surrender** our online spaces to those who spread hate, abuse, fear and vitriolic content, then **we will all lose**.

So our challenge as a society is to help shape an internet that is open and vibrant but also protects its users from harm. The UK is committed to a free, open and secure internet, and will continue to protect freedom of expression online. We must also take decisive action to make people safer online.

This White Paper therefore puts forward **ambitious plans for a new system** of accountability and oversight for tech companies, moving far beyond self-regulation. A new regulatory framework for online safety will make clear **companies' responsibilities** to keep UK users, particularly children, safer online with the most robust action to counter illegal content and activity.

This will be overseen by an independent regulator which will set clear safety standards, backed up by reporting requirements and effective enforcement powers.

Although other countries have introduced regulation to address specific types of harm, **this is the first attempt globally** to address a comprehensive spectrum of online harms in a single and coherent way.

The UK's future prosperity will depend heavily on having a vibrant technology sector. Innovation and safety online are not mutually exclusive; through building trust in the digital economy and in new technologies, this White Paper will build a **firmer foundation** for this vital sector.

As a **world-leader** in emerging technologies and innovative regulation, the UK is well placed to seize these opportunities. We want technology itself to be part of the solution, and this White Paper proposes measures to boost the tech-safety sector in the UK, as well as measures to help users manage their safety online.

We believe the approach in this White Paper can lead towards new, global approaches for online safety that support our **democratic values**, and promote a free, open and secure internet; and we will work with other countries to build an international consensus behind it.

Online safety is a shared **responsibility** between companies, the government and users. We would encourage everyone to take part in the consultation that accompanies this White Paper, and work with us to **make Britain the safest place** in the world to be online.

How are we to feel on reading this statement? Excited at the emphasised novelty and ambition of the plan? Proud that "Britain" is more innovative, more ambitious, in short, better than other countries? Convinced that technological progress brings danger? Concerned and horrified as we have been told to be – as we have been told we are – in the third paragraph? Ready for battle against behaviours that threaten the very core of society, as suggested by repetition of the metaphorical "undermine", the aspiration for building "a firmer foundation" and as the images of surrender and loss suggest?

Online safety is stated to be a shared responsibility. Earlier in the foreword, however, only companies are mentioned in relation to the new regulatory framework. Criticism is reserved for companies and bad actors. As in the debate on the murder of Lee Rigby, companies and criminals are collocated, aligned against a robust government that will enforce the defence of democracy as we know it on our behalf.

This tension between the professed aim "to address a comprehensive spectrum of online harms in a single and coherent way" and the focus on only one stakeholder group has not gone unnoticed by researchers. As Victoria Nash notes, the focus on technological cures for a range of social ills including child sexual exploitation and abuse (CSEA) material, hate speech, terrorist content, self-harm imagery, disinformation, and even content uploaded from prisons, neglects the non-technological manifestations of these problems.[23] As I have argued elsewhere, the efforts of technology companies can only be one part of an effective response to the public health issue of CSEA: without properly resourced and trained law enforcement, criminal justice and social work specialists, effective education and awareness programmes for children, deterrence and support mechanisms for offenders and potential offenders, and psychosocial support for those who have experienced abuse, the response will only ever be partial and therefore unsatisfactory.[24] Systematic mapping of the optimal response functions identifies at least nine relevant stakeholder sectors. Similar may be said of hate speech, the sharing of terrorist content, bullying and the other "harms" in scope: industry efforts alone will not remove certain individuals' desire to engage in these activities, nor the social conditions that prove fertile for others to fall victim. And while the Ministers state that they "want technology itself to be part of the solution", it is clear from the context that they are referring to the UK online safety industry, not US tech companies.

A further tension manifests in the foreword's antithetical depiction of technology. The internet is integral to our lives, but online harms are widespread. The digital revolution offers significant benefits, but also threatens an existential struggle against "hate, abuse, fear and vitriolic content". The UK "is committed to a free, open and secure internet" but the government is proposing to regulate. Elsewhere we have seen antithesis deployed to signpost the preferred choice of two options. Here, intentionally or otherwise, it highlights the difficulty of achieving all of the stated objectives, some of which are incompatible: "our challenge as a society is to help shape an internet that is open and vibrant but also protects its users from harm". The authors appear to have sensed this tension. The statement "Innovation and safety online are not mutually exclusive" reads as an attempt to address the uncertainty to which the foreword's content and very structure have themselves contributed. The text has an inconsistent voice, arguably at least two. In this respect, we do not need to see the Ministers' photographs and signatures to know that it has more than one author or guiding mind: its rhetorical construction betrays this.

A reader could reasonably object that there is nothing incorrect in an antithetical representation of the internet. It does indeed bring both great benefits and problematic behaviours. But there are alternative, more consistent, methods of execution. The most notable is seen in President Obama's address to the 2015 Cybersecurity and Consumer Protection Summit at Stanford University. This speech will be the focus of more detailed analysis in the next chapter. In the context of the current discussion, it will suffice to say that in close to 3,700 words, the benefits of the internet lead and dominate. When, after 840 words the President comes to address negative aspects of the internet, he refers to them neutrally as "cyber challenges", and tackles the paradox of benefits and threats head on:

> And it's one of the great paradoxes of our time that the very technologies that empower us to do great good can also be used to undermine us and inflict great harm. The same information technologies that help make our military the most advanced in the world are targeted by hackers from China and Russia who go after our defense contractors and systems that are built for our troops. The same social media we use in government to advocate for democracy and human rights around the world can also be used by terrorists to spread hateful ideologies. So these cyber threats are a challenge to our national security.

The President uses three successive antitheses with pointed repetition to illustrate the paradox cleanly. He then pivots to discussion of the threats, after which he sets out a four point plan, updates the audience on recent progress, and announces the signing of a new executive order. In stark contrast to the foreword of the Online Harms White Paper, he commends companies for "stepping up as well", thanks everyone for their partnership, and leaves the audience with an inspirational image that draws on his fondness for building metaphors: "if we keep working together in a spirit of collaboration, like all those innovators before us, our work will endure, like a great cathedral, for centuries to come". Recognising that a speech of nearly 3,700 words has greater scope for eloquence than a foreword of 550, nevertheless Obama's address at Stanford demonstrates that a consistent argument is possible *despite* the apparently essential benefit/threat paradox of internet technology. The White Paper foreword suffers by comparison. It is disordered, its effect potentially disorientating.

The White Paper's Executive Summary allows us to examine the rationale (*logos*) for the government's regulatory proposal. Its stated basis is in "the prevalence of illegal and harmful content online, and the level of public concern about online harms". As I and others have argued elsewhere, the paper's headline contention that

> Illegal and unacceptable content and activity is widespread online, and UK users are concerned about what they see and experience on the internet. The prevalence of the most serious illegal content and activity, which threatens our national security or the physical safety of children, is unacceptable.

is fundamentally flawed.[25] As Andy Phippen and Emma Bond note, a lack of clear definition of exactly what constitutes an "online harm" or "unacceptable content", and the range of illegal and otherwise harmful activities cited as examples in the document, preclude any kind of trustworthy measurement of the overall prevalence.[26] The only area for which prevalence data is presented in this paper is online CSEA. Prevalence for other activities identified as online harms cannot be extrapolated from these numbers. Logically, it is impossible to determine whether the prevalence is unacceptable if that prevalence is unknown.

Meanwhile, the argument for regulating in response to public concern is not proven by the evidence adduced in the document. For example, the White Paper's principal source of evidence for public concern, Ofcom's *Online Nation* survey, appears to show that people aged 16 or over are less concerned about child sexual abuse images than they are about having their data stolen.[27] Far from proving the case, appeal to this data appears to demonstrate a mismatch between public concern and objective measures of the gravity of harm. Indeed, it cautions us against relying on public concern as an indicator.

I am not alone in assessing the Online Harms White Paper as light on logical proof. Nash acknowledges that "a focus on improving platform governance could be justified if it demonstrated both a clear policy rationale and a carefully-calibrated set of proposals", but concludes, "arguably, neither of these is evident in the OHWP".[28] Phippen and Bond identify "throughout the paper, a problematic theme of rhetoric over evidence".[29]

This absence of evidence (*logos*) coincides with a penchant of the authors for appeals to morality (*ethos*) and the language of emotion (*pathos*). In addition to frequent usage of the vocabulary of responsibility, there are several references to "ethics" and its forms, including evidence from the 2018 Edelman Trust Barometer that "70% of Britons believe that social media companies do not do enough to prevent illegal or unethical behaviours on their platforms" (OHWP 37); there are multiple mentions of norms, specifically the government's "wider programme of work to establish the right norms and rules for the internet" (25).

Furthermore, the White Paper proposes the establishment of "a new statutory duty of care to make companies take more responsibility for the safety of their users and tackle harm caused by content or activity on their services" (41). This duty of care is envisaged not only as a moral responsibility, but as a legal duty enforceable by a regulator, with "substantial fines" and "liability of individual members of senior management" of companies among possible outcomes (7). The duty of care concept appears to seek to bestow on the companies legal responsibility for crimes and an unspecified number of non-criminal but undesirable behaviours committed on their platforms *by other people*. Nash notes that such a duty fails to engage with the problem of user responsibility;[30] Phippen and Bond, meanwhile, highlight a lack of clarity in the definition of this duty, and its potential relationship to the tort of negligence.[31] Recalling the depiction of Facebook as directly involved in the murder of Lee Rigby, the proposal is the natural policy counterpart to the rhetorical presentation of tech companies as lawless "others".

The tabloidisation of online safety

In addition to appeals to the morality of the reader, the White Paper makes frequent use of emotional and emotive language when describing some of the harms in scope. In this way, it not only presents how the government feels about these harms, but also seeks to generate the same feelings in the reader (appeal to *pathos*): for example, "The most appalling and horrifying illegal content and activity remains prevalent on an unacceptable scale"; and "Terrorists also continue to use online services to spread their vile propaganda and mobilise support" (12).

What each of us finds appalling or horrifying or vile is surely highly subjective. While we may agree with the deployment of these adjectives in conversation or at a press conference following an incident, their inclusion in a document designed objectively to present the evidence base for a legislative proposal is incongruous and unhelpful. By using these terms in a White Paper, the government seeks to set the tone for society's perceptions and responses: content and activity is branded as universally appalling, horrifying, and vile. Anyone who does not find it so is not "one of us". According to this scheme, the appropriate response to the class of online harms is shock and outrage, as opposed to careful consideration of the facts and merits of each case.

Antithesis of scale lends a hyperbolic flavour to our emotionally heightened state: the scale is big, companies' efforts too small (although neither is quantified by an objective measure), and we are to understand that we are not going to stand for it ("unacceptable"). Later in the document, platforms themselves are depicted as dangerous purely by virtue of their size: "the regulator's initial focus will be on those companies that pose the biggest and clearest risk of harm to users, either because of the scale of the platforms or because of known issues with serious harms" (54).

The word "vile" in any context is subjective, sensationalist even. It has been used before in the context of online harm, in comments made in 2013 by then Prime Minister David Cameron following the suicide of 14-year-old Hannah Smith, apparently after being bullied on social media platform ask.fm:

> The people that operate these websites have got to step up to the plate and show some responsibility in the way that they run these websites. Second point is, look, just because someone does something online, it doesn't mean they're above the law. If you incite someone to do harm, if you incite violence, that is breaking the law, whether that's online or offline. And I want to make sure we take as much action as we can. But also there's something all of us can do as well, as parents, and as users of the internet, and that is not use some of these vile sites. Boycott them. Don't go there. Don't join them. We need to do that as well. So I'm very keen we look at all the action we can take to try and help stop future tragedies like this.[32]

A subsequent police investigation found that Hannah had set up the accounts to verbally abuse herself.[33] That aside, there is much in these comments that is familiar: companies have to do more, be responsible because they are assumed already to be culpable. Identifying the technology itself as vile invites our revulsion, but here we are also explicitly asked to reject the platforms.

The word "vile" is popular with the tabloid media. Indeed, a search of news articles for the phrases "vile websites" and "vile sites" reveals a usage that predates Cameron's seemingly distinctive coinage. It first appears in relation to online safety on 12 December 1997, in an article in *The Sun* entitled "Pervert is Nailed":

> A FIREMAN exposed by The Sun for peddling filth on the Internet has been arrested by U.S. customs over the transmission of child porn.
> Ray Jones, 34, was held at Miami International Airport on a flight from London. Jones earned a fortune from his vile Internet website while on sick leave from Ealing Fire Station, West London. He believed he was immune from prosecution in the UK because his empire was based in America.

Here the phrase is associated with perversion, the distribution of child sexual abuse material made at once more graphic and to some extent trivialised by the use of a dirty metaphor ("filth"). The next appearance is in a *News of the World* article on 11 June 2000, entitled "Tartan terror threat to the Queen; Exclusive":

> Violent demo planned for Scots visit
> TARTAN terrorists are plotting May Day-style riots when the Queen visits Scotland next month.
> The Scottish Separatist Group hope to cause mass anarchy and disruption during the royal visit to Inverness.
> Crack SAS units have been drafted in after nuts posted details of the monarch's top-secret route onto a vile website.
> Some crackpots have also suggested bringing RIFLES to the visit and creating diversions to leave the Queen open to attack.
> FULL STORY - Pages 8 & 9

Here the invitation to turn to a double-page story marks this article as a front-page by-line designed to serve as bait. The designation of the website as "vile" serves, along with colloquial references to mental instability and hyperbole ("mass anarchy"), to pique our interest sufficiently to read further.

On 21 July 2013, two weeks before Prime Minister Cameron's comments on ask.fm, *The Sun* ran a double-page article on child sexual abuse material (bold emphasis added):

> HELP US, PM; FOR APRIL; TIA AND APRIL'S PARENTS IN PLEA TO CAMERON ON WEB CHILD ABUSE PICS
> THE parents of murdered schoolgirls April Jones and Tia Sharp have pleaded with David Cameron to help rid the internet of child abuse images.

> Coral and Paul Jones and Natalie Sharp and her partner David Niles quizzed the Prime Minister during a special 30-minute heart-to-heart at Downing Street, organised by The Sun.
>
> The parents of murdered April, five, and Tia, 12, said the **vile** online pictures are fuelling paedophiles' **evil** crimes and demanded search engine firms should do much more to prevent people posting and accessing the **shocking** images …
>
> Coral and Paul Jones, whose daughter April was sexually assaulted and murdered by **loner** Mark Bridger, produced a picture of a young teenage girl hugging an inflatable penis.
>
> They explained their daughter had found it five minutes after logging on to a website which was supposed to support April. A visibly **shocked** Prime Minister took the image from them and promised to crack down on the spread of **vile** images …
>
> Both sets of parents told Mr Cameron that search engine companies such as Google should be doing more to stop **perverts** getting access to the **shocking** snaps.
>
> Natalie, whose daughter Tia was abused and murdered by **warped** killer Stuart Hazell, told the PM that even an innocent phrase in Google can bring up indecent images …
>
> At the meeting, attended by Mr Cameron's web chief Claire Perry, the parents suggested ways the image production line could be halted. This included tracking pictures uploaded on the web, grading images and getting tough with search engines and **vile websites** …
>
> After the emotional meeting, the PM told *The Sun* he was determined to solve the problem and felt the tide of public opinion was turning against the big corporations on the issue. He said: "This could be a long-running **battle** but we have the public on our side."

Passing over the detail that *The Sun* appears to have orchestrated the meeting on which it is reporting, it is evident from the language used to describe the criminal activities in question that this article is far from neutral. It seeks to heighten readers' emotional response using exactly the same qualifiers as the Online Harms White Paper.[34] Both texts instruct us to join the government in shock, the appropriate response to vileness. Tellingly, the outcome announced by the Prime Minister is a war – or at least a battle – against search engines, here collocated and aligned with child abuse websites.

In the Online Harms White Paper, emotive and emotional language operates in dynamic interaction with appeals to ethics and logic. In the absence of compelling evidence (*logos*) of prevalence and public concern, the authors deploy morally and emotionally charged language (*ethos* and *pathos*). The result is a regulatory proposal that is focused on making companies *do the right thing*, and that – perhaps somewhat jarringly – seeks to simultaneously express and arouse horror and indignation. A close reading of the rhetoric of this text reveals this instance of policy-making to be less than rational, and certainly not objective. The very real risk of emotionally driven policy is that in failing to have a "clear eyed" appreciation of the problem, it may also fail to address it effectively.

The tabloid media of course goes further in developing a rhetorical shorthand for certain categories of "bad actor", particularly paedophiles and child sex offenders. A cursory review of UK newspaper articles this century reveals them to be "evil", "twisted", "beasts", "monsters", "sick", "paedos", "pervs", "sex fiends"; their activities are "sickening", "sordid", "horrors", "depravity", "too disgusting to report", "filthy"; when they are apprehended for a crime they are "snared", or "caged"; their victims are "hunted", "prey" and "preyed upon". There are a number of patterns discernible in the use of these terms. The offenders are certainly dehumanised, predatory, and themselves legitimate prey. Their characterisation as deviant sets them apart from "us", and their activities provoke specific reactions in right-thinking people. But at the same time, qualifiers like "filthy" and "sordid" have more problematic connotations, especially in this context. In combination with trivialising or otherwise crude language like "paedo", "sicko", "pics" and "snaps", and persistent use of the term "child porn" for child sexual abuse material (*The Sun* alone registering 2,634 headlines containing the phrase so far in the twenty-first century[35]), they may appeal to our instincts for gutter smut. While the language of othering provokes aversion, the clipped shorthand of tabloid titillation entices us to keep reading, and to turn to the double-page feature.

Such sensation-making representations have arguably contributed to the evolution of child sexual abuse into the ultimate emotional trigger for society at large, in Western societies at least. In the run up to the 2016 US election, the viral "Pizzagate" conspiracy theory sought to implicate senior Democratic party figures including presidential candidate Hillary Clinton in the trafficking and sexual abuse of children. Such was the currency of child sexual abuse as a trigger for outrage, that it prompted not only the sending of death threats to staff at the pizza parlour in question, but also led to a firearms incident on site. Despite this theory having been debunked, the association of the "liberal elite" with child sexual abuse has persisted. At the time of writing, the baseless QAnon conspiracy theory, that (among other things) Donald Trump is waging war against a Satanic cabal of Democrat child abusers, is gaining traction ahead of the 2020 US election using the hashtags #SaveTheChildren and #SaveOurChildren. Child sexual abuse has itself become a rhetorical device, and a politically useful one at that.

Big Tech as voiceless – silence as rhetoric

The study of silence – or the absence of speech – has a long history, particularly in the fields of linguistics, ontological philosophy, and criminal justice. In the field of criminal justice, the right to silence enshrined in many countries' criminal codes, which protects suspects from self-incrimination under duress, has become a familiar trope of police dramas on television. While a "no comment" response under questioning is itself neutral, one inference to be drawn is that there is information worth concealing. In this and other scenarios, silence can create a space in which other parties in an exchange can insert their own interpretations without challenge.[36] So, Quintilian observes on the practice of omitting inconvenient facts in court: "what sort of art is it that admits the weakness of a cause by silence?" (*Inst.Or.*4.2.66).

Silence is also of strategic utility to Classical orators. For Quintilian, it is a conscious act, whether an exercise of tact (8.3.39), a sudden break in speech which is left unfinished (*interpellatio*, 9.1.32) or a withholding of information (*reticentia*, ad loc. cit.). In all these cases, silence is not simply an absence of speech. What is unsaid is present "in the room": it may already be known to all and not require repeating; or it may be implied but not specified, leaving the audience to imagine their own version of events. Cicero identifies both *interpellatio* and *reticentia* as rhetorical devices (*De Oratore* 3.53.205). In his speech against the conspirator Catiline, he famously depicts the Roman Senate's silence as evidence of condemnation.[37]

Responses from US tech companies may also be deemed to amount to silence in cases where they consist – or largely consist – of formulaic statements that do not address the specifics of an issue of public interest.[38] Indeed, the very repetition of formulaic language like "We take the safety of our users very seriously" may have an effect opposite from that intended. Repetition risks being perceived as robotic (an accusation often levelled at tech company CEOs themselves), and drawing attention to that which has been left *unsaid*.

Edward Snowden's revelation in 2013 of alleged mass surveillance of online communications by the US National Security Agency was arguably the event that prompted some of the largest US tech companies increasingly to adopt a "no comment" approach to communications on security and safety issues, or to issue formulaic statements that amounted to the same. A number of companies were quick to issue public denials that they had granted direct access to their servers under the PRISM program.[39] These statements sought to distance companies from the notion of collusion with the government, and to emphasise their adherence to legal protections.[40] One by one, they introduced or renewed their focus on publishing transparency reports, detailing the number of government requests for user data.

Cooperation with government authorities on safety and security issues very quickly became the most sensitive subject for these companies. With little prospect of clarification from the governments themselves, none forthcoming on PRISM, and often hampered by legal restrictions on matters relating to ongoing criminal investigations, companies in the media spotlight had frequent recourse to stock phrases. So, *The Telegraph* article on the parliamentary debate into the death of Lee Rigby concludes:

> A Facebook spokesman said: "Like everyone else, we were horrified by the vicious murder of Fusilier Lee Rigby. We don't comment on individual cases but Facebook's policies are clear, we do not allow terrorist content on the site and take steps to prevent people from using our service for these purposes."

Three stock phrases have come to dominate responses from online service providers in the last decade. The first of these is "We take the safety of our users very seriously". A cursory Google search reveals over 30,000 results for this sentence, with the first page of results linked to public announcements and responses to press enquiries from numerous dating apps, the automated customer service response for reports to Kik Messenger service, and statements from apps for music creation, video creation such as musical.ly, the predecessor of TikTok, and various other social media platforms.[41] It is often combined with another formulaic phrase, "we have [a] zero tolerance [policy] for/towards X [behaviour, content]". For example:

> Musical.ly told BBC Trending: "We take the safety of our users very seriously and we have zero tolerance for inappropriate, illegal, or predatory behaviour on our apps. We urge our users to report any inappropriate activity to us."[42]
>
> A YouTube spokesman said: "We take the safety of our users very seriously and have a zero-tolerance policy towards content that incites violence."[43]

A third phrase, "There is no place for X [behaviour, content] on Y [app, platform]", is also a regular feature of company statements on safety issues:

> "There is no place for hate speech on Facebook and Instagram, and we don't want it on our platforms," Facebook said.[44]
>
> There is no place on Twitter for terrorist organizations or violent extremist groups and individuals who affiliate with and promote their illicit activities.[45]
>
> "The second thing I would say is we have zero tolerance, zero tolerance for hate speech and terrorism. There is no place for any of that on our platforms, and we have already made a commitment."[46]

Similarity of language across statements by executives, written policies, and automated customer service responses serve to render these phrases even more robotic and unhuman/inhumane. Through constant repetition they lose meaning. In some cases, they may seem dismissive of real-world harm and victimisation, as in the statement: "There is no place for grooming or child exploitation on our platforms, and we use technology to proactively find and quickly remove it."[47]

Formulaic responses may be read as a kind of silence in as much as they engage with profoundly human issues in a less than satisfactorily compassionate manner, and leave much of relevance unsaid. The publicised reluctance of tech company CEOs to attend government committee hearings on safety and security issues also points to a strategy of silence, when companies withhold the speaker requested. When Facebook CEO Mark Zuckerberg declined three requests to give evidence to the Digital, Culture, Media and Sport committee of UK parliamentarians in the wake of the Cambridge Analytica personal data scandal, the committee chair Damian Collins MP stated: "it is absolutely astonishing that Mark Zuckerberg is not prepared to submit himself to questioning … These are questions of a fundamental importance and concern to Facebook users, as well as to our inquiry as well. We would certainly urge him to think again if he has any care for people that use his company's services."[48] The silence of the person required and requested is perceived and presented as a lack of care and concern.

At the same time, the voice of the companies is effectively silenced through relegation to the background of public discourse. As in *The Telegraph* article on the parliamentary debate on the death of Lee Rigby, responses or statements from the tech companies are often consigned to the bottom of an article as an apparent afterthought, or omitted altogether. Balance and equal distribution of column inches are secondary considerations. The transparency reports introduced by the largest US companies following the Snowden revelations detail many thousands of instances in which they have assisted law enforcement with investigations into serious crime, including threat to life emergencies, but do not garner the same levels of media interest as reports that they are snubbing authority or refusing to cooperate – perhaps because they challenge that very narrative.

Edward Herman and Noam Chomsky's influential work *Manufacturing Consent* outlined a mass media propaganda model in which the withholding of column inches and airtime for marginal narratives is as important as the promotion of stories deemed to be useful to the media's owners and patrons.[49] Building on this, Huckin has advanced the concepts of topical silence and propaganda by omission: "Politicians, public officials, journalists, special interest groups, and others who use political discourse do so in ways that foreground certain information while backgrounding – or concealing altogether – other information."[50] Huckin's identification of propaganda by omission as "a phenomenon of entire discourses, not just of individual texts" finds analogies both in the silencing of tech companies through customary relegation in media coverage, and in the companies' self-silencing through parroting of formulaic responses.[51] According to this line of thinking, both activities undermine democracy by withholding information from citizens. As remedies, Huckin urges citizens to exhibit scepticism and acquire subject matter knowledge better to detect these strategic absences and ensure they are properly informed.

At once silenced and self-silencing, the world's largest technology companies contributed to the creation of a space in which their reputation and representation could be constructed by others – and as Others – largely without challenge.

The empire strikes back: end-to-end encryption

Another debate in which child sexual abuse has come to serve as a means to a persuasive end is that of end-to-end (E2E) encryption. Increasingly the default security measure for online communications services, this form of encryption scrambles the content of communications in transit. Unencrypted communications are only accessible on the users' devices, or endpoints – hence the designation "end-to-end".

E2E encryption poses a not insignificant challenge to the ways in which law enforcement has traditionally secured evidence in relation to online crimes, and intelligence agencies around the world monitor their targets' communications. In the eras in which postal, telegraphic, and wired telephonic communications were dominant, government authorities had the legal powers and the ability to intercept the content of any communication. In the first few decades of internet communications, traffic was either unencrypted in transit, or stored unencrypted on a central company server, from which it could be requested by the authorities.

Moreover, before the global dominance of US-based tech companies like Microsoft, Google, Facebook and Apple, authorities in the UK, for example, could request data from domestic email and internet providers using domestic legislation. Governments were able to exercise their sovereign rights over data-holding companies enshrined in their own territories. The rise of the US companies as global service providers challenged this method of evidence and intelligence gathering. Until 2018, US law – specifically the Stored Communications Act – prohibited Silicon Valley companies from disclosing the content of a users' communications directly to non-US authorities.[52] UK law enforcement was required to request the content of Facebook or Gmail accounts by means of international legal agreements, notably the largely paper-based and often lengthy procedure of Mutual Legal Assistance. Requests were submitted by foreign authorities to the US Department of Justice, who then instructed local courts in the US to issue search warrants on the providers. Waiting three, six, or even 18 months for evidence that could prove a serious offence was naturally frustrating for law enforcement, and in many cases a barrier to offenders being brought to justice. In this respect, international law was not fit for purpose.[53]

US tech companies would have violated US law if they had disclosed the content of their users' communications directly to foreign government agencies. This is not how high-profile cases were represented in the UK media. As just one example, these were the headlines for newspaper articles in relation to the Mutual Legal Assistance request for data material to the murder of 13-year-old Lucy McHugh in 2018:

> Evidence may have been lost because Facebook refused to hand over Lucy McHugh's Facebook data
>
> (*Daily Mail*, 18/07/19)

> Lucy McHugh's mum condemns Facebook for refusing to hand over murder suspect's password
>
> (*The Mirror*, 04/09/18)

> DEFACE-BOOK Facebook "adding to the pain of grieving families" like Lucy McHugh's by refusing them access to loved ones' profiles
>
> (*The Sun*, 09/09/18)

One could be forgiven for thinking that the company was being deliberately obstructive, when in fact it was constrained by US law from direct and more timely disclosure. The assumption of ill intent has continued into the encryption debate:

> BOOKED! Facebook plot to encrypt ALL chats "will help child abusers to hide", former police chief warns

> FACEBOOK risks helping child abusers to hide their sick online activities, a former police chief has warned.
>
> The alarm has been raised over Facebook's plans to encrypt more of our private chats – shutting out hackers, but also the police.[54]

There is much in this depiction that is familiar, including the alignment of a tech company with designated social outcasts and underhand behaviour, and the appeal to fear. But whereas previous security- and safety-related accusations levelled at US companies have often been met with silence or a generic statement from a spokesperson, relegated to the small print of media coverage, in the matter of encryption we see a reframing of the public discourse as a true dialogue, the companies reclaiming the moral high ground, and arguably a role in international order that further challenges sovereign authority. Ironically, a number of governments may themselves have accelerated this shift by their own public communications.

In October 2019, UK Home Secretary Priti Patel, US Attorney General William Barr, acting US Secretary of Homeland Security Kevin McAleenan and Australian Minister for Home Affairs Peter Dutton sent an open letter to Facebook CEO Mark Zuckerberg concerning the company's plans to apply to E2E encryption to all its services. Its focus was the impact E2E would have on current methods of identifying child sexual abuse material, which to date have largely relied on being able to review content for illegality. E2E makes centralised review technically impossible, because content is only visible "in the clear" on the end devices. It therefore threatens to put an end to Facebook's existing procedures for detecting, removing, and reporting to law enforcement millions of child abuse photos and videos per year (close to 15.9 million in 2019[55]).

The problem is real: it would be churlish and ill-considered to dismiss it. The reports made by Facebook concern the distribution of known images and videos of child sexual abuse, but also live grooming of children and young people to meet adults for sexual activity offline, or to produce new images and videos. Alerting the authorities in the relevant country has the potential to end ongoing abuse, bring offenders to justice, and prevent further offending. Deployment of E2E encryption makes this particular method of identification impossible.

E2E encryption is either "on" or "off". Not deploying E2E, or deploying a solution that allows for lawful access by government authorities, raises its own risks. Encryption prevents interception by criminals and hostile regimes alike. Media coverage of the extent to which some governments are prepared to use commercial spyware on their own and other countries' citizens, and reports of its use particularly against journalists and activists, prompts questions of how companies would identify which governments could be trusted not to misuse access, whether they would be required to choose between "good" and "bad" countries to have access, and whether it could ever be possible to prevent keys falling into the wrong hands, even if lawful access were technically feasible.

There also appears to be some public expectation that online communication be private. In 2016, a Reuters/Ipsos poll found that 46 per cent of Americans agreed with Apple's decision to oppose a federal court order requiring them to unlock the phone of the chief suspect in the San Bernardino terrorist attack: 35 per cent said they disagreed, while 20 per cent said they did not know.[56] A 2019 YouGov survey in the UK and US found that 64 per cent of respondents believed that end-to-end encryption could help protect their digital privacy.[57] A recent online poll conducted by *The Sun* on the same page as the "BOOKED!" article quoted above asked "Do you think Facebook should encrypt all chats?": 58.1% of respondents were of the opinion that they definitely should, 19.4 per cent voted "No, absolutely not", and 22.6 per cent "I'm not sure".[58]

Meanwhile, a YouGov survey in 2015 found that 53 per cent of UK respondents thought that "communications companies should be required to retain everyone's data – internet browsing history, emails, voice calls, social media interactions, and mobile messaging – for 12 months" and supported the police and intelligence agencies having access to this information for anti-terrorism purposes; 31 per cent opposed, and 16 per cent didn't know. Among the same set of respondents, 43 per cent opposed a ban on "encryption software that would prevent the security services from accessing someone's communications", while 29 per cent expressed support.[59]

The decision to deploy or not deploy E2E encryption is therefore at once technically binary and ethically complex. To put it crassly, the decision to protect the communications of activists and journalists may result in the continued abuse, physical harm, even death of children. On the other hand, a decision that prioritises child protection may result in more activists and journalists being persecuted and murdered. It is arguably the most difficult ethical decision the global community has faced in regard to internet technology, prompting some to consider a utilitarian approach that seeks to identify the greatest good for the greatest number of people.[60] This is understandably unacceptable to child protection specialists and child rights advocates, for whom each instance of child sexual abuse and each child death is one too many. It is far from a simple battle of right and wrong, good and evil.

This complexity is not reflected in the opening paragraphs of the 2019 letter to Zuckerberg from the Ministers of State (emphasis added):[61]

> We are writing to request that Facebook does not proceed with its plan to implement end-to-end encryption across its messaging services without ensuring that there is no reduction to user safety and without including a means for lawful access to the content of communications to **protect our citizens**.
>
> In your post of 6 March 2019, "A Privacy-Focused Vision for Social Networking," you acknowledged that "there are real safety concerns to address before we can implement end-to-end encryption across all our messaging services." You stated that "we have a responsibility to work with law enforcement and to help prevent" the use of Facebook for things like child sexual exploitation, terrorism, and extortion. We welcome this commitment to consultation. As you know, our governments have engaged with Facebook on this issue, and some of us have written to you to express our views. Unfortunately, **Facebook has not**

> **committed** to address our serious concerns about the impact its proposals could have on protecting **our most vulnerable citizens**.

It is immediately obvious that the Ministers see only one viable solution to the problem, namely lawful access. This is clearly aligned with the protection of citizens, whose vulnerability is emphasised. That Facebook has not yet guaranteed lawful access is portrayed as an unambiguous failure on their part.

At no point in this letter do the Ministers explicitly acknowledge the impossibility of simultaneously ensuring the security and integrity of E2E encryption and building backdoors for government agencies. Statements such as "We support strong encryption", and "Law abiding citizens have a legitimate expectation that their privacy will be protected" only serve to highlight the dilemma here: encryption is overwhelmingly a good thing, but the traditional intelligence methods of targeted surveillance are unfeasible in an environment secured by a "one for all" solution. When the Ministers state,

> We must find a way to balance the need to secure data with public safety and the need for law enforcement to access the information they need to safeguard the public, investigate crimes, and prevent future criminal activity. Not doing so hinders our law enforcement agencies' ability to stop criminals and abusers in their tracks.

what appears at first glance to be a more open-minded assessment based on general principles is reduced to the same demand for lawful access. The letter continues (emphasis added):

> Companies should not **deliberately design** their systems to **preclude** any form of access to content, even for preventing or investigating the most serious crimes. This **puts our citizens and societies at risk by severely eroding** a company's ability to detect and respond to illegal content and activity, such as child sexual exploitation and abuse, terrorism, and foreign adversaries' attempts to **undermine democratic values** and institutions, **preventing** the prosecution of offenders and safeguarding of victims.

Again, what appears to be a general statement about technology design becomes something of a more specific accusation in the context of this letter, addressed to Facebook, and Zuckerberg personally. The implications are that i) the recipient of this letter has somehow been directly involved in the design of E2E encryption, which is untrue; ii) E2E encryption itself (as opposed to bad actors using it) puts citizens and societies at risk; and iii) companies that deploy E2E, the recipient included, are deliberately hindering criminal justice and safeguarding. The geological and construction-related language of "severe erosion" and undermining encourages the reader to think of physical collapse; forensically, that phrase "undermine democratic values" echoes frequent usage in the UK Online Harms White Paper, and perhaps leads us to speculate on a common origin.

After another statement which appears to gloss over the technical impossibility of maintaining end-to-end encryption with a backdoor –

> We are committed to working with you to focus on reasonable proposals that will allow Facebook and our governments to protect your users and the public, while protecting their privacy. Our technical experts are confident that we can do so while defending cyber security and supporting technological innovation.

– the letter closes with the following paragraph (emphasis added):

> As you have recognised, it is critical to get this right for the future of the internet. Children's safety and law enforcement's ability to bring criminals to justice must not be **the ultimate cost** of Facebook taking forward these proposals.

The issue is presented as an existential moment. Where threats to democratic values, terrorism, and other illegal activities were included in the argued need for lawful access elsewhere in the letter, here we have returned to perhaps most emotive topic, children's safety. We are to understand that Facebook's decision to deploy E2E encryption could destroy the internet as we know it. The construction in the final sentence, meanwhile, reduces the debate to a binary choice between E2E on the one hand, and safe children and effective criminal justice on the other. Through this collocation, and again erroneously, the future of child safety and enforcement of law and order are depicted as hinging on Facebook's decision alone.

The lack of logical accuracy which pervades the ministerial letter leaves a clear space for a logical rebuttal. A letter of reply was posted to Facebook's website in December 2019.[62] Basic statistical analysis of the two letters reveals that while they are of a very similar length (1,156 words for the ministerial letter, 1098 words from Facebook), the Facebook response registers a higher readability score according to several measures, including Flesch-Kincaid, Gunning Fog, Coleman Liau, SMOG and Automated Readability. In particular, the Facebook text exhibits a lower number and smaller percentage of complex words than the ministerial letter (17.5 per cent as opposed to 23.5 per cent), and a smaller average number of words per sentence. These statistics accord with Flesch-Kincaid Grade Levels indicating that the Facebook text would be easily understood by 18- to 19-year-olds, the ministerial letter by 21- to 22-year-olds.[63]

As regards word frequency in the bodies of the texts, it may come as no surprise given the rhetorical focus of the ministerial letter that "Facebook" is the most frequent term that is not a conjunction or preposition (19 mentions). This is followed by "safety", "law", "content" and "child" (nine mentions each), "enforcement" and "children" (eight mentions each). The response from Facebook has a more diverse vocabulary, suggestive of a more general focus: 'people' (nine), 'safety' (eight), 'law' (eight), 'encryption' (eight) are the top scorers once conjunctions, prepositions, and pronouns are excluded.

Facebook's letter to the Ministers is also self-consciously a public communication. Where the ministerial letter bore the heading "OPEN LETTER: FACEBOOK'S 'PRIVACY FIRST' PROPOSALS", indicating that Zuckerberg was the addressee, but citizens of the world were permitted to read it, Facebook's text is entitled "FACEBOOK'S PUBLIC RESPONSE TO OPEN LETTER ON PRIVATE MESSAGING", signalling that we are the intended audience, just as much as the Ministers addressed. A close reading of the opening paragraphs reveals that the text engages with the problem by using identical or very similar language and concepts to that of the Ministers (emphasis added):

> As the Heads of WhatsApp and Messenger, we are writing in response to your public letter addressing our plans to **strengthen** private messaging for our customers ...
>
> **We all want people** to have the ability to communicate **privately and safely, without harm or abuse** from hackers, criminals or repressive regimes. Every day, billions of people around the world use encrypted messages to stay in touch with their family and friends, run their small businesses, and advocate for important causes. In these messages they share private information that they only want the person they message to see. And it is the fact that these messages are encrypted that forms the **first line of defense**, as it keeps them **safe** from cyber attacks and **protected** from falling into the hands of criminals. The core principle behind end-to-end encryption is that only the sender and recipient of a message have the keys to "unlock" and read what is sent. No one can intercept and read these messages - not us, not governments, not hackers or criminals.

Where the Ministers depicted the move to E2E encryption as creating vulnerability and as a safety risk, resulting in increased harm and abuse, here the same technology is a strengthening measure that keeps users safe and protected. Of note, Facebook adds hackers and governments to the list of sources of harm and abuse, where the Ministers identified only criminals. The company then makes clear that the Ministers' demands themselves constitute a threat to that safety and protection (emphasis added):

> Cybersecurity experts have repeatedly proven that when you **weaken** any part of an encrypted system, you **weaken** it for everyone, everywhere. The "backdoor" access you are demanding for law enforcement would be a gift to criminals, hackers and repressive regimes, creating a way for them to enter our systems and **leaving every person on our platforms more vulnerable to real-life harm**. It is simply impossible to create such a backdoor for one purpose and not expect others to try and open it. People's private messages would be **less secure** and the real winners would be anyone seeking to take advantage of that **weakened security**. That is not something we are prepared to do.

Here, it is the Ministers' proposal, not that of Facebook, that creates vulnerability, insecurity, and risk. The authors seek to persuade us of their logical acumen and ethical basis for action, and appeal to two authorities that are almost venerated in modern Western information society:

> Cryptography Professor Bruce Schneier said earlier this year: "You have to make a choice. Either everyone gets to spy, or no one gets to spy. You can't have 'We get to spy, you don't.' That's not the way the tech works." And Amnesty International commented: "There is no middle ground: if law enforcement is allowed to circumvent encryption, then anybody can."

Facebook's letter has provided members of the public with the introduction to E2E encryption that the ministerial letter omitted. In doing so, they are arguably more successful in engaging citizens in the deliberations. When they go on to describe how they already assist law enforcement, they are playing to the gallery, not the Ministers, who we may presume already know.[64] The authors align encryption with safety, and reframe the Ministers' prophecy ("it is critical to get this right for the future of the internet") so that encryption becomes the saviour of the internet, not its undoing ([emphasis added):

> **Keeping people safe** is one of our biggest priorities at Facebook and we are proud to be an industry leader in this area. **Our commitment to encryption is a continuation of our commitment to user safety**, as encryption vastly reduces incidents of common and serious crimes like hacking and identity theft. **This is critical as more of our information moves online.**

Where the Ministers letter ended with a demand - "Children's safety and law enforcement's ability to bring criminals to justice must not be the ultimate cost of Facebook taking forward these proposals" – Facebook's letter closes with a more collaborative tone that reflects a range of perspectives (emphasis added):

> We have spent considerable time over recent months meeting with **safety experts**, victim advocates, child helplines and others to understand how we can improve our reports of harms to children so they are more actionable for law enforcement. We have listened to our **users** who want an even more private experience. We have also heard from **governments** who want us to collect less data. As we move forward, it is our sincere hope that we can work together on solutions that **keep people safe** and their communications **private**. We recognize technological advances impact the way in which law enforcement operates and look forward to working with you to help ensure **the actions of government and companies are effective in keeping citizens safe**.

The authors remind the Ministers that the agencies they command are not the only stakeholders in child protection and citizen safety. Crucially, they leave us with an image of governments and companies working together *as equals* to keep citizens safe. Using the Ministers' own language and concepts, they reframe the debate, challenging the government orthodoxy while simultaneously seeking to appear more open to logical analysis and consultation. Taken as a pair, as two sides of a dialogue, we may feel that the Ministers, for all their moral backing, have come off the meaner.

In this exchange, E2E encryption is presented as simultaneously the most irresponsible choice and the most responsible; the safest and the least safe; the strongest and the most vulnerable; in citizens' best interests and their worst. Acknowledging that the binary nature of the technology may contribute to division and polar responses, we may still marvel at how it enjoys such diametrically different representations. One might say that it is a prime example of the power of rhetoric to reframe its subject to the outlook and persuasive aims of the speaker/author.

The format of the exchange may itself be suggestive of a rebalancing of power. While governments around the world continue to seek to impose sovereign authority on the largest US tech companies, and in some cases cast them as hostile non-state actors, there are some indications that they are operating like states and even being addressed as such. However much the text of the Ministerial letter seeks to exert pressure on Facebook, the very fact that Ministers of State have addressed an open letter to Mark Zuckerberg suggests that he is to be considered a counterpart of sorts. In September 2015, Zuckerberg addressed a meeting of the United Nations General Assembly focused on fostering economic growth, transformation, and promoting sustainable consumption and protection. His advocacy for universal internet access as a means to achieving the UN's Sustainable Development Goals received considerable media coverage.

In January 2020, Microsoft announced the opening of a permanent office for UN affairs, whose work "includes advancing global multi-stakeholder action on key technology, environmental, humanitarian, development, and security goals as well as helping to advance the UN Sustainable Development Goals (SDGs)".[65] This increased involvement in global governance and development, perhaps prefigured by the philanthropic public health efforts of tech grandees such as Microsoft founder Bill Gates, and the recruitment of political figures as senior executives, former UK Deputy Prime Minister Nick Clegg and Danish diplomat Ambassador Casper Klynge among them, point to the emergence of the largest US tech companies as a new class of supranational actor. The formulation of the letter to Zuckerberg by the Five Eyes Ministers betrays this ongoing shift in the balance of power.

The discourse analysed in this chapter imposes a rhetorical framing on the space between governments (primarily the UK government) and (primarily US) technology companies. In parliamentary debate constraining, antithetical presentations have combined with emotional language to portray companies and their representatives as irresponsible outlaws worthy of the public's indignation. Select outlets of the UK news media have endorsed and amplified the portrayal of companies as criminally responsible in the most graphic terms.[66]

Meanwhile, emotional language similar to that used by tabloid news outlets to sensationalise security and safety issues has appeared in government policy-making documentation whose evidence base is unsatisfactory and logically deficient. Its apparent purpose is to sensitise the reader sufficiently to be persuaded that "something must be done", and that the responsibility lies with the constructed Other, Big Tech. The companies' own avoidance of meaningful public communication on safety and security – their effective silence – has facilitated such a framing. But there are limits to the applicability and effectiveness of this rhetorical sensitisation and othering. Obscuring inconvenient technical considerations with moral and emotional arguments can backfire when technical expertise and logic is the other party's specialist subject. In the case of E2E encryption, the language of responsibility and vulnerability deployed by the government and the news media in harmony is repurposed by Big Tech to highlight dissonance and distortion.

Emotional policy- and law-making also risks constructing responses that miss their target because they are based on flawed evidence. This can lead not only to human rights and free speech abuses, but also to citizens being no safer than they were before, and even to the emergence of new vulnerabilities. Highlighting instances when communicators seek to influence our reactions to online safety issues is not to dismiss the merit of regulation or media coverage *per se*. The more we are able to question the language and presentation of statements on new threats, the better placed we are to evaluate these threats and respond appropriately. A close reading of the rhetoric of these exchanges yields more than an ability to identify flaws in this process. It enables us to spot signs of further power shifts to come.

Notes

1 Popular titles such as Alvin Toffler's *Future Shock* both highlighted the negative consequences of this fear of change, and heightened the sense of apprehension by billing itself as follows: "Brilliantly disturbing, it analyses the new and dangerous society now emerging and shows how to come to terms with the future." Alvin Toffler (1970) *Future Shock*, London: Pan Books. Frank Furedi's assessment is instructive here. Noting a propensity for technical explanations of risk "based on the commonsense assumption that the more we develop technology, the greater is the power to cause danger", he asserts that "change is seen not so much as a solution but as a cause of problems. Such reactions pertain not only to political experimentation. Initiatives in the field of science and technology are regarded with scepticism. Such scepticism is matched by the certainty that something will go wrong. The fear of side-effects … is the clearest manifestation of this association between change and danger." Frank Furedi (2006) *Culture of Fear Revisited*, London: Continuum, pp. 62, 67f.

2 Mary Shelley's *Frankenstein*, Stanley Kubrick's *2001: A Space Odyssey*, and James Cameron's *Terminator* series are a few of the most prominent and most cited representations of this.

3 David S. Wall (2008) "Cybercrime and the Culture of Fear", *Information, Communication & Society* 11.6: 861–884.

4 Wall (2008) p. 868.

5 Facebook Investor Relations (2020) "Facebook Reports Second Quarter 2020 Results", https://investor.fb.com/investor-news/press-release-details/2020/Facebook-Reports-Second-Quarter-2020-Results/default.aspx

6 Thomas Wiedemann provides a good précis of this polarity: "Apart from a lack of competence in Greek, the barbarian's defining feature is an absence of the moral responsibility required to exercise political freedom: the two are connected, since both imply a lack of *logos*, the ability to reason and speak (sc. Greek) characteristic of the adult male citizen." Thomas E. J. Wiedemann (2012) "barbarian", in *The Oxford Classical Dictionary*, Oxford: Oxford University Press. See also Edith Hall (1989) *Inventing the Barbarian: Greek Self-definition Through Tragedy*, Oxford: Clarendon; Paul Cartledge (1993) *The Greeks: A Portrait of Self and Others*, Oxford: Oxford University Press; and Emma Bridges (2015) *Imagining Xerxes: Ancient Perspectives on a Persian King*, London: Bloomsbury.

7 How much of this designation of the "other" is conscious and deliberate is a matter of debate. I use the term "construction" in this chapter advisedly, in reference specifically to its rhetorical presentation in public discourse on security and safety issues.

8 Peter Waldman and Hugh Pope (2001) "'Crusade' Reference Reinforces Fears War on Terrorism Is Against Muslims", *Wall Street Journal* 21/09/2001, www.wsj.com/articles/SB1001020294332922160; Peter Ford (2001) "Europe cringes at Bush 'crusade' against terrorists", *The Christian Science Monitor* 19/09/2001, www.csmonitor.com/2001/0919/p12s2-woeu.html

9 Timothy B. Lee and Kate Cox (2020) "Trump is Desperate to Punish Big Tech but Has No Good Way to Do It", *Ars Technica* 29/05/2020, https://arstechnica.com/tech-policy/2020/05/why-donald-trumps-war-on-big-tech-is-doomed-to-fail/; Paul Squire (2020) "Trump Finally Gets the War with Big Tech He's Always Wanted", *Digital Trends* 28/05/2020, www.digitaltrends.com/news/donald-trump-executive-order-social-media-war-big-tech/; James Pethokoukis (2019) "Trump's War on Big Tech is Getting Even Dumber", *The Week* 28/06/2019, https://theweek.com/articles/849384/trumps-war-big-tech-getting-even-dumber; Paul R. La Monica (2020) "Analysis: Trump's Crackdown on Big Tech is Misguided", *CNN Business* 28/05/2020, https://edition.cnn.com/2020/05/28/investing/social-media-stocks-trump-twitter/index.html

10 *The Telegraph* (2013) "Woolwich Attack: The Terrorist's Rant", 23/05/2013, www.telegraph.co.uk/news/uknews/terrorism-in-the-uk/10075488/Woolwich-attack-the-terrorists-rant.html

11 Hansard, *Murder of Lee Rigby*, Volume 588: debated on Tuesday 25 November 2014, Column 747.

12 Ibid., column 749.

13 Ibid., column 750.

14 Cf. the comment from the ISC's chair, Sir Malcolm Rifkind MP, later in the debate (column 754): "If that intelligence – the one hard piece of evidence that we have seen – had been available to the intelligence agencies at the time, it is at least possible that the murder of Fusilier Rigby could have been avoided."

15 Hansard, Vol. 588, column 754.

16 Peter Dominiczak, Tom Whitehead, Martin Evans, and Gordon Rayner (2014) "Facebook 'Could Have Prevented Lee Rigby Murder'", *The Telegraph* 26/11/2014, www.telegraph.co.uk/news/uknews/terrorism-in-the-uk/11253518/Facebook-could-have-prevented-Lee-Rigby-murder.html

17 Hansard, Vol. 588, column 761.

18 Tom Whitehead (2014) "Online Clues May Have Signalled Plans of Lee Rigby Killers Report Expected to Reveal; But Crucial Online Activities of Lee Rigby Killer Michael Adebolajo Was Not Flagged to MI5 Until after the Murder", *The Telegraph* 14/11/2014, www.telegraph.co.uk/news/uknews/terrorism-in-the-uk/11229367/Online-clues-may-have-signalled-plans-of-Lee-Rigby-killers-report-expected-to-reveal.html

19 At a seminar on security communication in 2019, a former senior Facebook executive revealed that a leading UK politician had described him as "functionally pro-terrorist" in a face-to-face meeting.

20 Freddy Mayhew (2020) "National Newspaper ABCs: Daily Mail Closes Circulation Gap on Sun to 5,500 Copies", *Press Gazette* 19/03/2020, www.pressgazette.co.uk/national-newspaper-abcs-daily-mail-closes-circulation-gap-on-sun-to-5500-copies/

21 UK Parliament (n.d.). "Glossary: 'White Paper'", www.parliament.uk/site-information/glossary/white-paper/

22 UK Government (2017) *Internet Safety Strategy Green Paper*, https://assets.publishing.service.gov.uk/government/uploads/system/uploads/attachment_data/file/650949/Internet_Safety_Strategy_green_paper.pdf; UK Government (2018) *Response to the Internet Safety Strategy Green Paper*, https://assets.publishing.service.gov.uk/government/uploads/system/uploads/attachment_data/file/708873/Government_Response_to_the_Internet_Safety_Strategy_Green_Paper_-_Final.pdf; UK Government (2019) *Online Harms White Paper*, https://assets.publishing.service.gov.uk/government/uploads/system/uploads/attachment_data/file/793360/Online_Harms_White_Paper.pdf

23 Victoria Nash (2019) "Revise and Resubmit? Reviewing the 2019 Online Harms White Paper", *Journal of Media Law* 11.1: 18–27.

24 Victoria Baines (2019) "Online Child Sexual Exploitation: Towards an Optimal International Response", *Journal of Cyber Policy* 4.2: 197–215.

25 Victoria Baines (2019) "On Online Harms and Folk Devils: Careful Now", *Medium* 24/06/2019, https://medium.com/@vicbaines/on-online-harms-and-folk-devils-careful-now-f8b63ee25584; Nash (2019).

26 Andy Phippen and Emma Bond (2019) "The Online Harms Spearmint Paper - Just More Doing More?", *Entertainment Law Review* 30.6: 169–173.

27 OfCom and Information Commissioner's Office (2019) *Internet Users' Concerns About and Experience of Potential Online Harms 2019*, www.ofcom.org.uk/__data/assets/pdf_file/0028/149068/online-harms-chart-pack.pdf

28 Nash (2019) p. 19.

29 Phippen and Bond (2019) p. 172.

30 Nash (2019) p. 24.

31 Phippen and Bond (2019) p. 171. Civil actions in the US provide a parallel for this approach: for example, the lawsuit brought against Google, Twitter and Facebook for "aiding, abetting, and knowingly providing support and resources to Isis" by a woman who experienced one of the November 2015 terrorist attacks in Paris.

32 ITN (2013) "Boycott 'vile' websites, says David Cameron – video", redistributed in *The Guardian* 08/08/2013, www.theguardian.com/society/video/2013/aug/08/boycott-websites-david-cameron-video

33 BBC News (2014) "Hannah Smith Inquest: Teenager Posted 'Online Messages'", *BBC News Online* 06/05/2014, www.bbc.co.uk/news/uk-england-leicestershire-27298627

34 Followers of UK politics may observe that a former tabloid newspaper editor once served as Mr Cameron's Head of Communications.

35 Lexis Nexis News search for "child porn", 01/01/2000 to 12/09/2020 inclusive, conducted 12/09/2020.

36 A. Jaworski (1993) *The Power of Silence: Social and Pragmatic Perspectives*, Newbury Park: Sage, p. 85: "it is more open for the audience to speculate about which assumption(s) the communicator had in mind to make manifest … in his or her use of silence".

37 *In Catilinam* 1.16: "convicted by the hostile verdict of their silence" (*gravissimo iudicio taciturnitatis oppressus*).

38 So Jaworski describes one perception of silence as "someone's failure to produce *specific* utterances" [original emphasis] ((1993) p. 73).

39 For the initial media coverage of the leaks, see for example Glenn Greenwald and Ewen MacAskill (2013) "NSA Prism program taps in to user data of Apple, Google and

others", *The Guardian* 07/06/2013, www.theguardian.com/world/2013/jun/06/us-tech-giants-nsa-data

40 "When Facebook is asked for data or information about specific individuals, we carefully scrutinize any such request for compliance with all applicable laws, and provide information only to the extent required by law"; "We disclose user data to government in accordance with the law, and we review all such requests carefully. From time to time, people allege that we have created a government 'back door' into our systems, but Google does not have a backdoor for the government to access private user data"; "We do not provide any government agency with direct access to our servers, and any government agency requesting customer data must get a court order" (Apple); "We provide customer data only when we receive a legally binding order or subpoena to do so, and never on a voluntary basis. In addition we only ever comply with orders for requests about specific accounts or identifiers. If the government has a broader voluntary national security program to gather customer data we don't participate in it" (Microsoft); cited by Frederic Lardinois (2013) "Google, Facebook, Dropbox, Yahoo, Microsoft, Paltalk, AOL And Apple Deny Participation In NSA PRISM Surveillance Program", *TechCrunch* 06/06/2013, https://techcrunch.com/2013/06/06/google-facebook-apple-deny-participation-in-nsa-prism-program/

41 Google Search, "We Take the Safety of Our Users Very Seriously", retrieved 27/09/20.

42 BBC News (2017) "Fears Over Fake Bieber and Styles Accounts", *BBC Trending* 24/04/17, www.bbc.co.uk/news/blogs-trending-39670673

43 Arthur Martin and Lucy Osborne (2013) "Google Cashes in on Hate Videos: Internet Giant Puts Ads Alongside Thousands of Terror Rants on YouTube", *Daily Mail* 27/05/13, www.dailymail.co.uk/news/article-2331832/Google-cashes-hate-videos-Internet-giant-puts-ads-alongside-thousands-terror-rants-YouTube.html?ito=feeds-newsxml

44 Huffington Post UK (2020) "Wiley Banned from Facebook and Instagram Over More Anti-Semitic Posts", *Huffington Post* 28/07/20, www.huffingtonpost.co.uk/entry/wiley-banned-facebook-instagram_uk_5f2054e6c5b6945e6e40a64e

45 Twitter "Terrorism and violent extremism policy", retrieved 27/09/2020, https://help.twitter.com/en/rules-and-policies/violent-groups

46 Michelle Castillo (2017) "Facebook: Zero tolerance policy on violent content 'does not mean zero occurrence", *CNBC* 20/06/2017, www.cnbc.com/2017/06/20/facebook-zero-tolerance-isnt-zero-occurrence-carolyn-everson.html

47 BBC News (2020) "Facebook Dominates Cases of Recorded Social Media Grooming", *BBC NEWS* 29/05/2020, www.bbc.co.uk/news/technology-52841358

48 Reuters Staff (2018) "Zuckerberg's Snub of UK Parliament 'Astonishing' Says Lawmaker", *Reuters Media and Telecoms* 27/03/2018, https://reuters.com/article/us-facebook-cambridge-analytica-britain-idUSKBN1H31QD

49 Edward S. Herman and Noam Chomsky (1988) *Manufacturing Consent: The Political Economy of the Mass Media*, New York: Pantheon.

50 Tom Huckin (2019) "Propaganda by Omission: The Case of Topical Silence". In A. Murray and K. Durrheim eds (2019) *Qualitative Studies of Silence: The Unsaid as Social Action*, Cambridge: Cambridge University Press, pp. 186–205. Cheryl Glenn identifies in silence and silencing "a power differential that exists in every rhetorical situation: who can speak, who must remain silent, who listens, and what those listeners can do" ((2004) *Unspoken: A Rhetoric of Silence*, Carbondale: Southern Illinois University Press, p. 9).

51 Ibid., p. 202.

52 The 2018 Clarifying Lawful Overseas Use of Data Act or CLOUD Act amended the Stored Communications Act to compel US-based companies to disclose data stored on servers in foreign states, but also provided the opportunity for foreign states to conclude bilateral agreements with the US for direct content data disclosure from US-based companies.

53 For more information on this process, see Kate Westmoreland and Gail Kent (2015) "International Law Enforcement Access to User Data: A Survival Guide and Call for Action", *SSRN* 08/01/2015, https://ssrn.com/abstract=2547289

54 Sean Keach (2020) "BOOKED! Facebook Plot to Encrypt ALL Chats 'Will Help Child Abusers to Hide', Former Police Chief Warns", *The Sun* 27/05/2020, www.thesun.co.uk/tech/11717886/facebook-encryption-crime-police-child-abus/

55 National Center for Missing and Exploited Children (2020), "2019 Reports by Electronic Service Provider (ESP)", www.missingkids.org/content/dam/missingkids/gethelp/2019-reports-by-esp.pdf

56 Jim Finkle (2016) "Solid Support for Apple in iPhone Encryption Fight: Poll", *Reuters Technology News* 24/02/2016, https://uk.reuters.com/article/us-apple-encryption-poll/solid-support-for-apple-in-iphone-encryption-fight-poll-idUKKCN0VX159

57 Tresorit Team (2019) "Trust in Tech Giants is Broken", *Tresorit Blog* 24/04/2019, https://blog.tresorit.com/trust-in-tech-giants-is-broken/. Data provided by YouGov Deutschland GmbH (2307 UK respondents, 1,273 US, between 03/04/2019 and 05/04/2019).

58 Keach (2020), accessed 22/09/2020.

59 Will Dahlgreen (2020) "Broad Support for Increased Surveillance Powers", *YouGov* 18/01/2015, https://yougov.co.uk/topics/politics/articles-reports/2015/01/18/more-surveillance-please-were-british; full results, accessed 22/09/20; https://d25d2506sfb94s.cloudfront.net/cumulus_uploads/document/wt26kxdn72/YG-Archive-Pol-Sunday-Times-results-160115.pdf (1,647 GB adults, fieldwork 15/01/15–16/01/15).

60 Morten Bay (2017) "The ethics of unbreakable encryption: Rawlsian privacy and the San Bernardino iPhone" *First Monday* 22.2, 06/02/2017, https://firstmonday.org/ojs/index.php/fm/article/download/7006/5860; Collin Duncan (2016) "For the Good of the Many a Few Must Die: How Encryption Became the Ultimate Utilitarian Thought Experiment", *Medium* 04/03/2016, https://medium.com/@BleachedSleet/for-the-good-of-the-many-a-few-must-die-how-encryption-became-the-ultimate-utilitarian-thought-94a95c512816; Irina Raicu (2016) "Ethical Questions About Encryption", Markkula Center for Applied Ethics at Santa Clara University, www.scu.edu/ethics/focus-areas/technology-ethics/resources/ethical-questions-about-encryption/

61 US Department of Justice (2019) "Open Letter: Facebook's 'Privacy First' Proposals", www.justice.gov/opa/press-release/file/1207081/download

62 Facebook (2019) "Facebook's Public Response to Open Letter on Private Messaging", https://about.fb.com/wp-content/uploads/2019/12/Facebook-Response-to-Barr-Patel-Dutton-Wolf-.pdf

63 Using WebFX's Readability Test Tool, www.webfx.com/tools/read-able/

64 "That doesn't mean that we cannot help law enforcement. We can and we do, as long as it is consistent with the law and does not undermine the safety of our users. You make strong points on this in your letter and we recognize the potential consequences end-to-end encryption can have on the critical work of the law enforcement officers you lead. We deeply respect and support the work these officials do to keep us safe and we want to assure you that we will continue to respond to valid legal requests for the information we have available. We will also continue to prioritize emergencies, such as terrorism and child safety, and proactively refer to law enforcement matters involving credible threats."

65 Microsoft Corporate Blogs (2020) "Microsoft Appoints Senior Government Affairs Leaders in Brussels and New York, Establishes New York Office to Work with the United Nations", https://blogs.microsoft.com/eupolicy/2020/01/17/senior-gov-affairs-leaders-appointed-brussels-new-york/

66 See also the BBC's repeated coverage of the suicide of teenager Molly Russell in 2017, especially the headline "Instagram 'Helped Kill My Daughter'", *BBC News* 22/01/2019, www.bbc.co.uk/news/av/uk-46966009.

4 The dark Wild West world war

Danger and incapability in the realm of cybersecurity

Fear of the dark

On 8 July 2015, the then FBI Director James Comey testified before the US Senate Judiciary Committee on the challenges for law enforcement to access encrypted electronic evidence. His concerns were identical to those expressed in the letter from the Five Eyes ministers to Mark Zuckerberg, discussed in the previous chapter. Unlike the ministerial letter, Comey referred to this as the "Going Dark problem".

A search of historical news items reveals that in the twentieth century the phrase "going dark" often denoted the literal dimming of the house lights at arts venues and, by extension, TV channels. For example, when MTV bought short-lived rival Cable Music Channel in 1984, *Communications Daily* ran with the headline "Going Dark at Midnight Fri.; MTV TO PAY $1 MILLION FOR TURNER'S CABLE MUSIC CHANNEL".[1] A step closer to Comey's usage is this application in a 1986 article from the Associated Press: "Satellite dish makers told the public Tuesday 'the skies are not going dark' even as Showtime-The Movie Channel Inc. began scrambling its signals full-time."[2] In the context of satellite broadcasts, darkness denotes inaccessibility.

We can therefore say that, by the time Director Comey gives his testimony, "going dark" already enjoys a metaphorical application to communications. Its application in the context of criminal investigations and counter-terrorism – Comey illustrating the necessity of access to internet communication with examples of technology's misuse by the Islamic State of Iraq and the Levant (ISIL), domestic extremists, and violent sex offenders – conjures up other images associated with darkness. The "dark side of the Internet" is a trope to which public figures and media outlets alike have frequently had recourse. It casts human activity, and the technology itself, as binary. While this may be appropriate for the code from which the tools are constructed, the light/dark polarity inevitably oversimplifies the range of possible internet-mediated experiences. Unlike the offline world, this construction does not permit the existence of shaded or half-lit spaces. In addition to an image of the dark side of the street loaded with fear of physical assault or mishap – so deftly and hyperbolically mapped in Ancient Rome by Juvenal – we may also think of the dark side of the human personality, and the

DOI: 10.4324/9781003028062-5

frightful transformations embodied by werewolves, Dr Jekyll and The Incredible Hulk. Darkness and light exist in all of us. Darkness predominant denotes humanity gone wrong, and primeval chaos.

When, in a 2006 speech entitled "Child Exploitation on the Internet: The Dark Side of the Web", Comey's predecessor Robert S. Mueller described "a dark side to this globalization" of information technology, asserting that an increasing amount of child sexual exploitation "takes place in the dark shadows of the internet – on websites and message boards, through file sharing and e-mail, and in real time with web cams and streaming video", and that those who investigate and prosecute these cases had "seen the darkest side of humanity", he makes full use of the metaphor's agility.[3] His designation of dark places on the internet also reflects a more specific usage, namely "darknet" or "dark web" for hidden or un-indexed online services. With the related, but not identical, term "deep web", they have come to represent spaces that are both criminal and lawless.[4] A couple of examples from news media will suffice to illustrate.

On 11 October 2013, *The Daily Mail* ran the following headline and subhead:

> The disturbing world of the Deep Web, where contract killers and drug dealers ply their trade on the internet
>
> - Dozens of "hitmen" are available for hire through the "Deep Web", or Tor
> - They all offer their services for a price paid in mysterious currency Bitcoin
> - One boasts: "I always do my best to make it look like an accident or suicide"
> - Others market services: "The best place to put your problems is in a grave"[5]

The reader will be able to identify immediately the tools of the rhetorical trade, including an appeal to emotion which effectively tells us how to feel, namely disturbed. An image caption later in the article likewise announces the activity to be "Chilling: So for those looking to bump off a difficult acquaintance, all they have to do is enter the Dark Web and search 'hitman for hire', such as this one". The ease with which offences are committed in this space is emphasised by the expansive "dozens", members apparently showing off, and trivialising language for murder. At the same time, we are given the distinct impression that at least some of this activity is beyond our understanding: digital currency Bitcoin's technical mystery makes it difficult for the ordinary reader, perhaps also the journalist, to grasp.

It is also a space in which law enforcement is deemed ineffective: "Such purchases are now so easy, in fact, that they can all be done from the comfort of one's home at the click of a button ... and there's almost nothing the police can do about it." One might think that law enforcement authorities would be keen to counter this narrative. But this is exactly the rhetoric they themselves have espoused. So, in widely reproduced quotes from a piece originally entitled "Dark Web Poses Challenges for Law Enforcement", Acting US Attorney for North Dakota Chris Myers states of dark web illicit drug retail that "The folks that are distributing these substances are using increasingly more sophisticated technology to remain anonymous, making our job that much more difficult"; this is contrasted with the ease of offending - "You can buy anything if you find the right website on the Dark Net … From tigers to hand grenades to controlled substances, it's there."[6] A 2017 joint report by the European Centre for Drugs and Drug Addiction (EMCDDA) and Europol described the Dark Net as "difficult to police yet easy to access".[7] Despite well-publicised and successful operations to disrupt the activities of large marketplaces such as Silk Road, Hansa, Alphabay, Valhalla and Wall Street Market, in strategic communications law enforcement in the US and Europe have persisted in highlighting the challenges of the dark web, and advertised their incapability. So, a public report produced by the RAND corporation on law enforcement needs identified that "lack of knowledge about what the dark web is and how criminals have begun to leverage it is a key problem".[8] Europol's 2020 threat assessment on cybercrime highlights in supersized font that "the Darkweb environment remains difficult to disrupt as developments are often challenging to anticipate. This adds to the law enforcement challenges with respect to this growing threat, which continues to function as a key facilitator for many other forms of crime."[9]

While the apparent honesty of these assessments is laudable, their negation of law enforcement capability will be received differently by different audiences. Policy-makers and legislators – arguably the primary audience of such threat assessments – may be minded to assist law enforcement with additional resources or empowering legislation. Criminals, on the other hand, may take heart from these public admissions of difficulty. What about members of the public? It is difficult to believe that they would find this representation reassuring; in fact, one might reasonably assert that it would generate a sense of insecurity. But it is very much consistent with the dominant visual rhetoric of cybercrime.

For a number of years until August 2020, a stock image greeted anyone visiting the FBI's public-facing cybercrime website (see Figure 4.1).[10] This image is typical of cybercrime iconography: darkness and blue light, cascading binary code, a faceless male figure in a hoodie. It is the graphic manifestation of the mystery of technology evoked by the *Daily Mail* (the hacker here in the guise of digital magician), of the global reach of cybercrime, as emphasised by the map backdrop, and of its rapacity (the hacker's hands being the only visible body part), of Western cultural stereotypes and, most of all, of the fear associated with darkness and the unknown. In terms of reassuring the public of their safety and security, it is a far from satisfactory image. Indeed, it is likely to have precisely the opposite rhetorical impact. The hooded figure is a stock feature of contemporary representations of hacking, but also of an older Western heritage of death personified as the Grim Reaper. The enduring impression is that cybercrime is something that is very threatening (perhaps mortally so), committed with impunity, and impenetrable to the ordinary citizen.

In this respect, linguistic and graphic darkness have the same effect: they generate fear. Its value has not been lost on cybercriminals, as a recent scam variant

Figure 4.1 Stock Image of Cybercriminal from FBI Website (until August 2020): Shutterstock, www.shutterstock.com/image-photo/computer-hacker-silhouette-hooded-man-binary-302442911

demonstrates. Sextortion is the popular name for a form of cybercrime that extorts monies on the premise that compromising footage of the victim has been obtained. While more sophisticated approaches use social media and video chat to generate said material for leverage, opportunist criminals engage in the mass distribution of emails that seek to play on the fears of anyone who may have an intimate secret:

> Subject – [*deleted*] @ hotmail.co.uk is hacked
> Hello! My nickname in darknet is [*deleted*]. I hacked this mailbox more than six months ago, through it I infected your operating system with a virus (trojan) created by me and have been monitoring you for a long time.
> I was most struck by the intimate content sites that you occasionally visit. You have a very wild imagination, I tell you! During your pastime and entertainment there, I took screenshot through the camera of your device, synchronizing with what you are watching. Oh my god! You are so funny and excited!
> I think that you do not want all your contacts to get these files, right? If you are of the same opinion, then I think that $805 is quite a fair price to destroy the dirt I created. Send the above amount on my BTC wallet (bitcoin): [*deleted*]. As soon as the above amount is received, I guarantee that the data will be deleted, I do not need it.

> Otherwise, these files and history of visiting sites will get all your contacts from your device. Also, I'll send to everyone your contact access to your email and access logs, I have carefully saved it! Since reading this letter you have 48 hours!

In this text, "darknet" is used rhetorically to generate fear, to contribute to an impression of the sender's technical and criminal sophistication, and to endorse the belief that they have been watching and manipulating unseen, much like the hooded hacker in the image on the FBI's website. Criminals and public defenders appear to subscribe to the same lexicon and iconography.

Catastrophe and compulsion in the cyber triumvirate

Equally intriguing is the discovery that criminal messaging borrows from law enforcement rhetoric on occasion. Cybercriminals engaged in delivering ransomware – malicious software that locks devices and encrypts files until a ransom is paid – some years ago began impersonating law enforcement with the presumed aim of increasing compliance. "Police ransomware", as it has come to be known, deploys a pop-up screen that makes use of highly localised branding and pseudo-legal references. Below are two instances. The first purports to be from US law enforcement, with an FBI badge occupying the right third of the screen:

> YOUR COMPUTER HAS BEEN LOCKED!
> This operating system is locked due to the violation of the federal laws of the United States of America! (Article 1, Section 8, Clause 8; Article 202; Article 210 of the Criminal Code of the U.S.A. provides for a deprivation of liberty for four to twelve years.)
>
> Following violations were detected:
> Your IP address was used to visit websites containing pornography, child pornography, zoophilia, and child abuse. Your computer also contains video files with pornographic content, elements of violence and child pornography!
> Spam-messages with terrorist motives were also sent from your computer.
> This computer lock is aimed to stop your illegal activity.
> To unlock the computer you are obliged to pay a fine of $200.

The second purports to come from UK law enforcement. In addition to stock logos for the now defunct Serious Organised Crime Agency (SOCA), Cheshire Constabulary, and The Metropolitan Police Service, it is framed by photographs of Queen Elizabeth II and former Metropolitan Police Commissioner Sir Paul Stephenson:

> Serios [*sic*] Organised Crime Agency
> Metropolitan British Police
> IP: [*deleted*]
> Country: GB Great Britain

> Region:
> City:
> ISP: [*deleted*]
> Operating System: [*deleted*]
> User Name: [*deleted*]
> ATTENTION!
> Your computer has been blocked up for safety reasons listed below.
> You are accused of viewing/storage and/or dissemination of banned pornography (child pornography/zoophilia/rape etc). You have violated World Declaration on non-proliferation of child pornography. You are accused of committing the crime envisaged by Article 161 of the Kingdom of Great Britain criminal law.
> Article 161 of the Kingdom of Great Britain criminal law provides for the punishment of deprivation of liberty for terms from 5 to 11 years.
> Also, you are suspected of violation of "Copyright and Related rights Law" (downloading of pirated music, video, warez) and of use and/or dissemination of copyrighted content. Thus, you are suspected of violation of Article 148 of the Kingdom of Great Britain criminal law.

In both texts, citation of legal instruments is intended to convey authority and the threat of a more severe punishment. The sender relies on the fact that the recipient's need to unlock the device and instinct to remain at liberty will prevent at least some victims from fact checking the legislation, which is of course erroneous. In the second case, professed capture of connection data serves to give the impression that the recipient has been watched unseen, while the right third of the screen shows both an active countdown clock – intensifying the sense of urgency – and helpful information on where to access the required payment methods.

That sense of urgency, and the constraining of the choice into no choice at all, echoes some of the antithetical security messaging we have seen elsewhere, but also the approach of some of the largest players in the cybersecurity industry, namely consumer anti-virus vendors. One advertisement shown in the US in 2019 exhibits features typical of the genre:

> [Male Voice] Today's digital world has a dark side. Because everyday things like shopping, banking, and even browsing online can expose personal information and make people vulnerable to cybercriminals. More than 850 million people in 16 countries were victims of cybercrime in the last year alone. Mobile ransomware attacks went up by 33 per cent; 86 per cent of adults may have put their information at risk using public wifi; and there's a victim of identity theft every two seconds.
>
> We believe that even though the digital world is constantly changing, people should always have the right to feel safe. So as cybercrime has evolved beyond just viruses, we've evolved too. Norton and LifeLock are now part of one company, to create all in one protection against today's new threats. New Norton360 with LifeLock combines Norton device security, VPN for online

> privacy, and LifeLock identity theft protection, backed by a million dollar protection package. With 50 million customers around the globe, we are the consumer ally for today's connected world: meeting the dangers of cyber-crime with the power of cyber safety; on a mission to secure the digital world just when it needs saving the most. Norton LifeLock – protectors of the digital universe.[11]

This advertisement is 1 minute 23 seconds in length. The first 32 seconds contain darkness, vulnerability, overwhelmingly large numbers, and a problem that is both high speed and getting worse. A soundtrack of choppy, synthesised strings heightens the sense of drama and urgency as they would in a tense thriller. Review of the voiceover text – a luxury not afforded to the first-time viewer – reveals conditional "cans" and "mays" that render the statistics less than definite and authoritative. Scrutiny of the very small print temporarily displayed on screen reveals that the 850 million victims have been estimated based on a survey of only 16,000 people, the victim every 2 seconds on a sample of just over 5,000.

The speed of change in the next section is illustrated and compounded by a rapid succession of images (11 in 15 seconds) and a repetitive piano soundtrack. The closing section, in which anti-virus software is depicted as a superhero, swells with a crescendo of drums worthy of an epic action adventure, and slows down the visuals to a rate of ten images in 36 seconds. We are to be rescued from the edges of our seats and the ends of our wits, when the situation is at its most desperate.

A similar approach is taken in the company's advertisement shown on UK television, in its announcement that "Today, your information is more exposed than ever. When you shop, sign in, or browse, you could be vulnerable to cyber criminals. More online threats demand more protection." We are to understand that the situation has never been worse: visuals suffused with blue light and showing people's personal data being broadcast on electronic billboards without their knowledge encourage us to make the logical leap from the possibility of vulnerability to a realised increase in threats.[12]

It is of course to be expected that organisations whose business is to sell a product will seek to persuade through advertising, and that a company selling security will do so by depicting the threat from which it promises to protect in dramatic, and arguably amplificatory, terms. It is the security equivalent of the cliché of the vacuum cleaner salesman emptying dirt out onto a potential customer's carpet in order to demonstrate the power of his product. What is perhaps more surprising is that government authorities, specialist law enforcement units among them, should use the same tactic.

For four years until August 2020, text displayed below the "faceless hacker" image on the FBI's cybercrime website described the threat from cybercrime as "serious - and growing. Cyber intrusions are becoming more commonplace, more dangerous, and more sophisticated". Readers will recognise the construction as a triad with *anaphora*, emphatic repetition of the leading word that is the verbal equivalent of striking the lectern. Later in the same paragraph, "pervasive and evolving" are the terms of choice. Ransomware is "insidious", and "the inability to access the important data [*sic*] can be catastrophic in terms of the loss of sensitive or proprietary information, the disruption to regular operations, financial losses incurred to restore systems and files, and the potential harm to an organization's reputation". Catastrophe literally denotes physical collapse and is therefore an exaggeration, an amplificatory metaphor, in the context of loss of data to a business. So, too, is the assertion that "the loss of access to personal and often irreplaceable items - including family photos, videos, and other records - can be devastating for individuals as well". Cyclones are devastating; while loss of sentimental items is upsetting, its depiction in language evocative of physical destruction is hyperbole.

Of computer and network intrusions we are told: "The collective impact is staggering. Billions of dollars are lost every year repairing systems hit by such attacks." As with journalistic usage analysed elsewhere in this book, the sensational adjective "staggering" (also metaphorical in origin) seeks to elicit shock in the reader as much as express that of the author. The gigantic but imprecise "billions of dollars" has the same effect as the very large numbers in Norton's advertising, to overwhelm the reader's imagination with the size of cybercrime.

Duly sensitised, the reader will immediately want to know how they can protect themselves. To reach the FBI's cybercrime prevention advice, they must scroll through a total of 16 paragraphs and 11 bullet points on the agency's key and related priorities, one of which is "Going Dark", rebranded as "Lawful Access" from July 2020. At the very bottom of the page, the FBI advises citizens in bold text to "Install or Update Your Antivirus Software … Install or Update Your Antispyware Technology … Keep Your Operating System Up to Date … Be Careful What You Download … Turn Off Your Computer". While the individual recommendations may be sound from a technical perspective, and the text under each heading provides some explanatory context, the relegation of citizen response to the endnotes, and a finale that is nothing short of bathetic defeatism – "turning the computer off effectively severs an attacker's connection" – results in a technophobic law enforcement narrative that disempowers the citizen. Moreover, the message to the citizen is the same, regardless of whether the speaker is a criminal, a vendor, or a public servant: you must click on a link and pay money for something you may not understand, or face the terrifying consequences. This rhetorical mechanism has in turn driven the emergence of "scareware": as the name suggests, the criminal ***modus operandi*** seeks to engage with consumers' fear of being hacked, manipulating them into buying rogue security software which is either useless or malicious.

In the interest of fairness, it should be noted that the FBI restructured this narrative in August 2020. The Cyber Grim Reaper no longer dominates the page, and a section entitled "What You Should Know" now sits in a more prominent position at the top. Under the sub-headings "Protect Yourself" and "Understand Common Crimes and Risks Online", cyber threats are explained in layperson's terms. Second place on the page is given to sharing information on how citizens can report cybercrime, either to the Internet Crime Complaint Center (IC3) or their local FBI field office. While much of the text is familiar – the impact is still "staggering" – there has clearly been an attempt to edit the most egregious examples of alarmism: on a linked mini-site, ransomware is no longer depicted as catastrophic or devastating. But most of all, this rewrite demonstrates the importance of arrangement to rhetorical effect. In this case, moving the sections around on the page empowers the citizen to learn about cybercrime, and play their part in countering it. Arrangement (*dispositio*) was recognised as a key component of rhetorical skill by Classical theorists, taking up an entire book of Quintilian's treatise. While it would be a stretch to suggest that the FBI may have developed a sudden fondness for the *Institutio Oratoria*, the arrangement of material on their website for persuasive effect certainly stands in a long rhetorical tradition.

The identification of changes in rhetorical tactic inevitably prompts the question of which is the more effective. Evaluation of the effectiveness and impact of different cybercrime prevention initiatives to date is almost entirely lacking;[13] indeed, measurement of the effectiveness of any crime prevention measure is fraught with difficulty. An obvious success metric would be a reduction in reported cybercrime as evidence of fewer citizens falling for scams. But an increased level of public awareness can just as easily lead to a larger number of crime reports, particularly where – as on the FBI's reworked website – reporting is actively encouraged. In this scenario, effective cybercrime prevention can actually lead to an increase in recorded crime that, taken out of context, could give the impression that the problem is actually getting worse, when the number of incidents may not have in fact increased.

As we have seen in Chapters 2 and 3, in the public security architecture, accurate assessment of the threat is at least a nominal prerequisite to the development of proportionate policy responses and the allocation of budget for protective measures. But quantifying the threat from cybercrime in a meaningful way has proved challenging. In many cases, relevant national legislation needs to be in place before law enforcement agencies can record a crime specifically as a cybercrime, let alone an internationally comparable one. Reports of scams by members of the public reflect only the suspicious behaviour that citizens have noticed and are minded to bring to the government's attention: technical measures such as widely deployed spam filters remove many criminal overtures from citizens' sight; many online frauds are likely to be reported to banks and payment providers in the first instance, corporate cyber-attacks to insurers. While advances in international data protection legislation – most notably the EU's General Data Protection Regulation – have driven the requirement for companies to notify regulators and affected subjects of individual data breaches, data controllers are understandably reluctant to risk further reputational damage by sharing overall statistics on cyber incidents. The cybersecurity industry is in possession of very large amounts of relevant data on attempted intrusions and the spread of malicious software, but this data set does not necessarily map to criminal offences as defined in national or international legislation. In the absence of comprehensive and verifiable statistics, and as apparent in Norton's advertisement above, very large numbers that do not reflect absolute incidence are able to gain currency and authority.

Lack of verifiable cybercrime statistics also opens up greater room for hyperbole. The tendency to cyber threat inflation has not gone unnoticed by political theorists and security scholars. Taking something of a constructivist perspective on the rhetoric of "cyber doom" and the prospect of a "cyber Pearl Harbor", in recent years several researchers – Myriam Dunn Cavelty, Jerry Brito and Tate Watkins, Sean Lawson and Erik Gartzke among them – have sought to draw attention to the way in which cyber threats have been hyped and securitised.[14] Securitised cyber threats align with a military response; desecuritised – or perhaps, rather, non-securitised – threats with a civilian law enforcement and community response.

The peculiar predicament of cyber threats, however, is that distinguishing between what constitutes a national security issue and what is organised crime is frequently a difficult task. The 2017 Wannacry ransomware incident is a suitable exemplar. Malicious software that ostensibly sought to generate profit through ransom payments impacted on poorly protected critical national infrastructure, including the UK National Health Service, with consequences for citizen healthcare provision. Subsequent investigation attributed the attacks to the state-sponsored North Korean Lazarus Group, whose operations have been identified by the US federal government as providing financial support to the country's illicit weapon and missile programs.[15] The profit motive situates the activity in the volume crime or fraud category, which would be the preserve of civilian law enforcement; impact on critical national infrastructure renders it a national security issue; alleged state sponsorship takes the incident into the realm of state interference, which traditionally would be met with a military response in the kinetic theatre; links to that state's nuclear armament programme transport it to the remit of international diplomacy and disarmament. Moreover, the nature of the activity can change as more information becomes available. It took seven months for Wannacry to be publicly attributed to North Korea.[16]

There is undoubtedly some truth in Brito and Watkins' assertion of the emergence of a "cyber-industrial complex" reminiscent of the military-industrial complex of the Cold War; as they note, the pre-eminence of traditional defence contractors' cybersecurity divisions in the provision of national security and intelligence support to governments is testament to this.[17] At the same time, practical difficulties in distinguishing between what should be treated as a national security issue, and what should be handled by civilian law enforcement – especially in the thick of incident response – create a space in which all cyber threats may be designated national security issues until proven otherwise. Or, as Hasian, Lawson and MacFarlane have observed in relation to the U.S.: "There is evidence that cyber war proponents recognize the rhetorical value of ambiguity and deploy it strategically when considering possible responses to cyber threats."[18]

Less attention has been paid to the impact of martial depictions of cybercrime and cybersecurity issues on citizens. This a worthwhile endeavour, particularly in light of the emergence of online influence operations as a widespread phenomenon in recent years. Once considered merely as targets that had to be protected from cybercrime, and arguably from themselves, citizens are now directly engaged in the spread of disinformation and misinformation on social media: to coin a military phrase, they are the first line of defence. Where previously the tactic of social engineering aimed for the most part to manipulate individuals in order to turn a profit – for example, by encouraging people to click on a link that would harvest personal data to be sold on to other criminals, or to steal intellectual property – there is now understandably greater focus on strategies for preventing people from sharing unverified social "news" items that have been tied to state-sponsored attempts to sow discord (e.g. surrounding the Black Lives Matter movement) and interfere in democratic process (the 2016 US election and UK Brexit referendum), and lending credibility to conspiracy theories. Technology companies are placed under pressure to suppress factually inaccurate content, fact-checking services have emerged as key stakeholders, and "critical thinking" has become the buzz phrase for efforts to improve citizens' distinction of fact from fiction. Given rhetoric's persuasive intent, representations of cybercrime and cybersecurity merit a close reading particularly in this space, where citizens have greater potential directly to reduce the threat to others and to the community.

So, when *The Times* ran with the headline "GCHQ in cyberwar on anti-vaccine propaganda" on 9 November 2020, we may reasonably ask what effect the declaration of war might have had on readers.[19] The body of the article reports on the UK intelligence agency's operations to disrupt targeted disinformation with links to the Russian government. While the debate around the exact threshold for offensive cyber operations is far from settled, it is safe to say that the operations described in this article do not constitute a war in the received sense of a kinetic conflict.

Nevertheless, the practice of cybersecurity abounds with military imagery and the language of warfare: at the most general level, even the very notion of "cyber-attack" – as opposed to "cyber-theft", "cyber-vandalism", or even "cyber-destruction" – exhibits martial leanings and conceives of IT operations as a military manoeuvre. Cybersecurity's lexicon includes breaches, logic bombs, "weaponisation" of data and programs, firewalls, adversaries, kill chains, Trojan horses (with a nod to ancient mythical conflict), to name but a few; use of the prefix war- for compound words denoting the clandestine scanning of telecommunications networks (wardialling, warchalking, wardriving, warbiking and warwalking) invites associations with military strategy exercises such as wargaming; the cybersecurity industry, meanwhile, has borrowed concepts from the military sphere, including Defense in Depth, red and blue teaming, Capture the Flag exercises and sandboxing, the last of which encourages association with the danger of an explosive device.

At the same time, frequent reference to cyber threat evolution and mitigation as an "arms race" claims cybersecurity for Cold War patterns of international relations rhetoric. This commonplace has transcended strict applications to digital military technologies, making its way into civilian law enforcement and consumer texts on cybercrime. A decade ago, I myself used the phrase in the European Union's cybercrime threat assessment: "In the ever escalating 'arms race' between cybercriminals and the authorities, vulnerabilities in people, processes and technology will continue to be exploited."[20] While taking some comfort in its appearance in quotation marks, I nevertheless offer it up by way of atonement.

While it may be expedient for journalists, vendors, and others to refer to cyber operations as a kind of warfare, there may be unintended consequences for a community's ability to respond to cyber threats. For the vast majority of the world's citizens in the early twenty-first century, war is waged by standing armies, at a step removed from direct experience. The "home front" emerged as a space distinct from the front line of battle in the two defining conflicts of the twentieth century. For families without serving military personnel and outside of conflict zones, war is physically and conceptually remote. Designation of cyber operations as war is therefore not only hyperbolical: it distances cybersecurity from ordinary human experience, and strips citizens of individual agency.

Close reading of cybersecurity vendor Crowdstrike's 2020 *Global Threat Report* reveals a heroising use of martial imagery and vocabulary that is notable for its consistency but by no means unique in the industry (emphasis added):

> This report provides a **front-line** view and greater insight into the cyber **battle** CrowdStrike's **seasoned** security experts are **waging** against today's most sophisticated **adversaries**, and offers recommendations for increasing your organization's cybersecurity readiness.[21]

Elsewhere in the report, security practitioners are termed "cyberdefenders", one of the company's software products is personified as engaged in daily "'hand-to-hand combat' with sophisticated adversaries", and its employees are recast as "threat hunters". In the lines above, some military allusions are more obvious than others. Use of the adjective "seasoned" in another context could have several possible reference points. Here, we may think of the commonly used phrase "seasoned veteran", sufficiently clichéd to have become an internet meme, and in turn of (particularly US) military veterans. The company's customers, employees and even its code are elevated by means of metaphor into combatants. The use of heroising martial language to depict the activities of the cybersecurity industry is the more intriguing given that the industry is one of the largest employers of military veterans. But this is not a war in the sense of a conflict that results in death or physical collapse – at least not directly.

Perhaps the most fascinating aspect of this technique is its similarity to the one used by Juvenal in the first century CE to describe the dangers of living in Rome. In this respect, the securitising instinct identified as so characteristic of the second half of the twentieth century may in fact have a much longer rhetorical history. Where Roman literature draws comparison with the mythical heroes best known to its audience, modern cybersecurity rhetoric looks to the military and to fantasy genres, among them the superhero franchises to which Norton's consumer facing marketing alludes. When it comes to visual rhetoric, the reader may also note the proliferation of shields among the logos of anti-virus companies, evocative of military defence. The impression persists that cybersecurity is the realm of specialists and superhumans: while it may make it more exciting as a career, the message to consumers is far from empowering.

Cyber and the unreal

The association with fantasy and science fiction is a key feature of what historians might call cybersecurity's foundation myth, its prehistory even. All compound words with the cyber- prefix trace their origins to cybernetics, the approach to studying animal and mechanical regulatory systems first expounded by Norbert Wiener.[22] Wiener's nomenclature itself harked back to the Ancient Greek *kubernēsis*, meaning steering, pilotage, or (metaphorically) government. In the second half of the twentieth century, popular science fiction abounded with cybernetic organisms, identified by the portmanteau "cyborg". Darth Vader of *Star Wars*, the Borg of *Star Trek, Doctor Who*'s Cybermen, *The Terminator*, and *RoboCop* all introduced cyborgs to the public well before cybersecurity gained currency as a popular concept.

The term "cyberspace", now regularly used in negotiations and texts on technology governance and international relations, was popularised by William Gibson in his 1984 novel *Neuromancer*. The subgenre in which Gibson was writing, cyberpunk, escaped the page to become a "real world" aesthetic. In something of a curious feedback loop, innovators raised on science fiction now name products in honour of their enthusiasms. One of Belgium's leading internet service providers has the same name as the rogue artificial intelligence in *The Terminator* movies (Skynet); Skynet was reported also to be the name given to the US National Security Agency's program for analysing communications metadata;[23] a Japanese robotics company took the name Cyberdyne from the same movie franchise.[24] A different frame of reference sees a UK accelerator for cybersecurity start-ups sharing a name with the chief villains of the *Battlestar Galactica* franchise (CyLon/Cylon).

Modern cyber- words are confections, neologisms in which a prefix with its origins in government/regulation has erroneously come to denote digital technology. In contrast to the less exciting but accurate alternative, "information security", cybersecurity and its oft-heard abbreviation "cyber" mean nothing at all without an understanding of this external heritage. In this respect, etymology aligns with the dominant rhetoric: issues related to cybersecurity are often represented as exclusive, inaccessible, and somewhat dystopian.

When cybercrime was new

President Obama's 2015 address at Stanford University includes the lines "The cyber world is sort of the wild, wild West. And to some degree, we're asked to be the sheriff."[25] In a similar vein, the FBI claimed to be "as comfortable chasing outlaws in cyberspace as we are down back alleys and across continents".[26] The Western Frontier is a peculiarly American frame of reference that has become something of an international leitmotiv in public utterances about cyberspace. The UK's National Society for the Prevention of Cruelty to Children's (NSPCC) lobbying activity for social media regulation is the Wild West Web campaign. In 2015, the then director of Europol referred to the need to "find a legislative balance so we don't allow the internet to become a Wild West in which criminals can act with impunity".[27] The World Economic Forum's former cybersecurity lead has made consistent and frequent use of the term in interviews from 2013, and as recently as 2020: "It's the Wild West and no rules or 'gentleman agreement' [*sic*] exists anymore due to geopolitical tension."[28] This imagery has also made its way into print media shorthand, as in this May 2020 headline in *The Economist*: "America rethinks its strategy in the Wild West of cyberspace".[29]

There is, of course, an element of machismo in this depiction of authoritarian lawmen seeking to impose order on a lawless environment. Dunn Cavelty notes the influence of the frontier image "in shaping the conception of an unruly and lawless place in need of order", and we may even discern in its international adoption a reflection of US dominance over both the substance and language of global technology policy.[30] Evocation of the frontier spirit also aligns with the rhetoric of novelty, insofar as cyberspace is consciously portrayed as a new territory. As we have seen in previous chapters, novelty and the related concepts of renewal and restoration are stock features of security rhetoric from the first century CE to the twenty-first century. In the context of cybersecurity and cybercrime, the novelty of the threat itself is emphasised, as in this 2018 statement by the governor of Rwanda's central bank: "The rapid expansion of networks and technologies, the opening of IT systems to external exchanges, the growing amount of electronic transactions and big data have caused the emergence of a new type of crime dubbed Cybercrime."[31]

Novelty is here associated with difficulty: in reference to cybercrime, the Mayor of London's website asserts: "The nature of crime is changing and raises new challenges where new crimes are often harder to detect, predict and prevent."[32] The challenge of novelty is sometimes emphasised at the expense of factual accuracy, as in this 2016 speech by a senior UK police officer:

> As traditional face to face crime decreases, criminality in the cyber sphere is on the rise. It is used to communicate, launder money, arrange illegal shipments and blackmail children from anywhere in the world.
>
> It has also opened up new crimes, such as distributed denial of service attacks and sharing of indecent images of children, plus the dark web, all of which never existed 20 years ago. The financial cost to UK businesses as a result of cyber crime continues to increase – we currently assess the financial cost of cybercrime to be well over a billion pounds a year.[33]

Consensus dates the first distributed denial of service (DDoS) attack to 1999 (denial of service more generally has a longer history), and the inception of the dark web is commonly traced back to the emergence of Freenet in 2000.[34] The sharing of indecent images of children, however, predates 1996 and indeed internet technology: while it is certainly the case that internet-mediated technologies have enabled the global proliferation of this material in digital form, it is entirely incorrect to state, as here, that the sharing of indecent images of children did not occur before their advent. In this instance, the emphasis on novelty appears to be more important than a factual evidence base.

The rhetorical association of novelty with difficulty presumes a natural state that is challenged by change. As something that evolves at speed, technology and its misuse are constantly "new", which perhaps goes some way to explaining the fondness for emphasis in public utterances on the novelty of cybercrime 20 years after its emergence. On the other hand, appeal to the shock of the new must surely have a limited lifespan as a rhetorical tactic. There will always be new aspects to cybercrime – new *modi operandi*, new technologies in use; but cybercrime *per se* is only new to those with a longer perspective. In 2020, anyone under the age of 30 has not experienced a world without it. For those younger members of society, declarations of novelty may not be as convincing. Indeed, they could conversely be taken as evidence that the speaker is struggling to keep pace.

Deconstructing the cyber pandemic

In addition to martial, frontier, and fantastic imagery, the lexicon of cybersecurity is heavily influenced by that of epidemiology: devices are "infected" by malware (a portmanteau for malicious software) that "spreads"; certain types of cybercrime are quantified and their gravity demonstrated by the number or rate of infections. This language is so pervasive in cybersecurity communication that it can be easy to forget that it is a metaphorical usage. Malicious software behaves *like a virus* because it self-replicates, but it is not (yet) an inherently biological problem. Texts examined in previous chapters have illustrated metaphor's capacity for making messages more vivid, immediate, and relatable. Their persuasive impact is in their ability to make the reader/listener feel as they might feel about the point of comparison. So, when Obama compares his cybersecurity strategy to the building of a great cathedral, the strategy is afforded the pride and wonder Americans would experience on seeing such an impressive building. How, then, might citizens feel about problems whose rhetoric is imbued with the language of virology?

The heritage of the viral metaphor is commonly traced back to Gregory Benford's 1970 short story "The Scarred Man", in which malicious software had the name "VIRUS", and the program engineered to remove it, "VACCINE".[35] Benford had worked on the precursor to the internet, the US Department of Defense's ARPANet project in the 1960s, yet another intersection between life and art, *praxis* and *mimesis*, science fact and science fiction. Researcher Fred Cohen is credited with introducing "computer viruses" to the academic world, in a much cited 1987 paper in the academic journal *Computers & Security*.[36] Cohen's definition was the blueprint not only for usage of the term "virus", but of a wider transferred lexicon:

> We define a computer "virus" as a program that can "infect" other programs by modifying them to include a possibly evolved copy of itself. With the infection property, a virus can spread throughout a computer system or network using the authorizations of every user using it to infect their programs.

> Every program that gets infected may also act as a virus and thus the infection grows.[37]

The hyperbolic potential of the metaphor is exploited from the outset. Cohen elaborates on the comparison as follows:

> As an analogy to a computer virus, consider a biological disease that is 100% infectious, spreads whenever animals communicate, kills all infected animals instantly at a given moment, and has no detectable side effects until that moment. If a delay of even one week were used between the introduction of the disease and its effect, it would be very likely to leave only a few remote villages alive, and would certainly wipe out the vast majority of modern society. If a computer virus of this type could spread through the computers of the world, it would likely stop most computer use for a significant period of time, and wreak havoc on modern government, financial, business, and academic institutions.[38]

There is much here that is familiar from doom-laden depictions of cyber-attacks. Also evident from the passage above is the capacity of the viral metaphor to elicit a response similar to that generated by a threat to human physical well-being at the level of the individual. The language of virology taps into our deep-seated fear of death and basic physiological needs. Its transferral to cybersecurity imbues computer problems with a sense of mortal danger. As Jussi Parikka has observed in his thorough study, *Digital Contagions*, viruses also "work as part of a certain imaginary of a health body of digital society and are territorialized as diseases of such a body"[39]

This chapter was planned well before the emergence of the COVID-19 novel coronavirus in 2020. As the discussion above demonstrates, cybersecurity problems have been associated with deadly viruses for many years. In the context of a global public health emergency, descriptions such as Cohen's may be uncomfortable reading to a public that has been presented with a very real viral threat to life, and that has been instructed to be on the alert.[40] Alarmist cybersecurity rhetoric at such a time is something of a gamble: target audiences may legitimately feel that they have bigger, more immediate threats to worry about; customary hyperbole may be indistinguishable from the noise of a large number of competing voices seeking to persuade citizens that they need their products "more than ever". But causing alarm is a default tactic of cybersecurity rhetoric, and old habits die hard. At the time of writing (late 2020), one vendor displays the following text on their website [original emphasis]:

> Preparing for the next global crisis - a cyber pandemic
> People and organizations have suffered greatly from the coronavirus pandemic. Many critical lessons are being learned, but none more important that another devastating crisis could be brewing. A catastrophic cyber event has long been envisioned, and with today's digitally connected world, a global cyber pandemic is now a reality.[41]

A banner at the top of the company's web pages bids visitors to "Prepare for a Cyber Pandemic. Secure your everything now". There are a number of possible reactions to this content: it could indeed trigger the alarm at which it is evidently aimed; it could be rejected as a cynical attempt to exploit an already heightened state of alert; it could likewise be seen as crass and insensitive by people who have been directly affected by the real virus.[42] We can perhaps be more definite about what this messaging is not, and that is empowering to the citizen. Governments in their communications on COVID-19 were keen to emphasise the role of ordinary people in controlling the spread of the virus, protecting themselves and others. In the text above, the only solution is to purchase the product offered by the vendor – no further protective advice is given. Moreover, eagle-eyed readers may recognise the hyperbolical adjectives (catastrophic, devastating) that the FBI saw fit to remove from their public messaging. The final assertion of the paragraph that "a global cyber pandemic is now a reality" is intrinsically meaningless, given that there is no such thing as a cyber pandemic in literal terms.[43]

On the same theme, a range of vendor solutions now promise "cyber-immunity". Some providers were quick to restate their allegiance to the concept while the global community was in the throes of the first wave of coronavirus infections.[44] This period also saw the emergence of a product claiming to be the world's first "computer vaccine".[45] Without the sales figures of these companies before and after such communication, it is impossible to gauge how successful these attempts to capitalise on the pandemic have been. Based on the evidence above, however, it is clear that COVID-19 has been used by some in the cybersecurity industry not only as a business opportunity, but also as a rhetorical device to persuade potential customers of the urgency and severity of cyber threats.[46]

Against predestination in cybersecurity rhetoric

Efforts to draw the reader's or listener's attention to hyperbolical representations of cybercrime and cybersecurity should not be taken as an attempt to dismiss the threat. Cyber-attacks can be serious and damaging, be it to reputations, finances, national security, and even personal wellbeing. Highlighting the way in which certain frames of reference are consciously chosen above others, however, and considering the potential impact of those on different audiences, especially the non-specialist public, can help us to identify alternative framings that may resonate with citizens while empowering them to protect themselves and others.[47]

One proposed approach seeks to harness lessons learned from public health. Rowe, Halpern, and Lentz have elaborated an intervention model that compares communicable and non-communicable cyber threats to communicable and non-communicable diseases, cyber risk behaviours to public health risk behaviours, and environmental exposures relevant to cybersecurity and public health respectively.[48] Following this model, communicable cyber threats such as email spoofing or unwittingly being the intermediary for an attack as part of a botnet of compromised devices are met with system-level interventions drawn from public health, including quarantine, mandatory reporting of new cases, educational information and guidelines for early detection.

A public health model also places importance on prevention: primary prevention seeks to minimise the threat by addressing risk behaviours and promoting generalised protections; secondary prevention seeks to reduce the impact of a disease or incident through targeted intervention; the aim of tertiary prevention, meanwhile is to manage long-term effects and reduce the risk of recurrence. A public health approach to cybersecurity could also legitimately adopt the language of virology, while at the same time giving agency to ordinary citizens. Individuals accustomed in the twentieth century to using a handkerchief through an understanding that "Coughs and Sneezes Spread Diseases", and more recently exhorted to save lives by wearing a mask, washing their hands, and keeping a distance from other people, are perfectly capable of basic digital hygiene as long as the rhetoric is accessible and the instructions are clear. As the analysis above has illustrated, too often cybersecurity rhetoric seeks to sensitise through fear and hyperbole, and constructs an antithesis whereby the only choice is between cybergeddon and buying a product. Transforming the well-worn framing of disease into one of community disease control, cyber public health has the potential to empower individuals to actively engage in cybersecurity without feeling overwhelmed by technical jargon or visions of inevitable doom.

Evidence of the possibility of alternative representations comes from what some may deem an unlikely source. While hyperbolical threat depictions do not easily accommodate humour, they are of course ripe for deflation. *Bathos* – as opposed to *pathos* – was a technique familiar to orators, dramatists, and poets in Ancient Greece and Rome. Then, as now, it was frequently used to cut people and things down to a more manageable, less threatening, less daunting size. It was a particular favourite of Juvenal, who had a fondness for undercutting his own hyperbolical portrayals of moral outrages.[49] Comical representation of an issue or ridicule of individuals likewise serves to diminish their grandeur and empower both the creator and the reader/listener.

A striking and rare example of comic deflation of cyber threats is proffered in a 2018 Disney movie. Firmly targeting a family audience, *Ralph Breaks the Internet* is an animated comedy in which lead characters Wreck-It Ralph and Vanellope von Schweetz enter the internet via a Wi-Fi router. Online platforms are depicted as physical locations and algorithms as creatures; the overall presentation is both accessible and non-threatening. Pop-up advertiser J. B. Spamley guides Ralph into the Dark Net to source a virus that will slow down a racing game with which his friend Vanellope has become obsessed: the aim is to make the game boring so that Vanellope will want to leave. In a scene reminiscent of visits to the Underworld in Greco-Roman myth, Ralph and Spamley descend in a lift to a dank, dimly lit, green-tinged street. This is the Dark Net, but not as we know it from prevailing cybersecurity rhetoric.

Passing a street hawker offering personal data for sale, the characters make their way to the premises of Double Dan, a Dark Net retailer. Dan is a Disney grotesque, a man-sized slug with more than a passing resemblance to *Star Wars*' Jabba the Hut and the voice of a cockney gangster:

Double Dan: Allow me to introduce you to Arthur.
[*Mechanical monster resembling a dragon or serpent bursts out of a toolbox*]
Easy there, boy! He's keen. Arthur's what I call an insecurity virus. Means he looks for little flaws and weaknesses that make a program insecure.
[*Dan crams Arthur back into the toolbox*]
You release him into that Slaughter Race game, Arthur will find some defect in the code. Then he'll copy that defect and spread it all over the game, till everything becomes quote unquote "boring", just like you want it.
Ralph: OK, just to be super clear here. No one gets hurt, right?
DD: Are you stupid?
R: Well, uh …
DD: Because the only way anyone gets hurt is if you are stupid. All you have to do is make sure the virus stays in Slaughter Race.

Naming the virus Arthur and depicting it as an unruly exotic pet situates the scene in a long tradition of comic shopkeeper routines, including Monty Python's "Dead Parrot" sketch and the purchase of the mogwai in *Gremlins*. Ralph's innocence and ignorance heighten the comedy, and there is an important moment of dramatic irony in Double Dan's almost prophetic warning. The dialogue deftly works a factual and informative explanation of the operations and impact of computer viruses into a brief exchange whose chief function is to progress the plot.

Arthur is by no means a cute pet, and his sudden explosion from the confines of his cage is surely intended to make a young audience jump. His dangerous potential is clearly signalled, but the comic setting, informal dialogue, and cartoonish rendering refashion the Dark Net and cyber threats as intelligible to mass audiences. As depictions of cybersecurity issues go, this is one of the most accessible and engaging. While its impact on the next generation of the world's adults remains to be seen, it nevertheless illustrates that what has become the default need not be the only, or even the most effective, rhetorical portrayal.

With imagery drawn from the military, Cold War diplomacy, fantasy and science fiction, virology, darkness, the Western Frontier, and other realms, one could be forgiven for thinking that cybersecurity suffers something of an identity crisis. Metaphorical inconsistency betrays uncertainty over whose responsibility cybersecurity is – the generals, the lawmen or the technicians as computer doctors. The same imagery is remarkable for its consistency in reflecting the interests of its constituency: it is predominantly a "Boys' Own" conception of how cybersecurity is practised, with inevitable impact on our understanding of who can practice it. A proliferation of portmanteaux – malware, malvertising, adware, scareware, ransomware, spyware, botnets, and cyber-compounds among them – advertise the discipline's impenetrability to non-specialists. So do terms such as spam, phishing, pharming, vishing, smishing, wabbits, and the like, akin to fantasy doggerel inasmuch as they require etymological deciphering. Fondness for constructing acronyms from specialist phrases – for example, APT (Advanced Persistent Threat), BYOD (Bring Your Own Device), DDoS (Distributed Denial of Service), RAT (Remote Access Trojan), XSS (Cross Site Scripting) – adds a further layer of obfuscation.

Cybersecurity is by no means the only discipline that requires learning of a technical language by practitioners. It is, however, arguably unusual in its requirement for an in-depth understanding of the terminology *before* a basic understanding of the subject can be grasped. One of the contentions of this chapter is that cybersecurity awareness and cybercrime prevention communications persistently fail to engage the public in meaningful protective measures, because a glossary is required to explain key concepts. To return to the COVID parallel, we do not expect citizens to be epidemiologists or healthcare professionals to fight the spread of a virus. We simplify the message with clear triadic instructions: "Hands, face, space".

In an age in which images and information are as "viral" as any software, there is a need to empower citizens to protect themselves and others from disinformation and technical disruption. Far from enabling capacity building, the dominant rhetorical features of public cybersecurity discourse are deployed in the construction of a threat that is huge, serious, complex and frightening, and a public that is powerless. The pervasive narrative is one in which cyber-insecurity is both the default state and catastrophic; cybersecurity, meanwhile, can be achieved only by means of a rescue by service providers or government authorities.[50] Consistent application to the threat of hyperbolical and heroising imagery only serves to heighten the citizen's sense of helplessness. Hitherto, this dynamic was to some degree effective: fear drove consumers to buy anti-virus software, which in turn prevented some cyber-attacks from succeeding. Now that we need ordinary people to understand what is happening online, and how to resist bad actors' attempts to use them as vectors for targeted influence operations, the old approach will no longer do.

Notes

1 *Communications Daily*, 29/11/1984.
2 The Associated Press, "Showtime Begins Scrambling; Dish Makers Seek Détente", 27/05/1986.
3 Robert S. Mueller (2006) *Child Exploitation on the Internet: The Dark Side of the Web*, speech to the Project Safe Childhood Conference, Washington, DC, 6 December 2006, https://archives.fbi.gov/archives/news/speeches/child-exploitation-on-the-internet-the-dark-side-of-the-web
4 "Dark Web" and "Deep Web" are often incorrectly used interchangeably in public discourse. The Deep Web is all of the World Wide Web that is not indexed by classical search engines such as Google and Bing. It therefore includes non-public spaces in social media, databases, cloud storage, and the like. The Dark Web consists of darknets (fora) that are inaccessible via a standard web browser.
5 Daily Mail Reporter (2013) "The Disturbing World of the Deep Web, Where Contract Killers and Drug Dealers Ply Their Trade on the Internet", *Mail Online* 11/10/2013, www.dailymail.co.uk/news/article-2454735/The-disturbing-world-Deep-Web-contract-killers-drug-dealers-ply-trade-internet.html
6 Sarah Volpenhein (2015) "Dark Web Poses Challenge for Law Enforcement", *Grand Forks Herald* 10/08/2015, www.govtech.com/gov-experience/Dark-Web-Poses-Challenges-for-Law-Enforcement.html

7 EMCDDA and Europol (2017) *Drugs and the Darknet: Perspectives for Enforcement, Research and Policy*, Luxembourg, p. 51, www.emcdda.europa.eu/publications/joint-publications/drugs-and-the-darknet_en

8 Sean E. Goodison, Dulani Woods, Jeremy D. Barnum, Adam R. Kemerer, and Brian A. Jackson (2019) *Identifying Law Enforcement Needs for Conducting Criminal Investigations Involving Evidence on the Dark Web*, Santa Monica: RAND Corporation, p. 2.

9 Europol (2020) *Internet Organised Threat Assessment (iOCTA)*, The Hague, p. 55, www.europol.europa.eu/iocta-report. Its 2019 report included a dedicated section on Common Challenges for Law Enforcement, namely loss of data, loss of location, challenges associated with national legal frameworks, obstacles to international cooperation, and the challenges of public-private partnership. Europol (2019) *Internet Organised Threat Assessment (iOCTA)*, The Hague, p. 56f, www.europol.europa.eu/activities-services/main-reports/internet-organised-crime-threat-assessment-iocta-2019

10 www.fbi.gov/investigate/cyber; archived site via https://web.archive.org/web/20200810050042/https://www.fbi.gov/investigate/cyber, accessed 30/10/2020.

11 Norton (2019a) "New Norton 360 with LifeLock", www.youtube.com/watch?v=vyQR4HovPnA, uploaded 31/05/2019, accessed 30/10/2020.

12 Norton (2019b) "Norton TV Ad September 2019 – UK", www.youtube.com/watch?v=bIfHEhKpS1A, uploaded 02/10/2019, accessed 30/10/2020.

13 As observed by Benoît Dupont (2019) "Enhancing the Effectiveness of Cybercrime Prevention Through Policy Monitoring", *Journal of Crime and Justice* 42.5: 500–515.

14 Myriam Dunn Cavelty (2007) "Cyber-terror - Looming Threat or Phantom Menace? The Framing of the US Cyber-threat Debate", *Journal of Information Technology & Politics* 4.1: 19–36; (2008) *Cyber-security and Threat Politics: U.S. Efforts to Secure the Information Age*. New York: Routledge; Jerry Brito and Tate Watkins (2011) *Loving the Cyber Bomb? The Dangers of Threat Inflation in Cybersecurity Policy*, Mercatus Center Working Paper, George Mason University; Sean Lawson (2013) "Beyond Cyber-Doom: Assessing the Limits of Hypothetical Scenarios in the Framing of Cyber-Threats", *Journal of Information Technology & Politics* 10.1: 86–103; Erik Gartzke (2013) "The Myth of Cyberwar: Bringing War in Cyberspace Back Down to Earth", *International Security* 38.2: 41–73.

15 U.S. Department of the Treasury (2019) "Treasury Sanctions North Korean State-Sponsored Malicious Cyber Groups", Press Release 13/09/2019, https://home.treasury.gov/news/press-releases/sm774

16 The White House (2017) *Press Briefing on the Attribution of the WannaCry Malware Attack to North Korea*, 19/12/2017, www.whitehouse.gov/briefings-statements/press-briefing-on-the-attribution-of-the-wannacry-malware-attack-to-north-korea-121917/

17 Brito and Watkins (2011) p. 24.

18 Marouf Hasian Jr., Sean Lawson, and Megan D. McFarlane (2015) *The Rhetorical Invention of America's National Security State*, Lanham: Lexington, p. 138.

19 Lucy Fisher and Chris Smyth (2020) "GCHQ in cyberwar on anti-vaccine propaganda", *The Times* 09/11/2020, www.thetimes.co.uk/article/gchq-in-cyberwar-on-anti-vaccine-propaganda-mcjgjhmb2

20 Europol (2011) *Internet Organised Crime Threat Assessment (iOCTA)*, The Hague, www.europol.europa.eu/activities-services/main-reports/threat-assessment-internet-facilitated-organised-crime-iocta-2011; see also Jussi Parikka (2016) *Digital Contagions: A Media Archaeology of Computer Viruses* (2nd edn), New York: Peter Lang, p. 252: "It is clear that the past 10 to 15 years have seen an intensified field of digital network security. It is normal to speak of the 'arms race' in cybersecurity while, at the same time, national organisations are justifying massive investments in cyberwar centers of various kinds."

21 Crowdstrike (2020) *Global Threat Report*, p. 6, https://go.crowdstrike.com/rs/281-OBQ-266/images/Report2020CrowdStrikeGlobalThreatReport.pdf

22 Norbert Wiener (1948) *Cybernetics: Or Control and Communications in the Animal and the Machine*, Paris: Hermann & Cie.

23 Cora Currier, Glenn Greenwald, and Andrew Fishman (2015) "U.S. Government Designated Prominent Al Jazeera Journalist as 'Member of Al Qaeda'", *The Intercept* 08/05/2015, https://theintercept.com/2015/05/08/u-s-government-designated-prominent-al-jazeera-journalist-al-qaeda-member-put-watch-list/

24 The lexicon of robotics points to an older history of technology imitating art: the term "robot" was first coined by Karel Čapek in his 1920 play R.U.R. – "Rossum's Universal Robots"; "robotics" is attributed to science fiction writer Isaac Asimov.

25 Barack Obama, speech delivered at Stanford University, 13/02/2015, https://news.stanford.edu/news/2015/february/cyber-obama-remarks-021315.html

26 www.fbi.gov/investigate/cyber; archived site via https://web.archive.org/web/20200810050042/https://www.fbi.gov/investigate/cyber, accessed 30/10/2020.

27 Paul O'Hare (2015) "Europol calls for greater online crime regulation as mafia gangs migrate to Dark Net", *Daily Record* 04/03/2015, www.dailyrecord.co.uk/news/uk-world-news/europol-calls-greater-online-crime-5270073

28 Farsight Security (2020) "5 Questions with Troels Oerting Jorgensen, Chairman of the Advisory Board of the Centre for Cybersecurity, World Economic Forum", https://info.farsightsecurity.com/5-questions-troels-oerting-jorgensen; cf. Christophe Lamfalussy (2013), "Épinglé", *La Libre* 22/10/2013, www.lalibre.be/international/epingle-5265f3ad3570dfa00783df92: "Troels Oerting, le chef de l'unité contre la cybercriminalité d'Europol, estime que le Net est aujourd'hui le 'Wild West'".

29 The Economist, "America rethinks its strategy in the Wild West of cyberspace", 28/05/2020, www.economist.com/united-states/2020/05/28/america-rethinks-its-strategy-in-the-wild-west-of-cyberspace

30 Myriam Dunn Cavelty (2013) "From Cyber-Bombs to Political Fallout: Threat Representations with an Impact in the Cyber-Security Discourse", *International Studies Review* 15: 105–122, p. 108.

31 John Rwangombwa, quoted in "Banks, Telecoms, Police in Joint Effort to Counter Cyber Threats", *The New Times* 20/01/2018, www.newtimes.co.rw/section/read/227957.

32 The Mayor's Office for Policing and Crime (2020) "Cyber Crime", www.london.gov.uk/what-we-do/mayors-office-policing-and-crime-mopac/my-area-0/cyber-crime, accessed 11/11/2020.

33 Royal United Services Institute (2016) "A Speech by Lynne Owens, Director General of the National Crime Agency", 10/03/2016, https://rusi.org/event/speech-lynne-owens-director-general-national-crime-agency

34 Emerging Technology from the arXiv (2019) "The First DDoS attack Was 20 Years Ago: This Is What We've Learned Since", *MIT Technology Review* 18/04/2019, www.technologyreview.com/2019/04/18/103186/the-first-ddos-attack-was-20-years-ago-this-is-what-weve-learned-since/

35 Republished by the author in 1999 at www.gregorybenford.com/extra/the-scarred-man-returns/, accessed 29/10/2020.

36 Fred Cohen (1987) "Computer Viruses: Theory and Experiments", *Computers & Security* 6: 22–35.

37 Ibid., p. 23.

38 Cohen (1987) p. 24.

39 Parikka (2016) p. 41.

40 UK residents, for example, were told to "STAY ALERT, CONTROL THE VIRUS, SAVE LIVES" in images that drew on the iconography of Hazchem warnings and crimes scenes, complete with incident tape.

41 Checkpoint (n.d.) "Protecting Against a Rapidly Spreading Cyber Pandemic", www.checkpoint.com/cybersecurity-protect-from-cyber-pandemic/, accessed 10/11/2020.

42 There are similarities here to the propensity for cyber war proponents to "piggyback" on non-cyber events (9/11, Pearl Harbor and the like), as identified by Hasian, Lawson, and McFarlane (2015) p. 142.

43 This does not preclude the possibility of a future cyber threat having human physiological impact, for example exploitation of vulnerabilities in brain-computer interfaces or other implantable devices, resulting in tissue damage or function impairment.

44 Among them Kaspersky, who first blogged about cyber-immunity in 2019, www.kaspersky.com/blog/applied-cyberimmunity/28772/, accessed 10/11/2020, and whose video releases in May and June 2020 headlined the concept, www.youtube.com/watch?v=BbhoVy9Y_LI and www.youtube.com/watch?v=odtbm1hj-Ls, both accessed 10/11/2020. In the last of these, personification of technology via direct address from an android voice consciously blurs the distinction between human and machine, physical and cybersecurity. See also Darktrace's September 2020 press release on the latest iteration of its Immune System product, www.darktrace.com/en/press/2020/332/

45 Atense (2020) "No More Anti-Virus Software - Atense Inc., a Cyber Defense Company Claims to Have Developed The World's First Computer Vaccine", company press release 17/06/2020, www.atense.com/Press_Release.html

46 See Deborah Lupton (1994) "Panic Computing: The Viral Metaphor and Computer Technology", *Cultural Studies* 8.3: 556–568 for discussion of earlier comparisons of computer viruses to HIV/AIDS; also Parikka (2016), p. 34. It may be no coincidence that, as noted by Parikka (ibid., p. 43), antivirus programs emerged around 1987–8 with names such as Flushot, Vaccine, and Aspirin.

47 So also Dunn Cavelty (2013) p. 119: "Awareness of the power of threat representation and the preferences that come with them can help to understand that it is neither natural nor inevitable that cyber-security should be presented in terms of power-struggles, war-fighting, and military action, and that there are always different, and sometimes better options."

48 Brent Rowe, Michael Halpern, and Tony Lentz (2012) "Is a Public Health Framework the Cure for Cyber Security?", *CrossTalk* 25.6: 30–38, www.crosstalkonline.org/storage/issue-archives/2012/201211/201211-0-Issue.pdf

49 As identified by a number of scholars including William Scovil Anderson (1957) *Studies in Book I of Juvenal*, Bloomington: Indiana University Press, p. 35; John Henderson (1995) "Pump Up the Volume: Juvenal *Satires* 1: 1–21", *Proceedings of the Cambridge Philological Society* 41: 101–137; Susanna Morton Braund in her commentary on Juvenal's first book of *Satires* (1996) *Juvenal: Satires Book I*, Cambridge: Cambridge University Press, pp. 18, 25f.; Jonathan G. F. Powell (1999) "Stylistic Registers in Juvenal", *Proceedings of the British Academy* 93: 311–334; and Catherine Keane (2015) *Juvenal and the Satiric Emotions*, Oxford: Oxford University Press, p. 121.

50 Cf. Dunn Cavelty (2013) p. 118 "The cyber-security discourse is particularly rich in metaphors, which emerge as powerful perception-shapers and anchoring devices, but also tools that are actively used in political discourse. In other words, discursive constructions are both setting the linguistic rules of the game and are being used instrumentally. On the one hand, viral metaphors were used by technical experts to allow laypersons to understand (complicated) technological issues. But viral metaphors and the virus-as-weapon also speak to deep-seated fears in the human psyche that make national security solutions the logical choice."

5 Epilogue

Pandemic rhetoric

For scholars of rhetoric 2020 has been something of a bumper year. While it is tempting to use the word "unprecedented", it is as well to be mindful that to do so would itself be an instance of the exceptionalist language so dominant in the context of the coronavirus pandemic. Doubtless the rhetoric of the latest public health emergency will in due course provide rich material for constructivist scholars, particularly those alert to the ways in which issues outside the realms of defence, national security, and law enforcement may be securitised. A parallel tradition of privacy and surveillance studies has sought to highlight the potential for mission creep of hastily introduced emergency legislation, and has subjected personal data and location-gathering COVID track and trace apps to warranted scrutiny.

Activists in both disciplines point to a long history of curbs on the freedoms of speech and movement under the guise of ensuring safety and security. So, it is unsurprising that 2020's batch of conspiracy theorists, anti-vaxxers, and self-styled freedom fighters in the mode of anti-lockdown protesters have both responded to and propagated the rhetoric of fear and insecurity, particularly in relation to privacy infringement and surveillance. What makes the current swathe of conspiracy rhetoric distinctive is the extent to which it has been co-opted by mainstream political figures, its cross- and self-referentiality, and its intersection with Big Tech. 2020 has been a year of recycled and snowball rhetoric, and much of it has been conducted in short form, on social media.

On freedom, security, and sacrifice

The association of freedom, sacrifice, and security has seen novel applications in recent months. Benjamin Franklin's oft-misquoted 1775 maxim "Those who would give up essential Liberty to purchase a little temporary Safety, deserve neither Liberty nor Safety" constructed an antithesis that has been widely referenced since. European Union policies aimed at creating an "area of freedom, security and justice" (AFSJ) enshrined in legislation may be seen as something of a theoretical challenge to this construction, in so far as they assert the compatibility of freedom and security.[1] Meanwhile, the customary rhetoric of Remembrance in

DOI: 10.4324/9781003028062-6

English-speaking countries has collocated freedom with sacrifice, inasmuch as the fallen are deemed to have sacrificed themselves for the freedom of their fellow citizens.

It is this association to which President-elect Joe Biden referred in a virtual roundtable on the impact of COVID-19, streamed live on 2 December 2020 [excerpt]:[2]

> When I have this mask on, it's less about me being safe. It's about me making sure that you're safe. It's a patriotic thing to do, it really is. You know, I hear all this about "Well, it's a great sacrifice of my freedom". Well, tell that to all the people who went to World War I and gave their lives, and World War II, and the Korean War, and talk – I mean, come on, you're helping other people.

Invoking the historical association of freedom and sacrifice as a reminder designed to humble, Biden here challenges an antithesis between freedom and mask-wearing constructed by anti-lockdown activists, of which US citizen Deborah Baber became one of the most prominent proponents when a video of her impassioned intervention at a board meeting of Ventura County council went viral on social media:[3]

> Are you going to be wearing masks when you come in? Are you going to obey that, City, and if not, then how in the world are you expecting us to obey anything that you say? I protest face coverings. I am a healthy American. I used to be free. I am not a terrorist. I am not Antifa. I am not a sex slave that wears masks. I am not into sadomasochism and bondage. I am not a burglar. I am not a pandering politician like we see [*gestures towards the council*] here, and here, and here, and here. I am a proud Trump Republican, Trump Republican, yearning to be free again. Who are you, victim or victor? If you are offended by anything I have said, by the masses of people, then I am offended by the masses of people who do not question your wholesale slaughter of our constitutional and inalienable rights. Shame on all of you. Let liberty ring [*rings hand bell, then singing*] God Bless America, land that I love, Stand beside her and guide her through the night with the light from above. From the oceans to the prairies to the mountains white with foam, God Bless America, my home sweet home, God Bless America, my home sweet home [*rings hand bell, then shouting*] Let liberty ring!

Viewed millions of times on Twitter alone, this intervention assumed the status of a global public communication, Ms Baber herself coming to be known as "Trump's #1 Karen", in a deployment of the current pejorative moniker for an entitled or demanding white woman. Leaving aside the speaker's political leanings, of interest to the scholar of rhetoric is her construction of an antithesis between freedom and mask-wearing, and her association of mask-wearing with social deviants and ideological others. She has by no means been alone in this. The same construction has been applied to the imminent prospect of vaccination, the following Twitter thread one of many on the subject:[4]

User 1, 04/12/2020
Didn't want to wear masks, didn't want to stay indoors, don't want to get the vaccine, what the hell do y'all want? Why is everything in America so fucking unnecessarily difficult
User 2, replying 05/12/2020
There's a difference between asking, and mandating, under threat of state force.
User 3, replying 05/12/2020
you can sacrifice a little personal freedom for public health
User 4, replying 06/12/2020
Not saying people shouldn't take the vaccine but YIKES, can't believe people are willing to sacrifice their freedom at all for the government lol

Perhaps tellingly, further down this thread User 2 quotes Benjamin Franklin and is taken to task by others for doing so out of context.[5] The exchange has not received the level of public engagement of Ms. Baber's intervention, but nevertheless demonstrates the extent to which the antithesis between human security in the form of public health measures and personal freedom has permeated discourse on social media. The simplifying, binary construction is perfectly suited to short-form speech constrained by character and upload limits. It exemplifies a tendency to prioritise pithy soundbites over debate in detail. But it is discernible also in the public addresses of political leaders concerning COVID restrictions, for example in this televised speech by UK Prime Minister Boris Johnson [excerpt]:[6]

> When the sickness took hold in this country in March, we pulled together in a spirit of national sacrifice and community. We followed the guidance to the letter. We stayed at home, protected the NHS, and saved thousands of lives. And for months with those disciplines of social distancing we have kept that virus at bay. But we have to acknowledge this is a great and freedom-loving country; and while the vast majority have complied with the rules there have been too many breaches - too many opportunities for our invisible enemy to slip through undetected.

As User 2 in the Twitter thread above intimated, the opposition of freedom and human security conceives of a Hobson's choice between two threats, between deadly disease and infringement on one's human rights. Johnson's echoes of military Remembrance – the "spirit of national sacrifice", and the characterisation of the novel coronavirus as an "invisible enemy" – are intended to rouse the nation to again meet the challenge of observing restrictions, including the wearing of face masks. So, too, does his heroising portrayal of common sense [emphasis added]:

> And I know that faced with that risk the British people will want their government to continue *to fight to protect them*, you, and that is what we are doing, night and day. And yet the *single greatest weapon* we bring to this *fight*

> is the common sense of the people themselves - the joint resolve of this country to work together to suppress Covid now.

Evocation of the spirit of the Blitz assimilates public health measures with military conflict. In doing so, Johnson's rhetoric contrasts with that of Biden, who seeks to distance mask-wearing from the defence of freedom. The two communications differ also in their intent: Johnson seeks to exhort, Biden to quell and de-escalate. The choice of military sacrifice as a frame of reference itself highlights the susceptibility of public health to representation as a security issue.

Sheeple and chips

The COVID pandemic has also given rise to rhetoric that conflates public health with perceived technology threats. A decades-old suspicion of mobile phone technology, itself building on a long-standing fear of radio waves, and the identification of China as the source of both the COVID outbreak and the home base of one of the leading suppliers of 5G infrastructure components (Huawei) have given rise to the promulgation of an erroneous link between the two. As Ahmed, Downing, Tuters, and Knight have observed, this belief converges with another popular conspiracy theory, that "the pandemic is part of a plan by global elites like Bill Gates or George Soros – in league with Big Pharma – to institute mandatory worldwide vaccinations that would include tracking chips, which would then be activated by 5G radiowaves".[7]

Conspiracy theorists position themselves as "truth seekers", the only members of society who can really see what is going on.[8] At a time of heightened global uncertainty and perceived information overload, the desire for answers has led a not insignificant number of people to seek to fill in the knowledge gaps for themselves. The notion that the release of the virus was intentional reassures as much as it disconcerts: without a plan to explain it, the pandemic must be appreciated as an act of nature, a random occurrence or a failure of human public health responses – in short, a phenomenon that challenges the human desire for order, the uncertainty of which ultimately makes us feel less secure at an individual level. Conversely, an explanation that implies order, however malevolent, not only entails a certain predictability in the notion that the rich and powerful cannot be trusted, but also bestows on the believer a sense of information superiority that paradoxically makes them feel in greater control of their destiny than one that requires advanced study of epidemiology.

The 5G COVID conspiracy theory compels by convoluting this need for knowledge, more precisely the security of knowledge, and distrust of the powerful with a fear of death, Sinophobia, and technophobia. The technological threat manifests as the belief that those vaccinated will in fact be implanted with tracking chips. Where George Soros has long been a target for anti-Semitism, Bill Gates' alleged membership of the malevolent global elite is awarded for other reasons, specifically his philanthropy in the area of public health and disease control. But it can be no coincidence that the Microsoft co-founder and Big Tech poster boy of yesteryear is the focus of a conspiracy theory involving computer and communications technology. Indeed, it is the "techiness" of Gates that makes him so ripe for targeting. It is a mark of the currency of these theories that Reuters and other mainstream media outlets have felt the need to publish fact-checking articles debunking claims that Gates is responsible for COVID-19 and is planning to use microchip implants to fight the virus.[9]

From a linguistic standpoint, use of portmanteaux such as "plandemic" and "sheeple", the latter's apparent earlier circulation on distributed discussion system Usenet, and its popularisation through comic art are suggestive of a similar *terroir* and developmental trajectory to that of cybersecurity rhetoric.[10] Similarity is also discernible in the aura of exclusivity and superior knowledge cultivated by these groups. While it is arguably premature to subject a lexicon still very much in its infancy to detailed investigation, comparative analysis of conspiracy and cyber vernaculars is a potential avenue for future research.

Meanwhile, democratisation of public discourse via social media challenges traditional prescriptions and restrictions on who can speak, and in what context. Historically, soapbox oratory has been spatially limited, restricted to Speakers' Corners, the letters pages of newspapers, and the occasional "Have Your Say"-style television programme. As Deborah Baber's intervention illustrates, local acts of civic engagement now have global transmission capability: statements enjoy an international audience as soon as they are recorded or transcribed. Broadcast and print media's increasing reliance on crowdsourced news content ensures that citizens have greater public exposure and input to discourse than ever before.

This produces something of a paradox as regards the current swathe of conspiracy theories, that has gone largely unnoticed by their proponents. Big Tech is both a target of insecurity discourse, as embodied by Bill Gates, and the means of its mass distribution. The latitude of their distribution in turn gives these theories the possibility of greater societal impact. Policy and legislative efforts to control conspiracy content and other speech deemed harmful are therefore ostensibly aimed at protecting society or, in other words, "our way of life". The phrase manifests in Donald Trump's National Security Strategy as "the American way of life", and in David Cameron's tribute to Lee Rigby – "He was a British soldier who stood for our country and for our way of life."[11] Given its conservative overtones and idealisation of the *status quo*, the extent to which control of (in)security discourse has the secondary aim of protecting a society's governing and rhetorical structures is worthy of further consideration.

Recycled rhetoric: the peculiar phenomenon of techno-nationalism

The main body of President Trump's 2017 National Security Strategy includes a section detailing his administration's plans to "promote and protect the US National Security Innovation Base".[12] It may not be immediately obvious from this series of abstract terms that they refer to the need to safeguard the country's security technologies. Putting to one side any (potentially legitimate) concerns we may have about the circularity of including in a security strategy the need to protect measures that are themselves designed to protect security, we will observe that one country is singled out as a particular threat in this regard:

> America's business climate and legal and regulatory systems encourage risk taking. We are a nation of people who work hard, dream big, and never give up. Not every country shares these characteristics. Some instead steal or illicitly acquire America's hard-earned intellectual property and proprietary information to compensate for their own systemic weaknesses.
>
> Every year, competitors such as China steal U.S. intellectual property valued at hundreds of billions of dollars. Stealing proprietary technology and early-stage ideas allows competitors to unfairly tap into the innovation of free societies. Over the years, rivals have used sophisticated means to weaken our businesses and our economy as facets of cyber-enabled economic warfare and other malicious activities. In addition to these illegal means, some actors use largely legitimate, legal transfers and relationships to gain access to fields, experts, and trusted foundries that fill their capability gaps and erode America's long-term competitive advantages.

Intellectual property theft is elevated to the status of warfare, the addition of the "cyber-" prefix for good measure perhaps also triggering the hyperbolic, mystifying effect we have seen in its application elsewhere. A series of antitheses is deployed to persuade the reader that the situation described is a binary opposition, and to close down nuance. The US is on the side of the law, while China is associated with illegal and unfair practices. The US is repeatedly described in terms that evoke strength, particularly the language of hardness; China is identified as both weak and seeking to cause weakness. In this antithetical framing, introduction of the imagery of the American Dream by implication casts China as a nightmare: the snap transition from a US-dominated paragraph to one focused solely on China encourages such a contrasting appreciation by means of arrangement (***dispositio***).

Construction of a simple polarity also creates a space in which common legitimate business activities are classified as security threats. This extension of the scope of security is both characteristic of securitisation and a test of its limits. It is only after China has been identified as the ideological Other that the concept of the National Security Innovation Base is defined:

> We must defend our National Security Innovation Base (NSIB) against competitors. The NSIB is the American network of knowledge, capabilities, and people – including academia, National Laboratories, and the private sector – that turns ideas into innovations, transforms discoveries into successful commercial products and companies, and protects and enhances the American way of life. The genius of creative Americans, and the free system that enables them, is critical to American security and prosperity.

The "NSIB" is depicted here as a pre-existing entity: indeed the very use of an acronym implies a customary usage that has developed over time. In fact, as commentators on US defence policy have observed, this is the very first appearance of the concept in a public document.[13] It is a prime example of constructivist or constitutive rhetoric, in as much as the act of referring to the NSIB gives it social reality.[14]

As in the earlier paragraphs, the required response to economic and technological competition assumes military overtones. In an appeal to the reader's emotion (*pathos*), intellectual property is characterised not as data, but as the genius of the people – in turn echoing the earlier first-person focus on "a nation of people who work hard, dream big, and never give up". The trademark language of freedom reappears here: depiction of the US' "free system" as security critical, and of the "innovation of free societies" as under threat from states like China, makes of this a familiar struggle between good and evil (*ethos*). In the security rhetoric of George W. Bush, freedom was set in opposition to tyranny and terrorism in order to justify military action. A close reading of one speech specifically in relation to the threat of Chinese technology suggests that its appearance in Trump's National Security Strategy is likewise intended to evoke existential conflict.

On 19 June 2020, US Secretary of State Michael R. Pompeo spoke on "Europe and the China Challenge" at a virtual meeting of the Copenhagen Democracy Summit.[15] Purporting to address "the idea that Europe is being forced to choose between the United States and China", the speech consistently presents a binary opposition of freedom and tyranny, even in personal anecdotes:

> I spent a few years of my life – it's been decades, when I was a young soldier serving in Germany – patrolling along the Iron Curtain. I've seen tyranny firsthand, and I have dealt with all manner of unfree regimes in my previous role as director of the CIA and now in my current role as Secretary of State of the United States of America.

The Chair of the summit, former NATO Secretary General Anders Fogh Rasmussen, is praised as "a friend of freedom-loving people all across the world". Pompeo's speech clearly aligns freedom with capitalism by means of not entirely unassailable statements that "Democracy is the only system of government that honors human dignity and personal freedom and progress for mankind. The corollary is that capitalism is the greatest anti-poverty program in all of history." When Pompeo uses the formulation,

> I know that there's fear in Europe that the United States wants you to choose between us and China. But that's simply not the case. It's the Chinese Communist Party's [*sic*] that's forcing this choice. The choice isn't between the United States [*sic*]; it's between freedom and tyranny,

the reader-listener's memory of the construction of an identical choice in identical terms in relation to the Iraq War may leave them unconvinced. The clear alignment of the US with freedom and China with tyranny situates the former on the side of right and the angels, the latter as an enemy to all right-thinking – or "freedom-loving" people:

> The party wants you to throw away the progress we in the free world have made, through NATO and other institutions – both formal and informal institutions – and adopt a new set of rules and norms to accommodate them within Beijing.

The final words of the speech - "Let's not leave any confusion about the choice between tyranny and freedom" - signpost the key message once more. Not only identical to George W. Bush's Iraq War rhetoric in terms of imagery and antithetical framing, Pompeo's presentation of the Chinese threat has the same effect of negating complexity, grey areas, and alternative approaches to foreign policy.

However flawed the logic and sweeping the rhetoric, Bush's construction of a choice between freedom and tyranny had a concrete, real-world security incident as its backdrop. Pompeo adduces evidence of the threat from China as follows:

> You've seen this all. Everyone in this room knows that the Chinese Communist Party strongarms nations to do business with Huawei, an arm of the CCP's surveillance state. And it's flagrantly attacking European sovereignty by buying up ports and critical infrastructure, Piraeus to Valencia. We must take off the golden blinders of economic ties and see that the China challenge isn't just at the gates; it's in every capital, it's in every borough, it's in every province.

The stated threat is of a techno-economic character, as in the 2017 National Security Strategy. In a further echo of that document, Pompeo depicts it as a physical enemy at the gates, and as a sinister infiltrator: in short, as a threat to both national and community security. Special mention is made of technology company Huawei, the proposed incorporation of whose components into 5G telecommunications networks the US government has sought to prevent in Europe, the Five Eyes and several other nations.

When President Trump signed a 2019 Executive Order prohibiting the incorporation of "information and communications technology or services designed, developed, manufactured, or supplied, by persons owned by, controlled by, or subject to the jurisdiction or direction of a foreign adversary", and describing such technology as an "extraordinary threat to the national security", it was evident to all that Huawei was the primary supplier in scope.[16] The Executive Order was techno-nationalist in its intent and impact, insofar as it created a space in which to exert diplomatic pressure on other nations to remove Huawei components from their telecommunications infrastructure.[17] Accordingly, Pompeo's Copenhagen speech refers to the United Kingdom's move "towards securing its networks from Huawei" as one of a number of "positive steps".

Whether Huawei components do in fact pose a security threat is of limited consequence to the discussion at hand. Regardless, the conscious construction of innovation and trade *as security issues per se*, and the extent to which leading political figures are prepared to borrow from recent and memorable security rhetoric to do so, necessarily calls into question the objectivity of the argument presented and the evidence adduced. A close reading of these texts also assists in our understanding of International Relations: it enables us to determine that the US – whose companies are so often the target of technological othering – itself appears to have recognised the geostrategic utility of a foreign tech threat. Here, too, the media have a role to play: taking their lead from the NSS, outlets have been quick to engage in hyperbole, characterising Sino-American tensions as a "tech cold war", and even a "new world war".[18]

Security rhetoric and muted groups

One of the failings of this book is the dominance of voices that, with one or two notable exceptions, are white and male. It is an unfortunate reality, but a reality nonetheless, that the Classical authorities on rhetoric, at least those whose works have come down to us, were all male: references to Aspasia of Miletus as a teacher of rhetoric in fifth century BCE Athens are exceptional in this regard. Likewise, the primary texts in Chapters 2 and 3 are male-dominated. This was certainly not a matter of choice. Indeed, had Hillary Clinton been declared the winner of the 2016 US election, her National Security Strategy preface(s) would have been analysed in Chapter 2. It is reasonable to assume that women will have had a hand in the production of at least some cybersecurity rhetoric. My own professional experience and the personnel composition of cybersecurity industry marketing departments speak to this. Identifying instances of female speech in unattributed organisational communications is an impossible task, however. Confined to English language texts, by default the research neglected the security rhetoric of long-serving female leaders such as German Chancellor Angela Merkel. While the dearth of female voices in this book arguably reflects wider societal dynamics around who gets to speak, and who is listened to – to some extent aligning with Ardener and Ardener's Muted Group Theory – there is clearly an opportunity for more extensive analysis of women's security rhetoric.[19] As New Zealand Prime Minister Jacinda Ardern's emphasis on shared humanity and unity in statements following the 2019 Christchurch terrorist attack may indicate, we could be entering an age in which patriarchal security rhetoric is increasingly challenged.

There has also been no attempt made in this book to look beyond Western rhetorical theory and security discourse. Scrutiny of American constructions of the technology threat from China, for example, inevitably prompts questions of how Chinese authorities and media frame technology threats and their responses to foreign security rhetoric, and whether there is a discernible Sino-American dialogue. As the analysis of government and tech company rhetoric in Chapter 3 demonstrates, public identification of another party as a threat is a provocation to respond, even if the response issued is largely formulaic. By the same token, and for the sake of completeness, there may be benefit in comparative analysis of the Bush Doctrine and relevant statements by Iraqi authorities.

Future considerations

The use and misuse of technology has been a consistent presence in this book. The proliferation in recent years of short-form security rhetoric, epitomised by the video address announcing Trump's 2017 National Security Strategy, and of influence operations and misinformation via social media, is testament to the propensity for developments in communications technology to be harnessed for legitimate and illegitimate activities alike. Current concern over so-called Deepfakes – the term yet another example of a "techie" portmanteau – centres on the premise that citizens will be unable to tell the difference between authentic and synthetic audio-visual content. By the end of 2020, predictions of their misuse in electoral campaigns have failed to be realised.[20]

The concern is understandable, however. The Generative Adversarial Networks (GANs) which create Deepfakes are becoming more sophisticated, and this progress coincides with the widespread qualification of contemporary politics, the world, and the current era as "post-truth".[21] Global technology leaders have invested in technical tools to detect synthetic media intended to mislead.[22] Meanwhile, the *Oxford English Dictionary*'s definition of "post-truth" as "relating to or denoting circumstances in which objective facts are less influential in shaping public opinion than appeals to emotion and personal belief" suggests that a greater understanding of how public figures appeal to emotion could be of use in efforts to improve citizens' critical thinking. This book has demonstrated that such appeals, and the techniques used to achieve them, are perfectly recognisable. It would be wildly optimistic to claim that a grounding in Classical rhetoric can defeat a malicious use of Artificial Intelligence by itself. But its facility for compelling us to interrogate discourse and its utility for detecting inauthenticity, recycled framing, and flawed logic, may give us reason to think that it is not yet time to give up on humans' ability to think critically.

Concluding thoughts

Application of Classical rhetorical theory as a key to understanding ancient and modern security communications has helped us in some cases to confirm suspicions about their production and content; in others, it has challenged our expectations, uncovered new lines of enquiry, and yielded surprising insights.

In Chapter 1, analysis of ancient models and antecedents for modern security rhetoric has revealed security's utility as a self-aggrandising mechanism, also as a means of reassuring the public and seeking reassurance of personal safety in return. Moreover, threat inflation is revealed to be by no means an entirely modern phenomenon. Through use of hyperbole and catastrophising metaphor, Roman source material inflates threats and heightens fears in order to intensify relief. But it is also capable of more complex, unresolved representation, as when Juvenal's speaker seeks to convince us that the only remedy for urban danger is flight.

Examination of US presidential security rhetoric permits the identification of remarkable consistency with that of Ancient Rome. The language and imagery of novelty and restoration, the latter most obvious in Trump's "Make America Great Again", is evident in security communications 2000 years apart. Trump's preoccupation with recording his achievements in the first person likewise finds an ancient parallel, in Augustus' *Res Gestae*. His engagement in threat inflation with the express purpose of rendering his achievements all the more dazzling echoes the Younger Pliny's contrast of the reigns of Domitian and Trajan. His comprehensive construction of a personal security cult marks him out in this respect as the most Roman of the twenty-first-century presidents. Other presidents, meanwhile, make liberal use of Classical rhetorical tropes and figures: abundant asyndeton, constraining antitheses that effectively remove choice from deliberative oratory, metaphors that inspire while they explain. Cross-comparison uncovers a presidential rhetorical code comprising preferred language, imagery, and rhetorical devices: through a close reading of its application, we have been able to discern tensions between rhetoric and content, and strategic paradoxes; also, that presidents speak to each other through these texts.

Use of alienating antitheses to construct ideological Others as exhibited by Pliny and George W. Bush also find a parallel in UK government communications and media coverage analysed in Chapter 3. In addition to tracing an assimilation of technology companies to terrorists, we have observed how the language of (ir)responsibility situates companies among the criminally culpable, in apparent agreement with a legislative proposal to establish liability through a "duty of care". Notable similarity in government and media representations of US tech companies is indicative of a shared lexicon, rhetorical attitude, and mindset. It would appear, moreover, to be a two-way exchange. Tabloid-style appeals to sensation and emotion are found to be prominent in policy whose evidence is less than robust. Communication by tech companies has been silenced by the media and by the companies themselves, leaving even greater space for promulgation of the dominant insecurity narrative. Close reading of recent communications that tackle government statements head on and in their own style prompts us to consider the extent to which these changes may reflect shifts in global power dynamics.

In Chapter 4, cybersecurity is confirmed as the preeminent locus of contemporary threat inflation.[23] Perhaps less expected was the extent to which the rhetorical proclivities and tactics of law enforcement and industry coincide with those of cybercriminals. Consistent amplification through metaphor and intensification of urgency simultaneously heightens fear and removes agency from citizens, while fantastic and exclusive representations of "cyber" culture situate its activities beyond their knowledge and capability. Alternative presentations are not only possible: they are necessary to empower citizens to prevent cybercrime, and to protect themselves and others from influence operations. As analysis of pandemic-related and conspiracy theory communications in Chapter 5 demonstrates, rhetoric grounded in fear can gain ground at times of insecurity, and even contaminate official messaging. Meanwhile, reuse of the Bush Doctrine's rhetoric in the context of techno-nationalism highlights the amenability of certain concepts to deployment in different security scenarios. Freedom, which for Pliny was the object of restoration and in the Emperor's gift, becomes a specialty of US presidential security rhetoric, a pole in antithetical oppositions between good and evil, right-thinking countries (led by the US) and Iraq, and right-thinking countries (led by the US) and China; but also a sacrificial victim at the hands of public health.

One of the most diverting and challenging aspects of security rhetoric is the relentless appearance of new objects of study. At the time of writing (late 2020), the world is still mid-pandemic, the transition period for the UK's exit from the European Union is just coming to an end, and a new US president is due to be sworn in, who will issue his own National Security Strategy in due course. The US will soon experience its first female, African American and Asian American Vice President. In this respect alone, US security rhetoric is about to become more representative of the society in which it operates. In time the global public health emergency will subside and take its particular brand of exceptional messaging with it. Emerging technological developments will present further opportunities for the democratisation of security communications, and will doubtless be the objects of fear and concern. But if the findings in this book are anything to go by, we can say for certain that there will continue to be security communications ripe for rhetorical analysis, and we can hazard an informed guess at some of their likely attributes.

Consistency across millennia, continents, and problems in the language, imagery, devices, and appeals deployed allows us to identify a *tradition* of security rhetoric. Against its own repeated claims of novelty and lack of precedent, we can attest that in fact there is little about it that is new; its techniques, objectives, and even its target selection have been seen before. Moreover, the artefacts examined in this book demonstrate that they are anything but neutral, factual depictions of safety and security issues. Security rhetoric plays on – and therefore depends on – insecurity at an individual, urban, national, and international level. As we have seen, insecurity can be generated if necessary where it does not already exist.

This, and security rhetoric's identified capacity for cross- and self-reference, endorses the belief that close reading of *how* public figures communicate security issues to us matters. It can reveal – even in the absence of an in-depth knowledge of the content – flaws in policy logic and process, and items worthy of additional citizen scrutiny. As keys for deciphering rhetorical practice, the works of Aristotle, Cicero, Quintilian, and others have served us well for centuries. We could do worse than to look to them for assistance in decoding twenty-first-century safety and security narratives.

Notes

1 EUR-Lex (n.d.) "Freedom & Security", *Summaries of Legislation: Glossary of Summaries*, European Union, https://eur-lex.europa.eu/summary/glossary/freedom_and_security.html, accessed 06/12/2020.

2 Joe Biden, "President-Elect Biden Hosts a Virtual Roundtable on the Impact of COVID-19", https://youtu.be/3Se0ouTAS1Y, accessed 02/12/2020.

3 Intervention of Deborah Baber, Ventura County Board of Supervisors 16/06/2020, transcribed from https://twitter.com/Katiehugscats/status/1272957475247931392?s=20, accessed 06/12/2020.

4 https://twitter.com/Jose__517/status/1335511135232040963?s=20, accessed 06/12/2020.

5 https://twitter.com/thebadrouter/status/1335439143938138112?s=20, accessed 06/12/2020.

6 BBC (2020) "COVID: Boris Johnson's address to the country in full", *BBC News Online* 22/09/2020, www.bbc.co.uk/news/uk-54255898

7 W. Ahmed, J. Downing, M. Tuters, and P. Knight (2020) "Four Experts Investigate How the 5G Coronavirus Conspiracy Theory Began", *The Conversation* 11/06/2020, https://theconversation.com/four-experts-investigate-how-the-5g-coronavirus-conspiracy-theory-began-139137

8 T. Hill, R. Canniford, and S. Murphy (2020) "Why 5G Conspiracy Theories Prosper During the Coronavirus Pandemic", *The Conversation* 09/04/2020, https://theconversation.com/why-5g-conspiracy-theories-prosper-during-the-coronavirus-pandemic-136019

9 Reuters, "Fact Check: Bill Gates is Not Responsible for COVID-19", 10/09/2020, https://uk.reuters.com/article/uk-factcheck-gates/fact-check-bill-gates-is-not-responsible-for-covid-19-idUSKBN2613CK; "False Claim: Bill Gates Planning to Use Microchip Implants to Fight Coronavirus", www.reuters.com/article/uk-factcheck-coronavirus-bill-gates-micr-idUSKBN21I3EC

10 Oxford Languages (2020) *Words of an Unprecedented Year*, Oxford: Oxford University Press, https://languages.oup.com/word-of-the-year/2020/; The Economist (2020) "Brave New Word: From Plandemic to Breadcrumbs: Conspiracy-theory Slang", *1843 Magazine* 17/09/2020, www.economist.com/1843/2020/09/17/from-plandemic-to-breadcrumbs-conspiracy-theory-slang; Christopher Polancec (2010) *Goodnight, Neverland! Redditors Need Apply*, www.goodnightneverland.com/?p=299, accessed 31/12/2020; Know Your Meme (n.d.) "Sheeple", https://knowyourmeme.com/memes/sheeple#fn9, accessed 31/12/2020.

11 Hansard, *Murder of Lee Rigby*, Volume 588: debated on Tuesday 25 November 2014, Column 747. See Philip M. Taylor (2003) *Munitions of the Mind: A History of Propaganda from the Ancient World to the Present Era* (3rd edn), Manchester: Manchester University Press, p. 252, for an instructive discussion of the following antithetical depiction of two "ways of life" in the 1948 Truman Doctrine: "One way of life is based upon the will of the majority, and is distinguished by free institutions, representative government, free elections, guarantees of personal liberty, freedom of speech and religion and freedom from political repression. The second way of life is based upon the will of a minority imposed upon the majority. It relies upon terror and repression, a controlled press and radio, fixed elections, and the suppression of personal freedoms."

12 US NSS (2017) p. 21.

13 Daniel Morgan (2018) "The New National Security Innovation Base: Charting the Course for Technology in War", Modern War Institute at West Point 20/02/2018. https://mwi.usma.edu/new-national-security-innovation-base-charting-course-technology-war/; Andrew Philip Hunter (2018) "A Strategic Approach to Defense Investment", Center for Strategic & International Studies 26/03/2018, www.csis.org/analysis/strategic-approach-defense-investment.

14 See, for example, Hasian, Lawson, and McFarlane (2015) p. 3; Juha A. Vuori (2017) "Constructivism and Securitization Studies", in Myriam Dunn Cavelty and Thierry Balzacq eds (2017) *Routledge Handbook of Security Studies*, London: Routledge, pp. 64–74.

15 US State Department (2020) "Europe and the China Challenge, Speech: Michael R. Pompeo, Secretary of State, Virtual Copenhagen Democracy Summit, June 19, 2020", www.state.gov/secretary-michael-r-pompeo-at-the-virtual-copenhagen-democracy-summit/

16 Executive Office of the President (2019) "Securing the Information and Communications Technology and Services Supply Chain, E.O. 13873 of May 15, 2019", www.federalregister.gov/documents/2019/05/17/2019-10538/securing-the-information-and-communications-technology-and-services-supply-chain

17 The concept of techno-nationalism pre-dates the current debate over the power and state proximity of the largest global tech companies. Originally used to denote twentieth-century nationalising stances towards (and rhetoric of) manufacturing, oil production, aviation and innovation in general, it now popularly refers to foreign policy

that seeks to leverage communications technology for a state's wider strategic aims, and is often seen as a reversal of the tendency towards globalisation. See, for example, S. Montresor (2001) "Techno-globalism, techno-nationalism and Technological Systems: Organizing the Evidence", *Technovation* 21: 399–412; Amol Rajan (2018) "Techno-nationalism Could Determine the 21st Century", *BBC News Online* 08/09/2018, www.bbc.co.uk/news/technology-45370052; World Economic Forum (2019) "The Rise of Techno-nationalism - and the Paradox at its Core", Annual Meeting of the New Champions 03/07/2019, www.weforum.org/agenda/2019/07/the-rise-of-techno-nationalism-and-the-paradox-at-its-core/; A. Capri (2020) "US-China Techno-Nationalism and the Decoupling of Innovation", *The Diplomat* 10/09/2020, https://thediplomat.com/2020/09/us-china-techno-nationalism-and-the-decoupling-of-innovation/

18 The Economist (2020) "Huawei and the Tech Cold War: China v America", *The Economist* 18/07/2020, www.economist.com/leaders/2020/07/18/china-v-america; Jill Disis (2020) "A New World War Over Technology", *CNN Business* 11/07/2020, https://edition.cnn.com/2020/07/10/tech/us-china-global-tech-war-intl-hnk/index.html.

19 Edwin Ardener (1975) "The Problem Revisited", in Shirley Ardener (1975) *Perceiving Women*, London: Malaby, 19–28. See also Cheryl Glenn on "systematic silencing" ((2004) *Unspoken: A Rhetoric of Silence*, Carbondale: Southern Illinois, p. 25).

20 Jeremy Hsu (2018) "Experts Bet on First Deepfakes Political Scandal", *IEEE Spectrum* 22/06/2018, https://spectrum.ieee.org/tech-talk/artificial-intelligence/machine-learning/experts-bet-on-first-deepfakes-political-scandal; Tim Hwang (2018) "Don't Worry About Deepfakes. Worry About Why People Fall for Them", Berkman Klein Center for Internet & Society at Harvard University, https://cyber.harvard.edu/story/2018-12/dont-worry-about-deepfakes-worry-about-why-people-fall-them

21 Oxford Languages (2016) "Word of the Year 2016", https://languages.oup.com/word-of-the-year/2016/

22 Microsoft (2020) "New Steps to Combat Disinformation", *Microsoft on the Issues* 01/09/2020, https://blogs.microsoft.com/on-the-issues/2020/09/01/disinformation-deepfakes-newsguard-video-authenticator/

23 Cf. Hasian, Lawson, and McFarlane (2015) p. 131 on the rhetorical utility of "a seemingly ubiquitous threat that is simultaneously present but invisible, potentially as dangerous as a physical attack but not, itself, amenable to defeat through traditional, externally focused means of national defense. This is a threat that is everywhere and nowhere and, thus, requiring the national security state to be everywhere and nowhere, too."

Index

Note: Page numbers in *italic* refer to Figures

For Product Safety Concerns and Information please contact our EU representative GPSR@taylorandfrancis.com
Taylor & Francis Verlag GmbH, Kaufingerstraße 24, 80331 München, Germany

www.ingramcontent.com/pod-product-compliance
Lightning Source LLC
LaVergne TN
LVHW021111300926
849160LV00009B/689

* 9 7 8 1 0 3 2 0 3 0 8 4 5 *